Performing Place, Practising Memories

Space and Place

Bodily, geographic, and architectural sites are embedded with cultural knowledge and social value. The Anthropology of Space and Place series provides ethnographically rich analyses of the cultural organization and meanings of these sites of space, architecture, landscape, and places of the body. Contributions to this series will examine the symbolic meanings of space and place, the cultural and historical processes involved in their construction and contestation, and how they are in dialogue with wider political, religious, social, and economic ideas, values and institutions.

PERFORMING PLACE, PRACTISING MEMORIES

Aboriginal Australians, Hippies and the State

⊰ ◆ ⊱

Rosita Henry

Berghahn Books
New York • Oxford

First published in 2012 by

Berghahn Books

www.berghahnbooks.com

©2012 Rosita Henry

Library of Congress Cataloging-in-Publication Data

Henry, Rosita.
Performing place, practising memories : Aboriginal Australians, hippies and the
  state / by Rosita Henry. — 1st ed.
    p. cm.
  Includes bibliographical references and index.
  ISBN 978-0-85745-508-6 (hardback : alk. paper) —
  ISBN 978-0-85745-509-3 (e-book)
  1. Aboriginal Australians—Australia—Kuranda (Qld.)—Ethnic identity.
2. Aboriginal Australians—Australia—Kuranda (Qld.)—Social conditions.
3. Aboriginal Australians—Australia—Kuranda (Qld.)—Government relations.
4. Counterculture—Australia—Kuranda (Qld.)—History—20th century.
5. Aboriginal Australians in popular culture—History—20th century. 6. Whites—
Australia—Kuranda (Qld.)—Social conditions. 7. Kuranda (Qld.)—History.
8. Kuranda (Qld.)—Race relations. 9. Kuranda (Qld.)—Social life and customs.
I. Title.
  GN667.Q4H46 2012
  305.89'9150943—dc23

                                                                        2012001674

British Library Cataloguing in Publication Data

A catalogue record for this book is available from the British Library

Printed in the United States on acid-free paper.

ISBN 978-0-85745-508-6 (hardback)
ISBN 978-0-85745-509-3 (ebook)

❧ CONTENTS ❧

᧧ FIGURES AND MAPS ᧠

Figures

Maps

◁ PREFACE ▷

This ethnographic study focuses on the small Australian town of Kuranda – marketed for tourists as 'the village in the rainforest' – and explores how political identities are generated. It is a study of the way people constitute themselves in relation to place, and the way they construct, communicate and contest the identities produced within the contexts of a bureaucratic state order and a network of global economic and political forces. The study is not about any particular culture or sub-culture in isolation – neither the various waves of European settlers nor the Aboriginal population – but the practices of all categories of people, viewed at the intersection of their socio-political constitution and engagement. The ethnographic task at hand is to explore the fields of sociality of people who call Kuranda home, in order to discover their various practices of place-making.

The book is built around a number of linked analyses of conflicts, or 'social dramas', that have arisen in the town in connection with both public and private spaces. In turn, these social dramas foster theatrical and other staged performances that allow people to reflect upon their social situations. I explain these performances as practices that enable people to celebrate the ways in which their particularistic identities articulate with universal values. Through public performances and everyday spatial tactics, people resist state projects, but they also contribute to the cultivation and propagation of state effects. They play with identities so as to produce a sense of local community – a sense of place – that works both with and against the state.

The role of the state in relation to Indigenous Australians has recently become an issue of intense debate among anthropologists and other scholars, following the heavy-handed intervention of the Australian federal government in Aboriginal communities in the Northern Territory after the release of the *Little Children are Sacred* report by the Board of Inquiry into the Protection of Aboriginal Children from Sexual Abuse (2007). In the wake of the report's release, anthropologists were quickly condemned for having spent years keeping silent about sexual abuse and other expressions of violence in Aboriginal communities, as well as for having written ethnographies that obfuscated the severe 'dysfunction' of many of these communities. Consequently, the pendulum has begun to swing in the opposite direction, and increasing attention is being paid to abjection and suffering in Aboriginal communities.

In contrast to this ethnographic trend, the present book concerns the entangled lives of the Aboriginal and non-Aboriginal residents of a community that one cannot define as remote. While this community's proximity to a thriving regional city does not guarantee that the people here are free from chronic health problems, poverty, violence, sexual abuse, and the effects of alcohol and drug addiction, my aim has been to give equal emphasis to the pleasure and the sense of joyful hope for a better future that Aboriginal people have conveyed to me.

Rosita Henry
Townsville, April 2011

৭ ACKNOWLEDGMENTS ৮

To acknowledge adequately the important intellectual and personal help of so many friends, colleagues and family members during the time in which this book has come into fruition is almost as considerable a task as writing the book itself.

First of all, I thank my parents, Ramona and Wolfgang Rusch, and my eight younger brothers and sisters, Rosemarie, Rozana, Ricardo, Rosalie, Rohan, Rainer, Rene and Ranjini, as well as their extended families, for keeping me in touch with the really important things in life and for being a continuing source of my fascination with the nature of human sociality. I thank my parents for their lifelong encouragement, their pride in their children, and their unwavering confidence in our ability to choose the right path and achieve whatever we might set our hearts on.

I decided that I was going to 'become an anthropologist' while I was still in high school. For this decision I owe a debt of gratitude to my friend Maggie Wilson (nee Leahy). As best friends through our high school years, we spent all our time together in the boarding school we attended talking about our families and our childhood days. I was fascinated by Maggie's experiences growing up in Papua New Guinea in a village near Mt Hagen. Over the years, Maggie continued to encourage me, even lending her expertise as a filmmaker to help me record festival performances while I was conducting fieldwork for this book, until she passed away suddenly in April 2009.

In my research and writing for this book, I have had the benefit of the generous support of many colleagues at James Cook University. I am indebted firstly to the late Jeffrey Clark, who helped reawaken my passion for anthropology after I had spent a long time away from academia immersed in mothering and child care. Even at the height of his illness, Jeffrey found the time to provide encouragement and advice about the early period of my fieldwork, begun in 1993.

Bruce Kapferer's steadfast encouragement and support – as well as his contagious enthusiasm for my research project and for the drafts of chapters I had written – provided me with the self-confidence I needed to continue at a time when I thought I would never get to where I was going. His intellectual fervour has been inspirational for me and I thank him for this, for his confidence in me and for the lively intellectual direction he provided.

I am deeply grateful to my colleague and friend Maureen Fuary for her concerted scrutiny, her meticulous reading, and her insightful and imaginatively constructive comments on early drafts of the manuscript, as well as to Douglas Miles for his always sound advice and for reading early drafts of several chapters. I am also indebted to Rohan Bastin, Mike Wood and the late Christopher Morgan for lively anthropological debate over the years and especially to Shelley Greer, a committed friend and colleague who has been one of my muses, protective, steadfast and untiring in her support. I am also deeply grateful to Russell McGregor for generously and collegially taking the time to cast a historian's expert eye over the penultimate draft of the manuscript and for providing invaluable feedback.

Michael Allen provided encouragement at a time when it was badly needed. His recognition of the value of my project and his encouragement to publish provided a tremendous boost to my confidence in my study as a worthwhile contribution. I cannot thank Michael enough for his continuing support as mentor and friend. Special thanks are due to Don Handelman who read early drafts of a number of chapters and who generously spent the time to provide expert guidance. I am especially grateful to Gillian Cowlishaw, Julie Finlayson and Jonathan Friedman for reading and providing invaluable feedback on an early draft of the manuscript, as well as to Barbara Glowczewski, John Morton, David Trigger, Judith Kapferer, Lissant Bolton, Edvard Hviding and James Weiner for their insightful comments and encouraging advice on various sections presented at conferences or published as papers over the years.

In addition, I must mention Louise Lennon, Robina McDermott and the late Lyn Burrows, all of whom helped me at one stage or another through the complexities of university bureaucratic procedure and whose administrative expertise facilitated the production of various drafts of the manuscript. Anthropologists Frances Claffey (who worked during the 1990s on the Djabugay native title claim) and Bruce White generously shared their insights and archival material with me at the height of my fieldwork.

Of course I also owe a great debt of gratitude to all the people in Kuranda who made my study possible. I thank sincerely all those who kindly gave of their time to talk to me, who provided me with documentary material, reports, photographs and newspaper clippings, and who were always willing to share a bit of village news. I am unable to name them all, but I particularly thank Brian Clarke, Eve Stafford, Gayle Hannah, Michael Quinn, Wendy Russell, Judy Andrews, Diane Moynahan, and the late Ritchie Trapnell, Jim Mealing, and Joan Dods.

For generously sharing their memories and also for facilitating my research with other Aboriginal people of Kuranda, I owe a special debt of gratitude to the late Lyn Hobbler, Marita Hobbler, Florence Williams, Selwyn Hunter, Steven and Mona Fagan, Ganger Snider, Lance Riley and Milton Brim. I thank Esther Snider, Joyce Riley, Carol Riley, Michelle Collins, Rhonda Duffin, Andy Duffin, Nola Donoghue, Flo Brim, Willie Brim, Winnie Brim, Rhonda Brim and all the Brim Family at Mantaka – in particular Sherry Ann Diamond, who took me under her wing.

I am grateful to my parents, brothers and sisters, and in-laws for all the help they gave me in Kuranda while I did my fieldwork, providing me with a network of contacts and keeping their eyes and ears open for me at times when I could not be there. I especially thank my sister Rosalie who provided me with accommodation and nurturing and spent many an evening with me lending her own insights into the people and place. Rosalie spent numerous hours helping me to transcribe taped interviews and in general acting as a most valuable research assistant. I am also especially grateful to my sister Rosemarie for her generous help over the years in photocopying material for me, providing me with contacts, and using her wonderful talents to draw the maps, as well as to my brother Ricardo for insights and archival materials on the Kuranda Amphitheatre.

Last, but of course not least, I thank Bob Henry and our children Roselani, Rurik and Rafaela. I thank Bob Henry for his absolutely unconditional love and steadfast support, for his unselfishness in slowing down his own career prospects to give me the opportunity to pursue mine, for supporting my freedom to choose my own way and for always being willing to compromise. I thank my children, source of comfort and joy, for making me feel that they were proud of me and never being resentful about the times I spent away from them either in the field or 'off the planet' while utterly engrossed in writing. Special thanks go to my son Rurik for preparing electronic copies of the maps in reproduction quality for this book.

I acknowledge the institutional support that I received from the Australian Institute of Aboriginal and Torres Strait Islander Studies (AIATSIS), which provided a grant for a small part of this study. James Cook University awarded several Merit Research Grants that made my fieldwork possible. A research fellowship at the Cairns Institute provided time and a quiet place for completion of the manuscript.

Portions of chapters 4, 6 and 7 in this book were published in journal articles (Henry 1994, 1998, 2000). These have been included courtesy of the *Australian Journal of Anthropology* and *Aboriginal History*.

❧ Introducing Place ❧

Fieldwork and Framework

The Kuranda Experience is a trilogy of the old, new and ancient,
a journey through time which begins at your doorstep and ends
in unforgettable memories.
                    —Tourist brochure, 'The Kuranda Experience', c. 1997

'Meet me at the bottom pub'. It was 1993 and I had telephoned to arrange
a meeting to discuss my research proposal with a person from the Kuranda
community. I had been advised by other townspeople to talk to her, as she
had a degree in anthropology and was said to know something about the
Aboriginal people of the area. I was keenly aware of the phenomenon of the
'white broker' as described by Collmann (1988) and that there were many
such brokers in Kuranda: non-Aboriginal people who competitively defined their own identities according to the relative length and depth of their
relationships with and knowledge of Aboriginal people. How would these
white interlocutors feel about my ethnographic study with 'their' people?
Would this woman see me as a competitor? By asking me to meet her at the
bottom pub, I felt she was testing me. How would I relate to the Aboriginal
patrons with whom she regularly drank and played pool in a side room attached to the main bar?

I have to admit that I did feel apprehensive, but this had nothing to do
with the woman or her Aboriginal friends. Rather, what worried me was
the culture of Australian pubs. It was a culture with which I was unfamiliar.
Would it be okay for me to order a glass of lemonade, since I do not particularly like alcohol? Should I offer to shout a round of drinks? What were
the rules of engagement?

In the end, the meeting with the woman and her Aboriginal friends went
well, perhaps partly because I quickly explained that my study was not going to be about any particular culture or sub-culture in isolation, but about
the town itself as a home-place. I stressed that I was just as much interested
in the various waves of European settlers as I was in the Aboriginal popula-

tion. One young woman in the group, eager to contribute to my research, informed me that while Djabugay was the tribe for Kuranda, more generally people called themselves Bama or Murri. She preferred to call herself a Murri, saying that Bama, which actually means 'the people', sounded too much like 'bummer'. She seemed taken with the idea that I was also going to focus my study on the *migaloos* (white people), who could be found mostly at the 'top pub', according to her. (The two hotels had names but locals referred to them in terms of their respective locations at the bottom and top ends of the town.)

Spatial Practices

This book presents the results of over ten years of intermittent fieldwork (very little of it in either of the pubs mentioned above) that followed that meeting at the bottom pub in Kuranda, a small town located in the hills above the city of Cairns in tropical northern Australia (see Map I.1). The ethnographic task I set myself was to explore how place is created through the spatial practices and public performances of protest and celebration by a people in intense socio-political engagement with one another.

At the time I began my research in 1993, Kuranda – also known as 'the village in the rainforest' – sat somewhat uncomfortably within the Mareeba Shire. The Mareeba Shire – which was, after my fieldwork was complete, amalgamated with neighbouring shires into the Tablelands Regional Shire – had an area of 52,585 square kilometres and a population of approximately 18,638.[1] Its economy is predominantly based on primary industry (beef and dairy cattle, tobacco, sugar, timber, mining, and fruits and vegetables, with orchard crops including mangoes, avocados and lychees), in contrast to Kuranda, where the major industry is tourism.

Australian ethnographies of rural towns by anthropologists are few (see for example Cowlishaw 1988, 2004; Merlan 1999; Babidge 2004, 2010). While anthropologists generally acknowledge that Aboriginal lifeworlds are constituted within the broader forces, structures and discursive practices of the Australian nation-state, at the local level most anthropologists have tended to focus their ethnographic attention specifically on the Aboriginal 'domain' (von Sturmer 1984). My aim in this book is to give equal attention to the deeply intertwined spatial practices of all people associated with Kuranda, both Aboriginal and non-Aboriginal, especially the settlers who arrived as part of the counterculture movement during the 1970s and 1980s.

I began fieldwork in Kuranda the year after the Australian Federal government passed the Native Title Act in response to the Australian high

Map I.1. Location Map.
Map drawn by Rurik Henry.

court decision in Mabo v. the State of Queensland (1992). The decision overturned the legal fiction that Australian lands had belonged to no one prior to European settlement. In the wake of the high court decision and the subsequent legislation, the Djabugay in Kuranda made an application (on 26 May 1994) for a determination that native title exists in the Barron Gorge National Park. This was the first native title claim in Australia over a national park. It was not until 17 December 2004, over ten years later, that the consent determination was finally made.[2] In this exciting time that promised dramatic change for Indigenous Australians, I wondered how people at the grassroots level in rural Australia were dealing with the idea of native title in relation to their hometowns. My research in Kuranda therefore turned to the dynamics of the relationship between people and place in the face of these legal and political changes and the state bureaucratic processes that were rapidly developing to deal with them.

Kuranda as 'the Field'

My connection with Kuranda goes back to my childhood, and members of my extended family have lived in the Kuranda area since the late 1970s. Both the spatial and temporal boundaries assumed in the anthropological concept of the field are here challenged. When, in such a situation, does fieldwork begin, and when could it possibly end?

Kuranda has been part of the world of my imagination since I was about five or six years old, when we lived in the Atherton tablelands and would regularly drive past the township to visit my grandparents in Cairns. I have vivid memories of travelling in the back of my father's old truck through the green tunnel of trees that enveloped the endlessly winding and stomach-churning single lane road down the range. This sensation of travelling through a green tunnel in order to get to or from Kuranda is one I have since found that I share with many local people. It is an important trope in the arrival stories of new settlers, and the preservation of this tunnel-like entrance and of the rainforest that surrounds Kuranda is a key issue of concern in planning disputes in the town.

I also remember many a railmotor (train) trip from the tablelands boarding school I attended during my high school years through the Barron Gorge to catch a flight from Cairns to Port Moresby, where my parents lived at that time. One of my friends at boarding school was from Kuranda. In our final year at school we would visit her family over the school holidays and her brothers would drive us to Cairns to go dancing at a nightclub called 'The House on the Hill'.

Kuranda was just a place I regularly passed through, yet it always held a fascination for me. As a child, I was drawn to the bewitching beauty of the waterfalls and the green fecundity of the rainforest, which I imagined to be a fantasy playground for fairies. As I grew older, it was the excitement presented by another world – the world of the hippies I saw lounging at the Kuranda railway station, mingling with Aboriginal people outside the post office and the Shell petrol station or hitchhiking to the beach and Cairns – that captivated me. I did not know then that Aboriginal Australians had long been the subject of many anthropological studies of Otherness. From the point of view of a teenage girl, it was the hippies who were the exotic Other. They represented not just localised primitive wilderness but the world outside, a somewhat dangerous, globalised and cosmopolitan world that offered an escape from parochial rural Australia and my repressive Catholic boarding school. By the 1970s, Kuranda had become a recognised destination along a global hippie trail, as well as a haven for the so-called counterculture. Eventually, even my own parents were to join the movement. With my eight younger brothers and sisters, they settled on a block of land at the edge of the rainforest, built a tin shed for a house, dug a pit toilet, cooked outside on a wood stove, used a battery operated television and solar power for lighting, planted fruit trees and a vegetable patch for subsistence, and sold their surplus at the Kuranda markets. But this all happened after I had left home to study anthropology at the Australian National University in Canberra and after I had already identified Kuranda as a potentially fruitful field site for future research.

Thus, while I did not officially begin fieldwork for this study until 1993, my ethnography is informed by a much longer history of connection with the town. Although I had never lived in the town, the fact that my parents and younger siblings had made it their home meant that I was considered a local. I had the trust of both the 1970s hippie settlers, whose experiences were similar to those of my family, and of the Aboriginal people who knew my parents and who were old school friends of my siblings, nieces and nephews. Therefore, my study could be classed as falling within the genre 'anthropology at home'.[3]

However, I did not see myself as going to Kuranda to study either an already defined place or a given category of people. Rather, I wanted to immerse myself in a field of sociality. The ethnographic task, as I see it, is to expose relationships and strategies of power by exploring the fields of sociality that give expression to them. The idea is not to start with a given totality or identity, whether real or conceptual, but to explore how such totalities (identities) are generated through performance and constituted through discourse so as to become materially powerful. I therefore see my research as an exploration of the 'articulatory practices'[4] which operate to partially 'fix' the Kuranda people/place nexus as 'an objective and closed system of differences' (Laclau & Mouffe 1985: 125). I have also argued elsewhere (Henry 1999) that doing fieldwork does not mean going to a particular geographical site. It means placing oneself in a field of sociality so as to enable one to understand how totalities come to be fixed as objective systems in the first place. Going into the field means we place ourselves within a 'situational field' (Van Velsen 1967; Gluckman 1971) and within a social network that allows us to more fully experience – and thus understand – the processes by which peoples and places are, in fact, made. My interest is in moments when social conflict and antagonism come to the fore because it is these moments that reveal the limits of how categorical identities can be fixed socially. It is in these moments that the self can be found in the other and the other in the self (Fuary 2000); and the other can be very close indeed: one's sibling, one's friend, one's spouse, one's neighbour.

Kuranda People

In terms of the population of Kuranda, the main categorical distinction that locals make is between Aboriginal and non-Aboriginal people.[5] However, I stress that although I use the terms Aboriginal and non-Aboriginal in this study (and indeed do compare and contrast Aboriginal and non-Aboriginal responses to particular issues), my project is not a culturalist exploration of two different value systems. Rather, my focus is the overall social situation in which, and through which, the oppositional categories of Aboriginal and non-Aboriginal are in fact constituted. The aim is to understand how categorical identities are produced and articulated, not to take them as given.

Non-Aboriginal residents of Kuranda tend to categorise themselves chronologically according to their length of residence and the values that brought them to settle in the area. There are the early settlers and their descendants who have lived in the area since the beginning of this century. There are the people who moved into the Kuranda region during the 1970s and 1980s – mostly from urban areas in the south of Australia and from Europe and America – in search of an alternative lifestyle. Then there are the more recently arrived residents who moved to Kuranda as a result of economic development and the growth of the tourist industry in Cairns. For some of these latter people, Kuranda is merely a dormitory suburb of Cairns. They work and play in Cairns and tend not to become involved in Kuranda activities. Others, however, particularly those who own businesses in Kuranda, have become big players in village politics.

In part, Aboriginal people categorise themselves and are categorised by others according to whether they are 'traditional owners' of the Kuranda area or 'historical people' displaced from their own tribal territories during the days of forced removal of Aboriginal people to reserves and missions. This distinction is made widely in Queensland and elsewhere in Australia. It is linked to contemporary land rights discourse as expressed in the Aboriginal Land Act of 1991 (Qld) and the Native Title Act of 1993 (Cwlth), which both make a distinction between traditional and historical association with land.[6] This distinction has been raised as a factor in a number of land disputes among Aboriginal people in Kuranda and elsewhere (see Finlayson 1997; Martin 1997; MacDonald 1997; and B. Smith 2000).

According to the 2001 Australian census, Kuranda has a total population of 1,456. About 15 per cent (214) of the town's population identified as 'Indigenous', which includes Aboriginal and Torres Strait Islander people (although only sixteen of these identified as Torres Strait Islander). However, as with the non-Indigenous population, those Indigenous people who identify with the town mostly live outside the town boundaries. Thus, the census figures for Kuranda represent only a portion of the people who identify with Kuranda as their place. Aboriginal people mostly live in small settlements along the Barron River at Kowrowa, Mantaka and Koah, as well as at the old Mona Mona mission site (Map I.2). On the basis of the number of Indigenous people counted in the census collection districts[7] in which these settlements are situated, the total Indigenous population relevant to my study is estimated to be 725 (of these, 61 identified as Torres Strait Islander). Non-Indigenous Kuranda people living outside the village are more widely spread than Indigenous people. They tend to live dispersed on rural properties or on acreages in rural-residential subdivisions. Some properties operate as tenancy-in-common or as group-title.

Taking into account the people who live outside the census collection district of Kuranda but who still associate themselves in one way or another with the town, I estimate the total population, significant in terms of my study, to be approximately 4,500. Yet there are many people involved in the making of Kuranda as a place who do not actually live there. Kuranda is not only made by its local residents, but also by the hundreds of thousands of tourists who arrive from all over the world each year, as well as the itinerant travellers and the network of so-called 'new agers' who turn up to squat, generally during the dry season.

Although many townspeople think of tourism as being a recent phenomenon, the town has been a well-known tourist destination since the turn of the century. Visitors came not only for the beauty of the rainforest environment but also to satisfy their curiosity regarding the Aboriginal people who were living in camps on the edges of Kuranda town until 1916, after which they were removed to the nearby Mona Mona mission. Erik Mjoberg (1918: 26), the Swedish entomologist who led a scientific expedition to Queensland in 1912–13, observed that Kuranda Aboriginal people were a curiosity to tourists who would 'visit their camps in order to buy for just a few coins, a boomerang, a woven basket or some similar object'. During the early twentieth century, the town became popular with adventurous honeymooners, who would travel up the Queensland coast by steamship and then to Kuranda by train to see the Barron Falls and go boating on the river or walking in the 'scrub', as the rainforest was then called. Other tourists came to Kuranda for the sake of the dramatic train journey past thun-

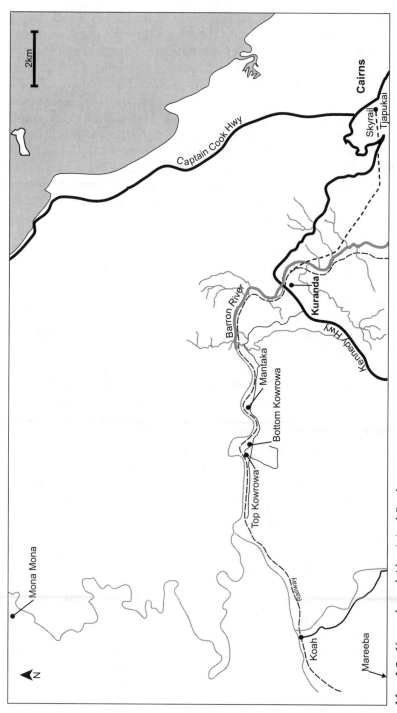

Map I.2. Kuranda and Aboriginal Settlements.
Map drawn by Rurik Henry.

dering waterfalls and through fifteen tunnels from Cairns to the Barron Gorge and beyond. During the 1950s, tourists were also encouraged to visit the Mona Mona mission as part of specially arranged bus tours in order to purchase arts and crafts produced for sale by the Aboriginal inmates.

The Village in the Rainforest

Kuranda has been marketed for tourists as 'the village in the rainforest' only since the late 1970s. This representation of the town as a village is significant in the Australian context, where even the smallest of country towns are not usually referred to as villages. The 'village in the rainforest' was partly a marketing ploy to attract tourists and partly a means by which new settlers to the area – refugees from the urban jungles of Australia and overseas – sought to redefine Kuranda as their home place. One could be tempted to argue that the village concept reflects their nostalgic search for some kind of Durkheimian *Gemeinshaft*. However, this would be too simplistic an explanation. Although, as Newton (1988: 55) notes, the counter-culture movement was heavily characterized by 'rural nostalgia', the village concept in Kuranda is an expression of a discourse that I suggest is best captured by the term 'rural cosmopolitanism'. While the village concept celebrates a notion of community and glorifies ideas of small-scale neigh-bourliness and homeliness, many of the 1970s and 1980s settlers dreamt of recreating Kuranda as a bohemian enclave in the fashion of the inner city villages of New York, London and Paris. The meaning that became at-tached to the concept of village in Kuranda exemplifies the way in which the global and the local actually assume and entail the existence of one an-other. The global is often defined in opposition to the local, but in fact only finds expression in the local. Similarly, while a cosmopolitan is thought to be a person of the world, a cosmopolitan identity is dependent on the exis-tence of local places.

While the village concept in Kuranda conceptually captures the global in the local, this rural cosmopolitanism – or rural bohemianism – masks an economic rationale. The marketing of Kuranda as a 'village' was also a strategic move on the part of the Kuranda Chamber of Commerce; and the village concept in Kuranda cannot be fully understood without a consid-eration of the essential role that business and attempts to capture the ever elusive tourist dollar play in the town.[8] In the wake of the tourists came de-velopers, entrepreneurs and other business people wishing to benefit from the industry. This book reveals how the townspeople confronted both one another and outsiders in their attempts to make and keep Kuranda as a home place.

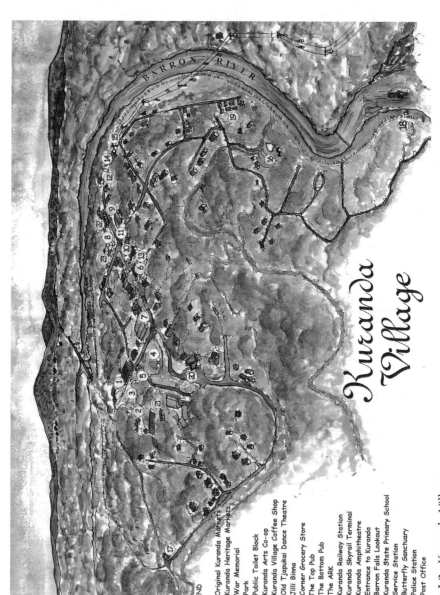

LEGEND

1. Original Kuranda Markers
2. Kuranda Heritage Markets
3. War Memorial
4. Park
5. Public Toilet Block
6. Kuranda Arts Co-op
7. Kuranda Village Coffee Shop
8. Old Tjapukai Dance Theatre
9. Jilli Binna
10. Corner Grocery Store
11. The Top Pub
12. The Bottom Pub
13. The ARK
14. Kuranda Railway Station
15. Kuranda Skyrail Terminal
16. Kuranda Amphitheatre
17. Entrance to Kuranda
18. Barron Falls Lookout
19. Kuranda State Primary School
20. Service Station
21. Butterfly Sanctuary
22. Police Station
23. Post Office

Map I.3. Kuranda Village.

Adapted from a watercolor by Rosemarie Rusch.

Social Dramas

The core of the book is presented in the form of a series of connected case studies, focusing on key 'hot spots' of social conflict in the town. These include an open air community performance venue, the local tourist market, the main street, a cable car route through a national park and a World Heritage listed area, and an Aboriginal dance theatre and cultural centre (Map I.3). The term 'hot spot' has been widely used with reference to areas and situations that have a concentration of crime and fear (Nasar & Fisher 1993: 187). I use it simply to convey the idea that competing discourses – local, national and global – concentrate at certain sites that then become the focus for political practice. I focus on those social dramas in Kuranda that generate moments of transformation from everyday practice to performance, since, I argue, it is in these transformative moments that identity politics comes to the fore. One of my key questions is how and why everyday political practice comes to be transformed into performances of cultural identity and difference. I argue that it is through the detailed examination of situated moments of transformation from practice to performance that the *substance* of identity politics can best be understood. In particular, my study focuses on issues of dispute in Kuranda regarding the planning and use of public space. I should make it clear at this point that the presentation of events and issues covered is selective. Although I have quoted extensively in an effort to present the views of Kuranda people as fairly as possible, my own editorial hand is obviously present in the overall pattern of presentation and in determining which dramas to cover and which voices to include. I suspect that some townspeople will object to the way I have represented particular issues. My project is not to tell the 'true' story of Kuranda, but rather to try to understand what the many and varied stories about Kuranda mean in terms of how identity categories are made and how community is envisioned.

I acknowledge and trace my approach to the influence of Turner's (1996 [1957]) concept of social drama and the extended case study method developed under the auspices of the Manchester School of Anthropology. This method has been discussed in some detail by Van Velsen (1964, 1967), who prefers to call it 'situational analysis'. Such case studies are not just a particular way of presenting ethnographic data; in themselves they provide a means of theorising the social. They do not simply provide illustration for more general abstractions; they are 'a constituent part of the analysis' (Van Velsen 1967: 140). The seeds of this type of analysis were sown by Gluckman (1971 [1940]) in his *Analysis of a Social Situation in Modern Zululand,* and grew into fruition in landmark ethnographies by Mitchell

(1956) on the Yao and Turner (1996 [1957]) on the Ndembu. Their focus on particular cases of dispute (or rather on a series of cases) within the villages they chose to study sprang from dissatisfaction with British structuralism. Yet they did not depart entirely from the idea of structure. As Van Velsen (1967: 141) puts it: 'We seek to relate the deviations from structural regularities to regularities of a different order, namely the interpretation of a social system in terms of conflicting norms.' This is where my analysis differs from theirs. I do not use the extended case study method and situational analysis in order to study either the relationship between behaviour and norms or the deviation of practice from structure. My case studies are not about 'norms in conflict' (Van Velsen 1967: 146) because they do not rest on any notion of norms as *a priori*. Rather, they are about practices of place and performances of identity as creative acts in themselves, both constitutive and challenging of structure. The situations I discuss are not simply assumed to occur *within* places, as in the Manchester School, but to be constitutive of them as well. My case studies are literally situational analyses because they are about the practices and performances that allow people to *situate* themselves in relation to one another *through* place, but within a social field of global interconnection. One of the fundamental aims of my study is to tackle the problem of understanding the relationship between local situations and wider political and economic contexts, including 'the rise of the network society' (Castells 1996). As Grewal and Kaplan (1994: 11) note, 'the parameters of the local and the global are often indefinite or indistinct – they are permeable constructs. How one separates the local from the global is difficult to decide when each thoroughly infiltrates the other'.

The Concept of Place

Edward Casey (1997) demonstrates how place came to be increasingly ignored in favour of space in Western philosophical thought. He attributes the demotion of place to the speculations of Newton, Descartes and others 'for all of whom space was conceived as continuous extension in length, breath, and width and, thus, as mappable by the three-dimensional co-ordinate system of rational geometry' (Casey 1997: 185). Places came to be conceived of as spatial sites and therefore as mere positions relative to one another. However, a renewed interest in place as *lived* experience surfaced in the writings of Merleau-Ponty, Heidegger and others. This renewed focus on place is based on the recognition of the capacity, both cognitive and corporeal, of human beings to constitute their own lifeworlds and to produce their own 'social space' (Lefebvre 1991). It is this capacity that I explore in this book.

Many fascinating analyses of Aboriginal Australian concepts of space and place and of time and temporality have been produced (e.g. Munn 1970, 1973; Myers 1986; Glowczewski 1989; Swain 1993; Rumsey and Weiner 2001). However, few ethnographers have focused on how concepts of and relationships to place are created and transformed in sites where Aboriginal practices of everyday life become utterly entangled with those of settler Australians and others. As Merlan (1999: 77) puts it, 'contemporary spatial practices, ways of living in place that are vitally relevant to its ongoing construction, [remain] insufficiently examined'.

Among others, Austin-Broos (2009), Babidge (2004, 2010), Rowse (1998), Povinelli (1993, 2002), Trigger (1992), Morris (1989), Collman (1988), and Sansom (1980) provide excellent studies of local and regional expressions of the dialectical engagement between Aboriginal peoples and the state. Strang (1997) compares and contrasts the place values and environmental ethics of Aboriginal people and pastoralists in Cape York. Finlayson (1991) examines Aboriginal families and households in Kuranda and how people harness the labour of white interlocutors or 'bosses' as a means of interfacing with settler society. Merlan (1999) considers transformations in the spatial practices of Aboriginal people in the town of Katherine in the Northern Territory, and Cowlishaw (1988, 2004) has addressed such issues in relation to the town of Bourke in New South Wales, as well as more recently in the western suburbs of Sydney (Cowlishaw 2009). Nevertheless, more of a balance is required in ethnographic description to account for the everyday practices and performances of non-Indigenous Australians in relation to the places that Indigenous people *share* with them.[9] Therefore, much of my study focuses on the spatial practices of the various waves of settlers in the Kuranda area. Through their spatial practices, these settlers created the networks of 'relatedness' that enabled them to imagine place as an encompassing local 'community'.

Spatial Practices and Performances

Anthropologists and other scholars have found it useful to investigate many different types of human activity in terms of performance. I use the term performance very generally to embrace events that are to various degrees planned and rehearsed before being presented. These include community meetings, protest demonstrations and marches, busking and street theatre, festivals, and sports matches, as well as community theatre productions, dance and music concerts, and ritual performances. The concept of frame – introduced by Bateson (1955) in his essay 'A Theory of Play and Fantasy' and adopted by Goffman (1974) – has been applied in the interdisciplinary field of performance studies to define performance as a mode of being that is distinct from everyday practice. Yet, as I reveal in the following chapters, in certain contexts the performative mode appears to dominate the very practice of everyday life.

It has been argued that what distinguishes performance from everyday practice is consciousness – in other words, that performance is a self-conscious activity. As Blau (1990: 250) writes, 'What is universal in performance ... are the marks of punctuation which are inflections (or economic indices) of *consciousness* even in performance which, like autistic play, speaking in tongues, or Sufi whirling, seems to occur without it.' The consciousness of practice that leads to performance, however, need not take the form either of a cognitive awareness of practice or of a situation reflected upon and explained through the use of language. Consciousness is also a particular orientation of the body in the world (Kapferer 1997: 222) fed by body memory and place memory. Consciousness does not necessarily refer merely to the cognitive awareness of the particular practice one may be performing at any given moment, but also to a bodily recognition of being *in connection* with a place and *in relationship* with others in that place.

In the process of their practices and performances, people bestow agency on places, so much so that they come to experience those places as inherently powerful and materially determinative of collective identity. This idea of identity in place I link to Heidegger's (1971) concept of dwelling (as explicated in his lecture-essay 'Building, Dwelling, Thinking') and Bachelard's (1969) notion of 'intense inhabitation'. Place-making is a practice of being-in-the world. Heidegger (1973) explores this concept as *Dasein* (human being as a 'there-being') in *Being and Time*. As Kule (1997: 102) observes, 'It is obvious that Heidegger's principal term *Dasein* incorporates this idea of belonging to place.' *Dasein* is not something that is already given, but is rather an existential possibility articulated through dwelling. To dwell is also to 'build', meaning not simply to construct something, but also to care for and cherish it. It is through dwelling that we make places. Heidegger (1971: 157) elaborates this idea as follows: 'To say that mortals "are" is to say that "in dwelling" they persist through spaces by virtue of their stay among things and locations. ... The relationship between man and space is none other than dwelling.' In other words, we make space significant by 'dwelling', by building, by investing time in it, so that it ceases to be space. Space is transformed into place by dwelling. Yet, what does dwelling entail? How do we dwell? I stress that dwelling can be nothing but human *social* engagement, and as much as it evokes notions of 'caring' and 'heeding', such engagement or being-in-the-world inevitably generates situations of social conflict in which the tensions and contradictions of identity politics come to the fore.

Identity and Difference

Collective identity is sometimes treated as a simple matter of free choice from a given corpus of traits, rather than as a dynamic and continuous process that is subject to structural constraints. In its contemporary use, the term 'identity' tends to be used to refer to characteristics that mark boundaries so as to create categories of difference. However, as Moore (1994: 2) writes, 'Identity and difference are not so much about categorical groupings as about processes of identification and differentiation. These processes are engaged for all of us, in different ways, with the desire to belong, to be part of some community, however provisional.' The social dramas I explore in Kuranda reveal that the very idea of 'community' itself generates social conflict. Kuranda people attempt to deal with difference by enveloping it or encompassing it in the sameness of community. Yet, these very strategies of power and practices of encompassment actually work to reproduce difference. Such processes of identification and differentiation can only be understood as historical processes; they are not divorced from the social situation or from the political and economic circumstances and modes of power which generate them.

Although both Aboriginal and non-Aboriginal people in Kuranda perceive Kuranda as a town relatively free of racial division, racialism is deeply imbedded in its history. Kuranda people represent their town as being harmonious in terms of race relations in contrast to other Australian places, and they work to make it so through various performance strategies. They attribute this harmony to the values and practices of the so called 'hippies', the new settlers of the 1970s and 1980s who identified with the global counterculture movement. This idea is celebrated in the documentary film *My Place, My Land, My People: People of Kuranda,* directed and produced by Mark Eliot (1989). The documentary features Aboriginal performer David Hudson, who states: 'Kuranda, the way white and black mix, it could be an example to other communities in Australia or throughout the world.' In the film, Kuranda is represented as a place where 'everybody works in harmony', where people are 'more open minded' and 'more accepting', and where there is 'an easier mix'. In this book I do not set out either to prove or disprove 'the truth' of such representations of Kuranda. Rather, my task is to show how, through their practices and performances, the townspeople work to create such representations and to cultivate Kuranda as a 'magic' place, benign and racially harmonious.

Kuranda Histories

Most Kuranda people readily direct anyone making inquiries regarding the history of the town to the Australian bicentennial publication *Kuranda: The Village in the Rainforest, 1888–1988* (Humston 1988). I visited many a Kuranda home in the course of my fieldwork and was continually referred to this book. Descendants of early settlers would bring it out and establish their authenticity by pointing with pride to the photographs and names of their forebears set in ink for all to see. In the typical form that local histories take, the book begins with a discussion on the origin of the name Kuranda, followed by a section on the physical environment and climate. This is followed by a chapter on the Djabugay people, the 'traditional rainforest Aborigines of the Kuranda area'. Here we see reprinted the relevant section from the anthropologist Norman Tindale's (1974) map of tribal boundaries in Australia and some photographs of items of material culture (huts, baskets, swords, shields). Also included, from the *North Queensland Naturalist*, is a paper by Douglas Seaton (1957) entitled 'The Initiation Ceremony of the Tjapukai Tribe'. In the second section of the book, Humston lists 'events around Kuranda before the first survey' in 1888. Among them are: the foundation of Cairns in 1876; the building of a road up the range suitable for dray traffic in 1877; the spearing of travellers and packers by Aboriginal people; a list of selectors who took up land in the area; the construction of different stages of the railway; and the opening of the first hotel. Other sections of the book concern the building of the railway line and the schools, the development of early industries such as timber, coffee, and tourism, a history of Mona Mona (the mission station to which Aboriginal people were removed under government legislation), and the impact of the World Wars. Although it recognises a prior and continuing Aboriginal presence in the Kuranda area, the book is primarily a celebration and legitimation of the history of white settlement.

Other publications on the history of the Kuranda area focus on the achievements of the early explorers' charting of tracks through the mountain range to the coast and the prospectors' discovery of gold and tin to the west; the establishment of timber industry; the building of the range road and the construction of the railway line from Cairns through Kuranda to the tablelands and beyond; the Barron Falls hydro-electric scheme; and the trials and tribulations of the settlers in establishing plantations, farms and stations (see, for example, Broughton 1991; Pike 1984).

Apart from these local histories, there are also reputable histories of North Queensland by scholars such as Bolton (1963). These accounts represent a history of economic development, of engineering feats, and of the construction of buildings, bridges, roads and railways. They celebrate origins and progress, 'man against nature' and the 'taming of the wild'. Such accounts are in general based on primary documentary sources that include government records such as the reports of the various Protectors of Aboriginals, as well as the diaries of explorers and other travellers and early newspaper reports. These primary sources portray Aboriginal people not only as a 'people without history' (Wolf 1982) but also as a people who, rather than *make* history themselves, have history *made for* them. Aboriginal people remain voiceless in these primary documents, their experiences blanketed by the all-powerful written word of colonial bureaucrats and lawmakers.

However, more recently there has been a trend among historians to make Aboriginal people present in their writings. For example, excellent histories of Aboriginal-European relations in the region have been produced by Loos (1982), May (1994), Reynolds (1982, 1987), and Bottoms (1999). Noel Loos (1982) addresses the issue by specifically searching the archives for evidence of Aboriginal resistance. His focus on resistance is based on his recognition that Aboriginal people expressed their own agency in the face of European invasion. Loos's work is a politically important resistance work in itself, and it must be read in the light of the fight against the discourse of *terra nullius* in the lead up to the Mabo decision (Mabo v. State of Queensland 1992) and the subsequent recognition of native title in Australia. Evidence of Aboriginal resistance to European colonisation implies a customary law of trespass and property rights in land.

Bottoms (1990, 1992, 1993, 1999) addresses the issue of inclusion of by liberally peppering his texts with Djabugay words and place names. Such a technique has recently become popular as a means of writing Aboriginal people into history and granting them a voice. Bottoms (1999) worked closely with Djabugay people to write his book *Djabugay Country: An Aboriginal History of Tropical North Queensland,* which is based on archival sources as well as on oral history. Its publication is authorised by members of the Djabugay elders group, whose signatures appear in the foreword.

History grants primacy to the written text, or more generally to an archive of material signs. Yet the repository of social memory is not just the texts and the material deposits. This is just one kind of transmission across time. Oral transmission of 'narrative knowledge' is another kind. There are also other ways of remembering that are not granted a hearing by the dominant discourse about what counts as knowledge.[10] Edward Casey (1987) distinguishes these 'mnemonic modes' as different forms of recollection – 'reminding', 'reminiscing', and 'recognizing', as well as 'body memory' and 'place memory' – which are 'beyond the confinement of the mind considered as the exclusive receptacle of remembering' (Casey 1987: 141). My analyses of social dramas in Kuranda and my discussion of various performances associated with key places in the town address these different 'mnemonic forms'. I liberally include throughout this book transcribed extracts of recollections that I recorded during field interviews with Kuranda people. My aim is to convey the flavour of the ways in which people reminisce about events in their lives, the turns of phrase they use to map their life journeys and voice their connections to place. These narratives are themselves a kind of spatial practice; they are 'spatial stories' that crystallise time in place. They 'carry out a labor that constantly transforms places into spaces or spaces into places' (de Certeau 1984: 118).

Narratives of Place

When I asked older residents of Kuranda what they knew about the settlement history of the area, their immediate response was to recall where particular buildings were located and who lived where. Their accounts were narrative maps of how the townscape has changed and about the flow of movements in, out and through this townscape. They expressed how difficult travelling used to be, telling stories of trips up and down the range by horse and dray, by car or by train, and of big wet seasons when the range was closed and it was impossible to get down to Cairns. People recalled – not just for me as ethnographer, but among themselves – images of the townscape and landscape and of their bodily experiences of being there. They related stories of dramatic accidental deaths in the community: someone killed when the bridge collapsed, a woman burned to death when her dress caught fire, a drowning in the Barron River, a suicide attempt in the Barron Gorge. Some of the more recent settlers who arrived during the 1970s and 1980s as hippies or alternative lifestylers enthusiastically related origin stories: how they first arrived in Kuranda, how they built their houses, and how they cultivated social relations with others in the town. They also readily told stories of their direct experiences of state power, stories of police drug raids and harassment by the shire council.

Mission Days

Aboriginal people responded to my questions by conveying an intimate knowledge of the changing townscape and of settlers' spatial practices. With older people, however, the focus of discussions tended to return again and again to accounts of life at Mona Mona mission. These stories were tinged with nostalgia and a yearning to return. Older residents mostly reminisced about growing up on the mission, including stories of the dormitory days and their memories of the 'old people', their parents and grandparents, who were living in camps on the mission and who were permitted to visit them only on Sundays. They fondly remembered hunting and fishing trips, treks across the range to the sea, holiday camps on the Barron River, rodeos on the mission, the Mona Mona rugby team and the brass band. Another common topic was the work experiences the people at the mission had as bakers, cooks, farm hands, timber cutters and millers, as well as outside in the forestry industry, on the railways, and as domestic labourers. People remembered how hard they worked and how little they received in return, as well as how the mission controlled access to their wages and allocated their spending money. They talked about living 'under the Act'[11], and those who had received exemptions from the legislative provisions readily produced their passes as proof of the regime.

Although there were recollections of cruelty and hardship, the days at the Mona Mona mission were remembered with wistful fondness. Few people who grew up on the mission expressed any bitterness they had harboured for wrongs done to them during the mission period. Such feelings tended to be more often articulated by members of the younger generation, many of whom never experienced mission life first hand. Younger people today think of themselves as the product of this history and as still suffering because of it. Since the closure of the mission in 1962, there has been continuing discussion and debate among Aboriginal people in Kuranda regarding mission life. The debate became public in 1996 when a woman who had grown up on Mona Mona revealed to a journalist from the *Cairns Post* (31 October 1996: 1–2) her experiences of disciplinary measures used by the missionaries. Her accusations against the missionaries created a furore among other people who had grown up on the mission. She claimed that she had witnessed public floggings and that as punishment for alleged misbehaviour her front teeth were forcibly extracted, her head was shaved, and she was forced to wear a sack to church over her bare skin. She also said that she had often been hungry, was regularly caned, and was locked in the community jail along with other children when she tried to run away. Other Mona Mona people were distressed that she had allowed this account of her experiences of mission life to be published. Her claims that the missionaries had treated Aboriginal people with 'extreme cruelty' were rejected in particular by many of the older residents, two of whom contacted the *Cairns Post* with a reply that was published the following day (1 November 1996: 2): 'Kuranda Aboriginal elders yesterday said disciplinary measures used by church missionaries at Mona Mona in the 1950s and 60s may have been severe, but they taught their people to respect the law … The elders spoke out yesterday after [a] former Mona Mona resident … claimed she had suffered extreme cruelty as a child at the hands of the missionaries.' One of the elders told me that some of the forms of discipline this former resident claimed to have experienced had indeed been practiced, but 'only in the very early days' of the mission.[12] She said that the woman had not experienced these punishments first hand but had constructed her account for the journalist from stories she had overheard her elders tell. Extraction of teeth, she argued, had never been carried out as a form of punishment, but only for genuine dental health purposes.[13] Yet the woman was not necessarily lying when she reported these experiences as her own. Her account might be interpreted as a traumatic memory of violence embodied through intergenerational transfer. Importantly, this debate reminds us that 'remembering is oriented not to the past, but to coming to terms with the past in a present that is continuously troubled by it' (Argenti and Schramm 2010: 17).

The disagreement about the oppressive nature of the disciplinary practices of the missionaries also reveals tensions among Aboriginal people concerning ideas of complicity and resistance. There is much concern, among younger people in particular, that the elders have been 'brainwashed' and that they do not recognise their own oppression. In Foucauldian terms, they see the elders as complicit in their own domination by their 'docility', caused by the 'disciplinary blockade' of the mission. One young man told me that in his view, many of the elders had been 'blocked' from seeing that they were treated badly during the mission days and that they continue to be oppressed today. Yet docility and resistance are not fixed or diametrically opposed ways of being in the world. Resistance and docility flow into one another. People who grew up on the mission have memories of the institution that are both happy and painful. The tension between docility and resistance is not just a tension between different people, or between categories of people. Individuals embody both docility and resistance simultaneously, and in their lives they have to deal on a daily basis with the ambivalent experience of being subjects of both power *and* autonomy.

Round-ups and Massacres

As well as reminiscences of life on the Mona Mona mission, Aboriginal people also recount narratives about 'round-ups' and 'massacres'. Such narratives are qualitatively different from the quasi-narrative reminiscences about the changing townscape. This narrative structure of massacre stories – together with the recognition that these stories are owned by particular families or are attached to people with the right to tell the story – marks their significance as part of a body of cultural knowledge for which Aboriginal people seek recognition as having a truth-value equivalent to written historical records. People whose ancestors were among those rounded up in the Kuranda area to be taken to the mission retell the stories the elders told them about places they used to hide,[14] about the violence of the police, and about the massacres of Aboriginal people by white settlers. Collins (1981: 20) was told the following story by Cecil Brim:

> The policeman (from Kuranda) came up there (Speewah). We were well known to him. Some people used to run away from the policeman. They didn't want to go to the mission in those days. The policeman caught us and we walked from there to Kuranda. We saw all the dilly bags and spears at the police station that the people had to leave behind. We then went up to the mission and saw our mob there and we started to talk language ...

Cecil Brim also told his eldest daughter, Marita, about how her ancestors were taken from Speewah to the mission. Other members of the Brim family know of the Speewah 'round up', but it was Marita to whom I was referred for oral history accounts of their family history before the mission days. Marita recounted a narrative passed on to her by her mother who had been 'kidnapped' by a policeman from a camp at Mt Carbine and taken to the Mona Mona mission. Her mother's father was a white man. He knew where she was camped, and came there one day with a 'black tracker' while the adults were away from the camp and only the children were home. The children had been told to hide from strangers. According to Marita, the policeman first called out and then set fire to the camp in order to make the children reveal themselves. The police took her mother because she was considered 'half-caste' and it was the practice to remove such children from Aboriginal influence. As Marita reasoned:

> My mother was half-caste, fair-skinned. In those days the mission was really the place for all the half-caste children. They said they had white man's brains and the government thought they might turn against them or something and they took them all off their parents (Marita Hobbler, pers. comm. 4 January 1995).

The recording of such accounts of round-ups and massacres are important to Aboriginal people in Kuranda not only because they tell 'their side' of the history of European settlement, but because they have contemporary currency in helping to establish rights to land. Through a politics of memory, people place themselves and thus contest the relations of power and domination that they experience and that determine the truth-value of the histories currently in operation. Massacre and round-up stories as a genre are part of a discourse of identity that celebrates Aboriginality on the basis of a shared experience of violence.[15] Another example of such a narrative is the massacre story based on the memories of Granny Buttercup, which is today told in the film screened for tourists in the history theatre at the Tjapukai

Aboriginal Cultural Park. In their narratives and reminiscences, Aboriginal people that I talked to in Kuranda generally framed their experiences in terms of a wider context of relatedness to one another and collective experiences of being in a 'state of domination' (Foucault 1988b:19).

The Politics of Memory

The politics of memory, as it plays out in Kuranda, expresses itself partly in terms of a conflict between history as a factual record of a given past and other forms of evidence of the connection between people and place. In *An Explorer's Guide to Kuranda*, a small booklet published for tourists, Ron and Anne Edwards (1994: 1) note that 'Kuranda does not have a great deal of history. It has plenty of gossip, in fact gossip is one of the town's main activities, but there is very little history.' Whether the authors were aware of it or not, this statement addresses an important issue of debate within the social sciences: What is history, and how is it different from other discourses about the past? How is history distinguished from gossip, and what is the relationship between the two? History carries an authenticity that is not granted to gossip. History assumes truth-value and social recognition as factual reality. It is thought of as being a record of a given real past, whereas gossip is thought of as an ongoing construction, an invention of the past motivated by interested human action.

Memory, similarly, is thought to be by definition 'a personal activity, subject to the biases, quirks, and rhythms of the individual's mind' (O'Meally and Fabre 1994: 5). This 'helter-skelter and dreamy impressionism of human memory' is not granted the same authority as is history with its events linearly ordered in time. It is not difficult to provide a list of defining features that distinguish history from memory. What is more interesting and important, however, is how the distinction between these two is *made*. History is given its authority over memory by the social recognition granted to it as objectively recorded reality. How is the truth-value of history *produced*?

The concept of history has been problematised by a number of social thinkers, including historians (see, for example, White 1973). Key issues that have been raised – and that continue to be debated – include epistemological questions regarding truth and objectivity, the relationship between history and human consciousness, the nature of 'events' and the link between disparate events, the relativity of historical knowledge, and the distinction between history and myth. With regard to the question of truth and objectivity, for example, Levi-Strauss (1966: 257) pointed out in *The Savage Mind* that 'historical facts are no more *given* than any other. It is the historian, or the agent of history, who constitutes them by abstraction'.

The distinction between myth and history has been addressed in connection with anthropological analyses of Aboriginal Australian narratives of colonial encounters (see for example Morphy & Morphy 1984; Rose 1984, 1994; Sutton 1988; Maddock 1988; Merlan 1994; Austin-Broos 1994, 2009; Beckett 1994; and Kolig 1995, 2000). Disregarding the finer definitional points in this debate, the emergence of the 'myth-history antinomy' (Merlan 1994: 151) as an issue for anthropologists is based on a questioning of the notion of a totalising History. This questioning has led to 'an awareness of the negotiability of history' and a recognition that 'narrative histories' are 'never, simply, factual accounts' (Austin-Broos 1994: 133, 136).

There has been a recent upsurge of interest in Indigenous history in Australia following public debate among historians and others concerning the truth-value of histories about European invasion and its consequences for the Indigenous population (see for example Attwood and Foster 2003). In what have become known as the 'history wars', Australian public intellectuals have responded to conservative historian Keith Windschuttle (2002), whose views echo anxieties among white Australians about the origin myth of frontier settlement as the basis of Australian nationhood, as well as about government policies concerning immigration, Aboriginal land rights and multiculturalism. However, it is not only the relationship between Indigenous peoples and settlers during the early colonial period that is fiercely contested, but also the very relationship between past and present. In seeking to explain social conditions in Aboriginal communities in the late twentieth and early twenty-first century, scholars continue to debate the causative relevance of colonial history (see Pearson 2000; Martin 2001; Sutton 2001, 2009). For example, Aboriginal scholar Noel Pearson (2000: 146) questions the taken-for-granted view that 'Aboriginal social problems' are but a legacy of a history of 'racism, dispossession and trauma' and argues that they are a factor of more recent government welfare policies.

Shaping the Past

Much has been written on the idea of the past as constructed in the present and of tradition and/or history as 'invented' (e.g. Herzfeld 1982; Hobsbawm & Ranger 1983; Handler & Linnekin 1984; Friedman 1992a, 1992b; Haley & Wilcoxon 1997). It is important to remember that while historical 'events' are constructed retrospectively, this does not mean that the phenomena we take as the substance for the events we construct did not have some real occurrence and material impact on people's lives. Moreover, such phenomena continue to be part of the reality of lived experience, for as Laclau & Mouffe (1985: 96) write, 'a discursive structure is not a merely "cognitive" or "contemplative" entity; it is an *articulatory practice* which constitutes and organises social relations'. Historical representation is grounded in people's shared experiences of events. Thus, I do not subscribe to a relativist perspective that renders all event-constructions equivalent. After all, 'history is itself a mode of demonstrating the relativity, temporariness, and temporality of phenomena' (White (1973: 79). To this I would also add the *spatiality* of phenomena. As Ulin (1995: 526) writes: 'Not all discourses of an imagined and relativised past have an equal chance of being advanced and recognised as authoritative. ... The effort to gain recognition for an interpretation of the past involves a political struggle for self-identity and mutual recognition that should not be trivialised by a postmodern equivalence of discourses'. The social dramas in Kuranda explored in this book reveal that not only is the *substance* of interpretations of the past contested, but there is also a question as to which interpretations should be granted discursive authority. In these dramas, protagonists struggle for the truth-value of their own histories to be recognized. The different narratives about the relationship between the past and the present, as elsewhere in Australia, are hotly contested as both Indigenous and settler Australians 'seek to appropriate their power' (Attwood and Magowan 2001: xi).

The Structure of the Book

In *The Order of Things* (1970), Foucault argued that his investigations are understandings of the present, as opposed to explanations of the past. They are concerned with the descent (*Herkunft*) as opposed to the origin (*Ursprung*) of practices (Foucault 1988a: 140, 145). Foucault calls his approach to history a 'micro-physics of power' (1977: 139), and it is with this approach to history in mind that I write the first chapter of this book. My task is to make present practices and social dramas in Kuranda intelligible by tracing their descent. I rely not only on primary and secondary documentary sources, but also on the 'narrative knowledge' and recollections of Kuranda residents since, as Taussig (1992: 163) notes, it is in 'the coils of rumour, gossip, story, and chitchat where ideology and ideas become emotionally powerful and enter into active social circulation and meaningful existence'. However, narrative knowledge is not just a matter of words and of representation, but also of practice, as expressed through bodily actions, habitus, and performance.

In Chapter 1, I trace the transformation of the lifeworld of Aboriginal people in the Kuranda area through European colonisation. I discuss the colonising and disciplinary practices that were and continue to be directed at an erasure of place memory. I argue that such practices in effect operated to mutilate memory[16], so as to make Aboriginal people subjects in a state of domination, or 'docile bodies' (Foucault 1977: 135). In other words, the mission worked as an instrument of both corporeal and 'symbolic' violence in an attempt to generate a new Aboriginal habitus (Bourdieu 1990: 53).

I move on, in Chapter 2, to consider the second wave of European settlement in the Kuranda area, which began in the late 1960s and continued throughout the seventies and into the early eighties. I discuss the context of the arrival of these new settlers, as well as the relationships they developed with the established residents of the area, both the older settlers and the Indigenous people. I examine the practices these new settlers – some of whom were then called 'hippies', 'hairies', 'counter-culturists', or 'alternative lifestylers', among other less complimentary names – used to construct place. Emplacement for these people was, I argue, the freedom to practice individual autonomy within the embrace of a particular concept of community. In order to reveal the political and historical conditions for this practice, I examine the relationship the settlers had with the local shire council regarding building regulations and alternative land tenure arrangements (such as tenancy-in-common and group title). I explore the responses of Aboriginal people and the already established settlers to the place-making activities of these new settlers.

The next chapters of the book constitute a series of linked case studies, or situational analyses, of social dramas connected with particular places in, or associated with, Kuranda. I analyse these social situations in terms of performances that address tensions between identity and difference as well as place and product. The first of my case studies, Chapter 3, focuses on the construction of a community performance venue, the Kuranda Amphitheatre. I analyse this social situation in terms of two types of performances associated with the amphitheatre – performances produced specifically for the stage and social dramas generated beyond the stage – through both of which people attempted to place themselves in relation to others in the town.

In Chapter 4, I focus on disputes regarding the village marketplace as another hot spot of contested identity in Kuranda. I trace the metamorphosis of the markets from periodic community events – ones run by 'hippies' who existed outside of a monetary economy – to the key privately owned tourist attraction in the town. The social dramas associated with the development of the Kuranda tourist markets reveal the tensions that arose between the hippies' attempts to make Kuranda their own and the forces of commodification already established in the town. The changes in the markets articulate political and economic forces that Kuranda people experience as originating on the outside, in the global realm, and that they attempt to accommodate as well as to resist. In chapter 5, I explore processes of town planning and management in Kuranda by relating a series of disputes that arose in relation to the main street and the development of the town as a tourist village. Through such explanation, I reveal how place becomes an ongoing and dynamic agent in a politics of memory through which people make and remake themselves as social beings and negotiate the future of their home town. Planning, however, is also a form of disciplinary practice. While demonstrated engagement in strategic planning people allows people to achieve recognition of their claims, this very process draws them further into the structure of state governmentality. Ironically, Kuranda townspeople, both Aboriginal and non-Aboriginal, have found themselves increasingly swept into this disciplinary process in their attempts to achieve some autonomy of control over their placeworlds.

Chapter 6 focuses on the connection between performance and identity politics in the context of the Tjapukai Aboriginal Dance Theatre in Kuranda and its development into the Tjapukai Aboriginal Cultural Park in Cairns. I discuss the strategies and relationships of power that gave birth to this tourist attraction, as well as the cultural performances by means of which Aboriginal people both accommodate themselves to categorical identities and redefine themselves within a political context that demands that they establish their authenticity in terms of cultural continuity. These performances became an opportunity for Aboriginal people to challenge the paradigm that requires cultural continuity to be established and evidenced through the rules of classical customary law in order to achieve state recognition of native title. Dance and other performances assert the embodied nature of culture and glorify the forms of remembering that this paradigm neglects. I refer here to what Casey (1987: 147) has termed 'body memory … how we remember in and by and through the body'. Because cultural performances emphasise this embodied acquisition of culture, Aboriginal people use them to assert the continuity of connection to place that is otherwise denied them.

In Chapter 7, I explore the articulation of different Aboriginal and non-Aboriginal responses to a tourist development: the Skyrail, a cable car from the bottom of the range to Kuranda through the Barron Gorge National Park and Wet Tropics World Heritage Area. I focus on a particular moment of protest action within the Skyrail dispute. Such moments, I suggest, are the key to understanding how political identities are made. In my analysis of this protest situation, I show how place is produced situationally within the performance of a dialectical play between processes of identification and differentiation.

Finally, Chapter 8 provides a discussion of the contradictions that link the various social dramas and staged performances that I examine in this book. I conclude that these dramas give expression to processes of differentiation and identification in which social actors engage with one another politically in order to define themselves in relation to the various agents, projects and effects of the state (bureaucratic and corporate), as well as to claim a role in constituting their own place-worlds.

NOTES

1. Estimated resident population as of June 2003. Australian Bureau of Statistics, 'Regional Population Growth, Australia and New Zealand, 2002–03' (ABS cat. no. 3218.0).

2. This is the first claim over a national park in Queensland to be successful without litigation. The consent determination states that under their traditional laws and customs, Djabugay People have *non-exclusive* native title rights and interests in Barron Gorge National Park. There are 'other interests' that, in the event of a conflict, prevail over Djabugay native title rights. The other interest holders in Barron Gorge National Park include: the State of Queensland, the Wet Tropics Management Authority, Skyrail Pty Ltd, the Cairns City Council and the Tablelands Shire Council, Powerlink, Ergon Energy Corporation, Stanwell Corporation, and the public who can access the Barron Gorge National Park for recreation purposes.

3. As the virtues and limitations of focusing one's ethnographic lens on one's own society have already been well debated, I do not dwell on them here. See Messerschmidt (1981), Handler (1985), Rabinow (1986), M. Strathern (1987), Eipper (1990), Okely (1992 and 1996), Morton (1999). This literature can be linked to works on 'indigenous anthropology', the idea of the 'native anthropologist' (see, for example, Fahim 1982; Choong 1990; Narayan 1993; Hastrup 1996; Motzafi-Haller 1997), and the 'auto-critique of our own knowledge constructions' as relates to self/other, subject/object dualism (Moore 1996: 8).

4. Laclau & Mouffe (1985: 96–142) define an 'articulatory practice' as a discursive structure which 'constitutes and organises social relations'. Because there can be no such 'real object' as society, no 'essentialist totalisation', articulatory practices operate to constitute society only through the partial fixing of meaning achieved through the construction of 'nodal points'. Articulatory practices work in tension against the 'polysemy that disarticulates a discursive structure'.

5. I mostly use the term Aboriginal in preference to Indigenous in this book, as Indigenous Australians include both Aboriginal and Torres Strait Islander people. There are few Torres Strait Islander people living in the Kuranda area, and this study particularly focuses on Aboriginal people. Aboriginal people in Kuranda sometimes used the terms Aboriginal and non-Aboriginal when talking to me, particularly in the more formal context of recorded interviews. More casually they would use terms such as *bama* or *murri* (Aboriginal) and *migaloo, white* or *whitefella* in reference to non-Aboriginal people. The term *migaloo* tended to be avoided by Aboriginal people when I was in their company, and on a number of occasions people apologised for using it, as the term is considered derogatory.

6. Section 4.03 (1) of the Aboriginal Land Act lists 'traditional affiliation' and 'historical association' as two of the grounds on which a land claim may be made. The Native Title Act, on the other hand, excludes historical association as a basis for claim, unless historical association can be shown to amount to native title.

7. Queensland Census Collection Districts CD3030303, CD3030304, CD3030305, CD3030311, CD3030312, CD3030314.

8. The re-imaging of Kuranda as a village can be compared in this respect to the south Australian town of Hahndorf, which is marketed as a pioneer German village. I have heard tourists in Kuranda make this comparison.

9. See McIntyre-Tamwoy (2004) for an excellent discussion of the issue of shared places in relation to cultural heritage values.

10. I use the term 'hearing' here intentionally to refer indirectly to a social context in which Aboriginal people are forced to provide evidence of their rights to land in tribunal hearings or courts of law.

11. There were actually several legislative instruments: the Aboriginal Protection and Restriction of the Sale of Opium Act of 1897, which provided for the official creation of reserves and for the removal of Aboriginals to such reserves (sections 4(a), 4(b), and 9); its successor, the Aboriginals Preservation and Protection Act of 1939; and finally the Aboriginal and Torres Strait Islander Affairs Act of 1965, which, although it repealed some of the earlier 'protection' provisions, still maintained the reserve system in Queensland.

12. Mission policy, with regard to the actual form that punishments took, changed according to the superintendent in charge at any given time. Finlayson (1991: 114) notes that an ex-resident recalled having her hair shaved several times as punishment for swearing, and another remembered that the policy at one stage was for someone from the child's own family to be forced to publicly administer twenty cuts on the back with a cane. Other punishments meted out included up to two weeks in the mission gaol on a diet of bread and water. For what were considered more serious offences, such as illegitimate pregnancies, offenders were sent away to Palm Island. According to Finlayson (1991: 115), marriages were sometimes held in private in response to illegitimate pregnancies. No family members were allowed to attend, and the expecting mother was forced to wear sackcloth and to have her head shaved.

13. I have tried to protect the privacy of individuals by avoiding naming them, unless they have given their consent for me to do so.

14. For example Syd Gray, son of Djabugay elder Mrs Enid Boyle, recorded in 1981 that his mother and her husband, Mr Jimmy Boyle, talked about a waterfall where people would run to hide from the white man. See Gray, S. (1981). 'Oral history about Mona Mona mission and Kuranda area' (outline of taped interview held at the Australian Institute of Aboriginal and Torres Strait Islander Studies, Canberra; archive numbers 006690 - 006691; collection number: GRAY_S01).

15. Accounts of the removal and institutionalisation of Aboriginal children and first hand accounts from members of 'the stolen generation' have been docu-

mented by the Human Rights and Equal Opportunity Commission's National Inquiry into the Separation of Aboriginal and Torres Strait Islander Children from their Families. The report (Wilson 1997) led to a renewed effort on the part of some settler Australians to take part in reconciliation measures, among these the circulation in Australia of 'sorry books' that settler Australians were encouraged to sign, the emergence of 'National Sorry Day', and finally the government apology delivered by Prime Minister Kevin Rudd on 13 February 2008.

16. The phrase 'mutilated memory' has also been used by Gruzinski in the title to his paper 'Mutilated Memory: Reconstruction of the Past and the Mechanisms of Memory Among 17th Century Otomis' (1990).

ᴥ Chapter 1 ᴥ

Colonising Place

The Mutilation of Memory

Memory is usually thought of as having to do with the temporality of mind (Halbwachs 1992; Douglas 1995) rather than with the materiality and corporeality of place. Yet as Casey argues:

> [Memory] is the stabilizing persistence of place as a container of experiences that contributes so powerfully to its intrinsic memorability. An alert and alive memory connects spontaneously with place, finding in it features that favour and parallel its own activities. We might even say that memory is naturally place-oriented or at least place-supported … Unlike site and time, memory does not thrive on the indifferently dispersed. It thrives, rather, on the persistent particularities of what is properly *in place:* held fast there and made one's own (Casey 1987: 186).

The link between memory and place is realised through the agency of the lived body (Casey 1987). Places are constituted and animated by the social and political engagement of human beings with one another. However, people make place within social processes and structures that have already been moulded and that continue to be shaped by others. It is in this sense that place is already 'pregnant with the past' (Ingold 1993: 153), pregnant with practices of power and domination. However, as we store our memories in places, we store places in memories (Casey 1987). Thus, removing people from places does not necessarily mean forever losing the memory of the places themselves. Lost places may be commemorated, and people may feel homesick or nostalgic for ancestral places they have never actually inhabited. Such memories may even be transmitted to later generations. Nevertheless, to remove a people from a place means to deny them the embodiment of those memories that are triggered and cultivated through actual social engagement and corporeal experience with that place. This can result in a profoundly disorienting mutilation of memory.

Paths and Pockets: The Colonisation of Aboriginal Places

Before European colonisation of North Queensland, the Aboriginal people of the rainforest region around Kuranda made 'systematic and sustained' use of clearings in the rainforest that were connected by a network of pathways (Loos 1982: 89). Evidence for this can be found in the journals of early explorers and prospectors such as Christie Palmerston, who made an expedition from Herberton to the Barron Falls in December 1884 and January 1885,[1] and James Venture Mulligan, who made an expedition through the area in 1875 (Loos 1982: 89). The explorers provide fascinating accounts of the intensive occupation of the North Queensland rainforest[2] region by Aboriginal people prior to European settlement:

> Traversed this creek only one mile seeing a great number of native tracks, also a number of shields painted and laid along its banks to dry ... we could hear the aborigines talking on both sides of the creek, and passed through several camps from which they had scampered away leaving everything on seeing us: native blankets in dozens, bushels of red berries cooked and uncooked; I believe there was a hundredweight of newly crushed meal heaped up on their greasy looking blankets. Long ungainly swords and shields scattered about in all directions; scores of small fishing nets ... (Palmerston in Woolston & Colliver 1968: 28).

> At the end of the creek on which we are camped struck a blackfellows' track or road; we followed it for over two miles round to the west end of the scrub. The track is well beaten, and runs between the hills and the scrub ... A splendid track, the best native track I ever saw anywhere. There are roads off the main track to each of their townships, which consist of well thatched gunyahs, big enough to hold five or six darkies. We counted eleven such townships since we came to the edge of the scrub, and we have only travelled four miles along it. At certain seasons this must be a crowded place with blacks, which seem to live principally on nuts, for there are barrowfuls of nutshells at their camps (Mulligan 1877: 6).

A descendant of one of the early settler families told me that when the settlers rode through 'the scrub' down to the coast before the range road was built, they would picnic and/or camp overnight in 'pockets' in the scrub that he thought Aboriginal people had made. He named a number of such pockets: McKenzie's Pocket, Christmas Pocket, Cedar Pocket, Read's Pocket, Dinner Pocket, and Welcome Pocket (Maurie Veivers, pers. comm. 16 January 1996). The names indicate their importance in the European settlement of the rainforest area, and it is clear that the settlers recognised them not only as landmarks but also as havens in what was to them a broad expanse of endless and unwelcoming scrub. These pockets were not only obvious places to camp, but also sites from which to begin settlement of the area. Loos (1982: 89) notes that all the pockets in the rainforest discovered by explorers and made use of by early settlers 'were probably Aboriginal camp or ceremonial sites'. The following account by Christie Palmerston could be taken as evidence of this:[3]

> I continued my journey along this large path, making great progress ... and also through many native camps, saw many paths leading from and junctioning with this one. In two miles it led me to a small pocket or open space of about an acre or less. ... This corroboree ground presented a clean orderly appearance, the smallest shrub even having been plucked out by the roots, to all appearances the preceding day. ... Large paths, similar to the one followed by me, branch from this pocket in all directions (Woolston & Colliver 1968: 29).

About thirty years later, naturalist Erik Mjöberg (1918: 168) wrote of the rainforest peoples: 'They often cut out a large circle in the rainforest, before they put up their humpies, partly to get some sunshine and partly to avoid the old branches falling down on them.'

It is important to note that Europeans did not simply move into the rainforest country, but that they actually appropriated Aboriginal pathways through the forest and chose to occupy specific sites that Aboriginal people had cleared. This is significant and shows the immediate and traumatic impact that European settlement must have had on the Aboriginal population of the rainforest. Aboriginal oral history corroborates this occupation of their home sites by the settlers. Some of these pockets were associated with particular family groups, while others were places where different family groups met for socialising, for ceremonial activity and for exchange. The Djabugay name for these places is *bulmba,* a term that can be qualified to refer to particular types of places, such as grounds for fighting or for ceremonial corroboree meetings, as well as to refer to people of the same place. In other words, the term *bulmba* refers not simply to a bounded place, but also to the general concept of home or homeland, and it may be extended to mean 'the world, land, sea, sky and even time itself' (Banning & Quinn 1989: 73). In the process of her linguistic study of Djabugay, for example, Cassells recorded the following (my emphasis):

> Gulu *bulmba* ngandji binangunday yaluguli
> camp/home 1pl. listen today

Today we listen to the people at home
Bamulu *bulmba* djurawala ngundaying
person-ERG home wrong-now see
and we see people doing wrong now

. . .

gulu ngandjin *bulmba* nyiwul yiringan
1p. home one belong
This is our only home here, this land
Bulmba ngandji binangundalum
camp, home, land pl. listen-PURP
Let's listen to the old people
gadjagadjar ngandjinda *bulmba* djanang burmu wala
spirits-REDUP-WITH 1pl.DAT home stand still now
Everything is standing still now

. . .

gulay *bulmba* guragura wala
home, people great grandfathers, ancestors now
All the old people are gone now

. . .

gulaywu *bulmbawu* bibunbaywu
these – ALL camp – ALL child, young – ALL
For all these young ones
bulmba ngandji yiringanu wanggaruwanggaru nguru
home 1pl. belong east – ALL
This is our home, stretching all the way east, right up
ngunbaywu ngunbaywu wanggaru nguru guwulu wuru
Kuranda – ALL-REDUP Speewah
To Kuranda, and right back to Speewah,
yalngiri wuru guyangga wuruwu wubulu wuru
Crystal Cascades PLACE NAME PLACE NAME
and Crystal Cascades; up to guyangga and down to wubulu,
djulanuwu wuru gulu guludu wuru djulanu
PLACE–ALL Dove Creek PLACE NAME
and right on to djulanu and Dove Creek,
marandjaru wuru garadjuruwu wuru gudjay *bulmba*
Bebo Mountain PLACE–ALL those places
Bebo Mountain, and garadjuru

. . .

bulmba: guragurawu wala mayngalawu wala
old people last of the line now nothing-ALL now
We, the old people, are the last ones left, we are going soon (Cassells
    1977).

This text, from which I have only selected small sections, describes not just the extent of the land that the informant considered home, but also the informant's sense of 'home' as a relationship with others through shared place.

The European settlers first moved into the very heart of Aboriginal rainforest country. In other words, colonisation was not simply a case of settlement of the Aboriginal people's general territory, but of occupation of their actual dwelling places, their homes, their hearths and their network of paths (or 'pads' as they are locally known). Thus began the mutilation of place memory.

It can be inferred that townships like Kuranda and other smaller settlements in the area, such as Kowrowa and Mantaka, began and grew from these pockets – that is, from the *hearth* lands of Aboriginal country.[4] Mantaka and Kowrowa were known to the early settlers as 'Welcome Pocket' and 'Dinner Pocket' respectively. Djabugay people told me that there were camps at many places like these along the banks of the Barron River and its tributaries, some of which they continued to use after European settlement of the area:

> You see my grandparents used to work in Kuranda, and that's when I was about three or four. I used to walk from the mission [to] the camp where we stayed. They used to walk with me and we used to pad down the riverside right down to past that bridge there, Kuranda Heights. Go past there. And we had a little camp just further down there, down the quick side, Barron River. In the thirties, camp at the thing; and we had a little track going up to the railway and just had a little gate we can go through. And we used to go up in town then; and they be working for the Veivers [original settler family] (Esther Snider, pers. comm. 18 June 1996).

Particularly well remembered are the camps on the river at Kuranda Heights, at Oak Forest and near the Kuranda Railway Station.[5] The concentration of population along the river and its importance in terms of identity is evidenced by the name 'the Barron River Tribe', which was given to the people in the early literature and which became the name they used themselves between European settlement and the 1980s, at which point Djabugay and other tribal or clan names began to take on political precedence.

Although Aboriginal people on the coast had begun to experience the devastating affects of the *beche de mer* fishing industry as early as the 1860s,[6] the first Europeans to move into the rainforest region were timber gatherers during the 1870s. Prospectors, miners and selectors soon followed, creating an impact upon the rainforest peoples from all directions.[7] As Loos (1982: 93) writes: 'While timber-getters and selectors were encroaching upon the rainforest Aborigines from the east, denying them the rivers and river flats of the Daintree, Barron, Mulgrave, and the Johnstone, miners and newly-established small cattle stations on the west were restricting their access to hunting grounds and freshwater fishing.'

The first of the cattle stations to be established close to Kuranda was 'Emerald End' on the Barron River, which was owned by John Atherton. However, direct contact between Aboriginal people and the settlers intensified during the main construction phase of the railway line and the roads through the range. Settler communities of railway workers and farmers sprang up along the railway sidings as more and more land was made available for selection.[8] Many of the selectors found it difficult to make a living from farming alone and supplemented their income by working in the timber industry, on the railways, or through prospecting and mining.

According to Loos (1982: 3), European encroachment on the land reduced Aboriginal access to traditional food sources to the point that the tribes were actually starving. In his annual report (Queensland, Parliament 1900: 2), Northern Protector of Aborigines W. E. Roth, provided support for this:

> As each new block of country becomes taken up, the blacks are forcibly hunted off their water supplies and hunting grounds both in it and in its immediate neighbourhood. *According to their own laws of trespass they are prevented from seeking fresh pastures*, except at the cost of fighting ...[9]

However, the rainforest was a formidable enough barrier to the settlers to provide some Aboriginal people with a relatively safe haven from which to mount a campaign of resistance, as well as to supplement their diet with settler cattle. According to Bolton:

> The dense forests between the Atherton Tableland and the coast hid the comings and goings of cattle-killers only too well. John Atherton estimated his average loss as a bullock a day for five years, and once or twice a spear was aimed at him (Bolton 1963: 94).

Bolton does not mention any retaliation on the part of Atherton. Yet according to Aboriginal oral history, he ordered and participated in a massacre of Aboriginal people who had stolen one of his horses in lieu of payment of the bullock he had promised them for showing him a way across the range to the coast.[10]

Loos (1982: 93) argues that resistance to European settlement from rainforest Aboriginal people 'was so effective that it led to the evolution of a completely new government policy' to 'pacify the Aborigines' by providing food rations. This policy, which was initiated and supported by some of the settlers themselves, replaced the earlier policy of violent 'dispersal' of Aboriginal groups using the native police force. According to Loos (1982), the native police force had proved to be ineffective in the face of the large-scale resistance of rainforest peoples. Rationing meant that Aboriginal people who had previously been repelled from areas of white settlement were now 'let in'. Writing at that time, Eden (1872: 211) defines 'letting in' as allowing, and indeed encouraging, the Aborigines 'to come and make themselves useful, shepherding a few sheep, chopping wood, stripping bark, and a thousand odd jobs to which they are adapted, receiving in return protection as long as they behaved well, and little presents of blankets, tomahawks etc.'. In other words, not only Aboriginal land but also their labour was now to be appropriated. The new policy meant that camps on the edge of European settlements grew rapidly, including several camps in the Kuranda vicinity. There was a ration station at Kuranda and a depot at Myola, a few kilometres from Kuranda, that distributed food and tobacco to Aboriginal people camped in that area (Queensland, Parliament 1896: 8–9). There were also Aboriginal camps on a number of settler cattle stations, plantations and farms in the area. Some Aboriginal families continued to occupy the same camping places that they had before the settlers arrived, but since these camps were now located on European 'properties', they were classified as 'fringe camps'.

During this period, Aboriginal people were given (and adopted for themselves) the names of the particular European settlers for whom they worked. For example, the Matthisens, a Djabugay family, adopted their name from Thron and Elizabeth Matthisen, who settled beside the railway line at Dinner Pocket (now Kowrowa) in about 1907. Charlie and Rosie Matthisen lived on the Matthisen property and worked for the family. Even after they were removed to the Mona Mona mission, Charlie and Rosie continued to work for different members of this particular settler family for many years (Hughes 1982: 3).[11] Similarly, the Aboriginal family named Street took their name from the settler Alfred Street who began to grow coffee on their land in 1896.[12] Other Aboriginal surnames that can be traced to settlers include Hobson, Hobbler and Newbury.[13] Some Aboriginal people took their surnames from the explorers and government officers posted to their areas. Connolly writes of an Aboriginal leader, Dick Palmerston, who took his name from the explorer Christie Palmerston:

> The Mowbray Valley was the hunting grounds of the Chabbuki [Djabugay] Tribe of Aborigines, and about 40 of the old tribe continued to move through the Valley on their hunting trips on walk-about, between the Port Douglas camp, and the camp at Mona Mona, near Kuranda. Their King

was called Dick Palmerston, who claimed to be one of Christie Palmerston's guides (Connolly 1984: 44).[14]

Similarly, the Aboriginal surname Donoghue was taken from a policeman stationed in Kuranda during 1915–1916.

This practice of taking or being given the names of European settlers meant that in cases where families were separated or where individuals worked for different settlers, members of the same patriline sometimes found themselves with different surnames. According to Marita Hobbler (nee Brim, pers. comm. 4 January 1995), her father, Cecil Brim, was separated from his brothers during the police 'round-up' at Speewah. They never saw each other again. Her father had worked for a Brim and went by that name, while one of his brothers, who had escaped the round-up, adopted a different surname. His descendants, therefore, have that name. According to Marita, she met this side of her family for the first time during the 1990s. Her cousin had seen a funeral notice in the paper for a Brim and had come to meet his relatives. As Marita noted, 'They usually pass on, you know. They pass on that knowledge. He's got that name ... but yet he still know he's a Brim.'[15] The replacement of the names of Aboriginal people and places with those of the European settlers worked to erase the Aboriginal rights to and identity in places from settlers' memory. Yet Aboriginal people's adoption of names associated with particular settlers also operated as a way for Aboriginal people to maintain their connection to the places from which they had been removed. One means Aboriginal people have used to seek recognition of their relationship with particular settled places is to appeal to settler memory of Aboriginal connection to these places through the names they share.

Fringe-Camps and Missionisation

After Meston visited Kuranda during his 1896 inquiry into the 'conditions of the Northern Aboriginals', he estimated that about fifty or sixty Aboriginal people were receiving regular supplies, distributed under the supervision of the police, from the ration station at Kuranda. In support of the policy of rationing, he notes that 'they have regarded the food as an act of friendship from the Government, and responded by being peaceable and friendly with all the settlers in the neighbourhood, giving no trouble whatever' (Queensland, Parliament 1896: 10). Meston noted, however, that at Mareeba food was scarce for the Aboriginal people and that he himself 'mustered about 100 blacks and gave them flour, beef, and some tobacco' (Queensland, Parliament 1896: 11).

The policy of providing Aboriginal people with rations and blankets heralded what is known as 'the protection era' in Australian government relations with the Indigenous population of the country. By the end of the nineteenth century, the different Australian colonies had begun to introduce more comprehensive legislation to 'protect' Indigenous people. Queensland's Aboriginals Protection and Restriction of the Sale of Opium Act of 1897 was arguably the most comprehensive of such 'protection' legislation. An examination of the history of the disciplinary regime legitimised under this legislation makes intelligible the bureaucratic practices of power that continue to operate today with regard to Aboriginal people.

The 1897 'Protection' Act provided for the extensive regulation of the lives of Aboriginal people in Queensland.[16] A key feature of the legislation was that it enabled the creation of special reserves for Aboriginal people, as well as their segregation from settler society. The act provided for the appointment of Protectors of Aboriginals, superintendents for the reserves, and other officers, the removal of Aboriginal people to reserves, the control of Aboriginal people on such reserves, including their disciplining and punishment and the suppression of their languages, rituals and beliefs, the supervision of their property and money, the control of their employment and conditions of employment, the supervision, custody and care of their children, the exclusion of unauthorised persons from reserves, the control of marriages with non-Aboriginal people, the issue of blankets and rations, and the restriction of the sale of liquor or opium to Aboriginal people. In other words, the legislation sought complete control over their lives, from birth to death. This was the beginning of a regime that continues to this day, in spite of changes in government policy and legislation. Aboriginal affairs in Queensland, as Kidd's (1997: 346) archival study of government files has exposed, 'has operated since its inception as a closed, secretive and highly defensive agency of government'.[17] In 1898, two Chief Protectors, Archibald Meston and Walter Edmund Roth, were appointed under the act, one each for southern and northern Queensland respectively. The commissioner of police, William Edward Parry-Okeden, was also appointed as a Protector for both districts, and police officers and clerks of petty sessions acted under the direction of the Protectors. Aboriginal people had no avenues through which to appeal the administrative decisions of these state agents.

Besides setting up its own government-run reserves, the state of Queensland actively encouraged Christian churches that were eager to undertake missionary work to operate their missions as officially recognised reserves. In exchange for reserve land and government contribution to mission costs, the various Christian churches were harnessed into the service of the state to help implement its protectionist policy. The superintendents of the missions were appointed as local Protectors of Aboriginals under the act, turning missionaries into direct agents of the state. By 1905, the Northern Protector, W. E. Roth, was able to note that 'the mission stations are year by year becoming of greater assistance to the State in dealing with the pauper aboriginal waifs and strays, adults and children, on the most economic lines' (Queensland, Parliament 1905: 13).

The Carceral System

In the Kuranda region, it was not until after the Seventh Day Adventist Church established the Mona Mona mission in 1913 that Aboriginal people began to be systematically relocated to missions and reserves.[18] Well before this time, however, their camps were visited by missionaries from Yarrabah on the coast south of Cairns (Kidd 1997: 40). In his report for 1899, the Northern Protector of Aboriginals, W. E. Roth, wrote:

> The missionaries continue to visit the aboriginal camps in the surrounding districts, and have thus come into personal touch with some 282 blacks distributed along the Barron River, the Mulgrave River, and at Kuranda.

Figure 1.1. Aboriginal Camp at Kuranda, 1904.
Collection: John Oxley Library, State Library of Queensland.

In addition to the spiritual advantages accruing from this peripatetic method of holding religious service, Mr. Gribble does a great deal of good in relieving sickness and disease with his case of medicines ... and loses no opportunity of proclaiming the benefits of the Mission station. By those means he picks up many a little waif and stray, and, with the consent of the parent, brings them into Yarrabah. Similarly, some of the older Mission boys have been trained for this particular kind of work, and parties of these young men, independently of Mr Gribble, have brought several little children into the station (Queensland, Parliament 1900: 6).

Aboriginal people from the Kuranda area were also removed to other reserves. Most people from the Kuranda region, however, continued to live in camps along the Barron River until 1916 (see Figure 1.1).

News of the establishment of the Mona Mona mission was not well received among either the Kuranda settlers or – according to one of them – by the Kuranda Aboriginal population. A local publican, E. Hunter of Hunter's Barron Falls Hotel, wrote to the Protector of Aborigines on 8 September 1913 as follows:

News has been received to the effect that a Mission Station is to be established a few miles from Kuranda. The blacks are very much upset over the matter as they do not favour the Mission. Will you kindly advise me what authority these seven days missioners have – if any – *to take these blacks against their wishes* [original emphasis].[19]

The missionaries were not able to persuade Aboriginal people in the Kuranda camps to join the mission voluntarily. However, the Chief Protector of Aboriginals, J. W. Bleakley, considered that they must be removed regardless of their wishes, referring to them in his report of 7 September 1915 as 'a poor destitute lot ... and an eyesore to the numerous visitors to this beauty spot in the North'.[20] It is interesting to compare his report with that of his predecessor, R. B. Howard. After visiting Kuranda in 1912, Howard noted in his annual report:

On reaching Kuranda, I found between 50 and 60 natives camped on the river; they were all in good health, and several are working under agreement. These people are a very quiet and contented lot; no opium, drink, or disease is found amongst them, and they are spoken of as excellent workers (Queensland, Parliament 1913: 8).

Could there have been such a dramatic decline in less than three years? The reference to visitors and to the identity of Kuranda as a tourist destination is also significant. The Kuranda publican's letter and the Protector's comments reveal conflicting sentiments regarding the value of Aboriginal people to tourism in the area. A number of the Kuranda Aboriginal people were under work agreements. They also earned some money from the tourists who visited their camps and were considered a good tourist attraction for the town, much like today. On 6 March 1916, the publican, E. Hunter, was once again inspired to write on the matter of their removal, this time to the Hon E. Theodore:

> I have just heard that the Kuranda blacks are very shortly to be removed to the Mission Station. I must ask you to enquire into this for us as they are very interesting to tourists in their natural homes. They are a pure and the only increasing tribe known in the north. They are of great service to the inhabitants and give no trouble to the police.[21]

Clearly, there was a disjunction between the demands of the bureaucratic state and local white interests in maintaining the symbiotic relationship that had developed between them and the Aboriginal people. After the removal order came through, a total of sixty four Aboriginal people from the Kuranda camps were forcibly removed to the mission, including – without warning to their employers – those under work agreements. This was in spite of the fact that the Chief Protector had issued an instruction that workers could be removed at a later date 'at the discretion of the Protector'.[22] The removal was not achieved in one go, however, as many of the people escaped police capture. In a memorandum to the commissioner of police dated 14 June 1916, Senior Sergeant Kenny reported:

> The removal of the tribe has not been effected. Up to the present 36 of them have been removed. The others are scattered about the district and always evade capture as they do not care to go to the mission. The remainder will be rounded up as soon as possible.[23]

According to Collins (1981: 20), the Aboriginal people he interviewed told him that some of the people eventually picked up by police at Kuranda had fled the earlier round-ups at Mareeba and elsewhere in the Tablelands and were sheltering in the Kuranda camps. In general, camps connected with ration stations tended to be 'filled with Aboriginal people from different districts all suffering the destitution and impoverishment accompanying European economic development' (Finlayson 1991: 48).[24]

People from the Mareeba and Kuranda areas comprised the majority of inmates of the mission. Although, as noted above, people from further afield were also removed to Mona Mona,[25] in comparison to other reserves

to which people were removed from all over Queensland (such as Palm Island and Yarrabah), the Aboriginal population of Mona Mona was relatively
homogeneous. After the intake of the large groups of Aboriginal people
from the camps in Mareeba and Kuranda between 1914 and 1916, people
tended to be removed to Mona Mona only irregularly as individuals or as
small family groups. Some of these were transferred from other reserves
for various alleged transgressions, while others were removed as 'neglected'
children, and so on. From reconstructions based on place of removal and
the linguistic affiliation remembered by people today, it can be concluded
that three main language groups were represented on Mona Mona: Djabugay, Muluridji, and Kuku Yalanji. Of course, political and linguistic affiliation does not necessarily coincide. Norman Tindale, an anthropologist who
visited Mona Mona in 1938 (26 August – 5 September), lists approximately
twenty-one different tribes as being represented on the mission.[26] However,
of these, the dominant ones – in terms of the number of people Tindale
interviewed – were Djabugay, Muluridji, Kuku Yalanji, Kuku Imudji, Djirbal, and Yidiny.[27] This indicates that Mona Mona pooled a relatively locally
based population of neighbouring peoples. Tindale also recorded that a
number of his informants identified as Buluwandji (Bulway speakers). Bulway is linguistically classified as having been a dialect of Djabugay spoken in
the Kuranda area on the south side of the Barron River, and some Kuranda
people today choose to identify specifically as Buluwandji.

The confinement of Aboriginal people to reserves and mission stations
meant that they could no longer regularly return to the *bulmba* (home
places) that enabled the transmission of place memory to the younger
generation. Only when free to move along their network of paths and return to their camping places were people able, as part of this 'dwelling',
to rekindle and 'build' memories for transmission to the next generation.
Place constitutes a fundamental mnemonic tool for Aboriginal Australian
peoples, as numerous scholars have argued (e.g. Myers 1986; Glowczewski
1989; Swain 1993; Rumsey 1994; Merlan 1999; Rumsey and Weiner 2001;
Magowan 2007; Austin-Broos 2009). Memories are not cognitively confined, but reveal themselves through being-in-the-world. For Mona Mona
people, the sight of a particular tree (often the mango, today, a tree introduced to the region) might trigger, for example, a mother's memory of having given birth there and prompt her to relate her memories of this event to
her child. Waterholes, rocks and mountains enfold narrative memories of
the Dreaming. The sounds of corroboree, of clap sticks and the pounding of
the earth recall the old people. The cracking of nuts recalls a grandmother
preparing meal to bake bread for the children and a story she might have
told them while she worked. The smell of damper cooking in the hot ashes,
the damp cold of a misty mountain morning, the comforting warmth of the

campfire, the soft touch of long grass brushing against one's legs, the pain inflicted by the leaves of the stinging tree or the thorns of the lawyer cane palm that flourished beside the walking pads, the cool water of the Barrron River on a hot day, the taste of freshly caught fish or wild bees' honey – all this is the substance of place memory. It is from this that Aboriginal people were removed.

A Disciplinary Regime

The following extracts from various police station charge books[28] exemplify the discipline and punishment which defined the Protectionist regime in Queensland:

> A *sentence of detention* for seven years ... *convicted of a charge* of being a neglected child.
>
> Aged 7 years. *Arrested* on removal order at Ashmore Station to be sent to Mona Mona.
>
> *Arrested* for unlawfully leaving Mona Mona [my emphasis].

The use of the phrase 'removal' is telling. Although the stated rationale behind the reserve system was to protect Aboriginal people, in practice the protectionist regime served the interests of the European settlers with respect to land – although not with regard to cheap labour – by 'removing' the possibility of any contested rights in such land. Once removed to the mission, Aboriginal people effectively became prisoners. By law they could not leave unless the mission superintendent gave special permission, or unless they were granted certificates of exemption from being 'under the act'. People who chose to leave Mona Mona and other such reserves without permission were 'arrested' or 'captured' as 'absconders', 'deserters', or 'escapees'.[29] Punishment for escaping was banishment to a mission or government reserve even further removed from one's home country and one's family and friends.

In their camps along the Barron River, people had lived in dwellings constructed in the traditional manner. After they were removed to the mission, they rebuilt their camps on the mission in the same style, as the mission had only just been established and not enough mission houses had been built.[30] According to a number of past residents of Mona Mona, there were for many years two such camps on Mona Mona: one of Djabugay speakers, the core of which came from the old camps on the Barron River at Kuranda, and one camp of Muluridji speaking people, the core of which came from the Granite Creek Camp at Mareeba (see also Finlayson 1991: 51; Collins 1981). Only older people and very young children lived in the camps, as after the age of four or five boys and girls were removed to segregated dormitories. A number of one and two bedroom houses were built each year on the mission and allocated to married couples on the basis of their compliance with Christian doctrines and the disciplinary program of the mission. According to Finlayson (1991: 52), some of the older Aboriginal people 'clung tenaciously' to their independence and lived out their lives in the camps, refusing mission housing even when it became available to them. The system by which mission housing was allocated, however, served to promote a hierarchy among Aboriginal families that was reinforced by the privileges attached to particular employment opportunities. According to Finlayson (1991: 48), 'much status accrued to those individuals selected to perform special roles in church services', such as singing in the choir and reading Scripture.³¹ Other favoured positions included jobs in the Mona Mona community police, supervising the dormitories, working in the store, teaching in the school and playing in the brass band.

People's experiences of life on Mona Mona parallel the experiences of other Aboriginal people in Australia who were similarly institutionalised under this 'protectionist' regime (see, for example, ethnographic studies relating to north Queensland missions and reserves by Martin 1993, Trigger 1992, Anderson 1983 and Chase 1980). Finlayson (1991: 287) includes

Figure 1.2. The Mona Mona mission before it closed in 1962.
Collection: John Oxley Library, State Library of Queensland.

a history of the Mona Mona mission and a detailed account of the disciplinary practices 'by which the mission imposed its own cultural and religious perspectives on the Aboriginal inhabitants'. These included practices such as those Foucault (1977) discusses in *Discipline and Punish*: spatial segregation or 'the art of distributions', temporal control of activity, and the constant and hierarchical observation of behaviour. The mission was deliberately laid out so as to keep Aboriginal people separate from white society, an intention reinforced by rules that made the missionaries' houses out of bounds to Aboriginal inmates unless they worked there as domestic workers or on certain other special occasions. Children were kept segregated from their elders and from each other in dormitories with a strictly enforced visiting code.[32] Christian couples were segregated in neat rows of wooden houses from their 'wild' Aboriginal relatives living in the camps on the periphery. According to Finlayson (1991), residents were deliberately kept segregated even in the seating arrangements in the refectory. Adults who had been allocated houses were forced to eat in the communal dining room along with the dormitory children until they went on strike about the issue.[33] As Finlayson (1991: 116) argues, being forced to eat in the refectory symbolised to the Mona Mona inmates their 'lack of status and their position as dependents'. All mission residents, except those in the camps, were required to adhere to a strict timetable organised around supervised activities: sleeping, eating, working, schooling and church attendance. Even leisure time was strictly organised. Nevertheless, there were times when inmates were able to be free of this strict disciplinary regime. They were permitted regular visits to traditional camping grounds such as Oak Forest during holiday periods, and some had access to the outside world through work permits. Men in particular were able to maintain their connection to the country and to networks of kin outside the mission confines through their work in forestry, the railways and the cattle industry. In addition, as mentioned above, throughout most of the life of the mission there were people living in camps on the mission who were not subject to the same regimen as those who lived in the mission houses and dormitories.

Language Loss

The most profoundly colonising practice of all was the removal of children from their parents and their segregation in dormitories. It was this practice more than any direct prohibition that resulted in the muting of Aboriginal orality and the erasure of Aboriginal ritual practices. Isolation in dormitories meant that the younger generation no longer had access to the sources of power that lay in the use of language and in the participatory practice of ritual performances. The missionaries were mainly concerned about Aboriginal rituals, but it was the impact of their policies on the use of Aboriginal languages that Aboriginal people consider the most profoundly disempowering affect of institutionalisation. According to some accounts, older people who spent time as children in the camps of their parents managed to learn some of the language, but many of the old people said they were afraid of speaking their language in front of their children. The missionaries taught the children to read and write in English and forbade the use of 'language'.[34] Both missionaries and Aboriginal people saw literacy in English as a new form of power, one that would help Aboriginal people deal with the new world that they now had to confront. Yet literacy is also a mechanism of state power. As Levi-Strauss (1992: 299) observed in *Tristes Tropiques*, 'the fight against illiteracy is ... connected with an increase in governmental authority over citizens. Everyone must be able to read, so that the government can say: Ignorance of the law is no excuse'.

The key point I wish to make about the muting of Aboriginal orality on the mission was that it denied Aboriginal people the ritual power that they recognise as being inherent in language and that connects them to places and to Dreaming ancestors. Djabugay people say, for example, that they are afraid to visit particular places because they do not have or do not know the right 'language' to make themselves safe in those places. It is a generally held belief that in order to be safe in certain places, one should be able to call out in 'language' to the ancestors before approaching. With the muting of everyday language, the special powerful words and phrases to do this were also lost, words and songs that through their very utterance allowed people to act upon their world. This is language in its performative mode, where orality is practice and where saying something means doing something.[35] In other words, speech and ritual practice are inseparable. It is the actual words – or combination of words as sounded in the particular language and ritually applied – that contain the power to bring the world into being. Taussig discusses the nature of this 'mimetic magic' in a different ethnographic context with respect to Cuna medical chants. He writes:

> The simulacrum here is created with words, not objects! In fact two mimetic movements are involved. One is the duplication in song of the spirits ... The other mimetic movement depends upon this invocation of the spirits because, since they duplicate the physical world, then to bring them forth by means of song is to mimetically gain control over the mirror-image of physical reality that they represent (Taussig 1993: 105).

Since it is not just the act of uttering but the utterance itself that is considered to be powerful, there is no possibility of translation. Loss of language thus means loss of the ritual power to deal with ancestral places. This loss is keenly felt by Aboriginal people who today are called upon to demonstrate continuity of their connection to the country, for example in the context of native title claims. They themselves value knowledge of language as demonstrating connection to place, but they also know that this sort of knowledge is accepted within the discursive field of native title and heritage as a 'cultural fact'. It is such cultural facts that are taken into account when the legal bases of their claims to land are assessed.

Younger people bemoan the fact that their elders did not pass on their language. They put this down to the fact the missionaries forbade them to speak their own languages. However, it was not simply that the older people were silenced, but that the young people were *made unable to listen.* A number of elders complained to me that until recently, the younger people did not come to them to listen and learn. Cassells also noted this frustration and despair among older people. The following text is selected from her transcription and translation of a recording of Gilpin Banning speaking in Djabugay, and it also demonstrates Banning's concept of the oneness of language, place-memory and being-in-the-world:

> Those children make our mouth tired (from talking and not being listened
>   to).
> They won't follow our words, what we say.
> . . .
> Let's listen to the old people
> Everything is standing still now
> There is no goodwill now
> Many people have passed away
> The rules are not adhered to
> All the old people are gone now
> I am old now, I nearly cry
> for all these young ones.
> . . .
> All these place names we don't listen to now
> Come and get the words that come
> from those far-away, old people who are long gone.
> Come and get the words/language for all those places
> Come and ask us the names
> We must give it out now
> We, the old people, are the last ones left, we are going soon.
> The young ones do not listen now
> The young ones take other paths now
> Not the one path

The people are listening to bad things,
No more do they listen or perform corroborees, or practice *burayi*[36]
They break our law
After us (after we are gone) the young ones will see
Then they will get a fright, and they will be alone.
I say to you, the words are gone, past. That's all now (Cassells 1977).

From Incarceration to Assimilation

The Queensland government further extended the powers of the Aboriginal Protectors with the introduction of new legislation, the Aboriginals Preservation and Protection Act of 1939. As Wearne describes the situation on missions like Mona Mona and other reserves:

> Enormous power to control and direct was given by the Act to the superintendent. Aboriginal courts on reserves could consist of the superintendent sitting alone – and he need not have legal training. So broad and ill-defined were his powers that he could hear as an offence almost any matter of which he disapproved ... The newly established Aboriginal police force, also under the superintendent's control, was wide open to manipulation by him through police 'trustees', and, hence, to abuse of individuals at his direction. His responsibility also extended to the reserve gaol. So not only did the superintendent represent the authority of the Protector/Director; under the Act, he was appointed policeman, judge and gaoler – a situation which completely negates the normal process and principles of justice (Wearne 1980: 15).

The gaze of the state was legitimised by the appointment of medical practitioners who regularly examined the health of Aboriginal people on the reserves.[37] Sections twelve and thirteen of the act empowered the Protector of Aboriginals to order Aboriginal people he suspected of being infected with a contagious disease to submit to medical examination. In 1937, Aboriginal people on Mona Mona were examined by Sir Raphael Cilento, director general of health and medical services, in response to fear of an outbreak of Hanson's Disease (leprosy). Sir Raphael found three cases of the disease and ordered that these people be removed to the leprosarium at Peel Island.[38] In April 1939, 247 Mona Mona residents were again examined by a medical officer. The officer found one 'positive case' of leprosy, one 'doubtful case' and nine 'suspect' cases.[39] By September 1940, however, there were thirty-five suspect cases noted,[40] and the Shire Council wrote to the director general of health and medical services expressing concern over the lepers at Mona Mona and requesting that adequate action be taken to prevent 'possible spread of the disease'.[41] Could it be that reactions to this 'outbreak' of leprosy expressed public fear not just of the disease itself, but of the potential infection of the social body through the assimilation of Aboriginal people? It certainly resulted in further disciplinary practices. In August 1938, the Chief Protector of Aboriginals wrote to the superintendent of Mona Mona regarding the prevalence of leprosy on the mission. He reminded the superintendent of the provisions in the act that gave him the power to entirely prevent the admission of visitors to the mission and to prevent the Aboriginal inmates from leaving the mission.[42] In 1939, a separate leprosarium was established for Aboriginal people at Fantome Island, near Palm Island. A number of people were subsequently removed from Mona Mona and placed into confinement there. In *Madness and Civilization*, Foucault (1967: 6) argued that long after leprosy had virtually disappeared in Europe during the Middle Ages, 'the values and images attached to the figure of the leper as well as the meaning of his exclusion' remained. He showed how the leprosarium of the Middle Ages and earlier was used centuries later to confine 'poor vagabonds, criminals, and "deranged minds"' (Foucault 1967: 7). In relation to Aboriginal people in Queensland, the outbreak not of leprosy itself but of *fear* of the disease is, I suggest, an expression of the last gasp – and grasp – of their 'great confinement' (Foucault 1967: 38).

It was not until the 1950s that assimilation policy began to have some practical effect on the lives of Aboriginal people in Queensland. However, the government was still able to justify maintaining its reserve system. The director of native affairs in his annual report (Queensland Parliament 1960: 2) noted: 'Mindful of the difficulties associated with the ultimate assimilation of the aboriginal race into the white community, the Queensland Government's policy of preparing native personnel toward such assimilation by education, trade, and domestic training, proceeds'. It became easier, however, for Aboriginal people to be granted exemptions from the provisions of the legislation, and during the 1950s increasing numbers of Aboriginal people sought employment outside the mission. The Mona Mona mission administration began to pay a cash wage for work on the mission during this period.[43] Nevertheless, the administration maintained control over wages because residents were forced to spend their cash at the mission store. Moreover, under section 12(10) of the Aboriginals Preservation and Protection Acts of 1939–1946, which provided for the establishment of trust funds for 'the control of the savings of aboriginals, estates of deceased and missing aboriginals and unclaimed moneys', amounts were deducted from the pay packets of Aboriginal workers to be 'saved' for them.[44] For example, out of a total weekly pay of eight pounds, a worker might only get three pounds 'pocket money' in hand from his or her employer, with the rest being sent directly to the Protector for banking.[45] Often employers deducted from the 'pocket money' payment for such items as clothing, tobacco and rations supplied to their workers, so that some people under work agreements actually saw little or no cash.[46]

In 1955, the state government took over responsibility for Mona Mona from the Seventh Day Adventist Church, and the director of native affairs was appointed trustee of the reserve.[47] However, the Seventh Day Adventist missionaries continued to manage the reserve. In the case of Mona Mona, fast tracking the assimilation process had a particular urgency because of plans to build a dam in that area. In his report to the director of native affairs, Mr C. C. Lister, the superintendent of the Mona Mona mission, wrote:

> A big proportion of our men are working out as stockmen, with the Forestry Department and on cane farms. As they assume responsibility for caring for their families, their self-confidence is growing. While more are employed off the Mission, our activities about the Station are diminishing, because less labour is available. Forty-three exemptions have been granted since March, 1962, in keeping with Departmental policy, and nine more are pending. Natives are becoming more willing to leave the protection of the Mission and take responsible places in society (Queensland Parliament 1962: 12).

The Mission was closed on 1 January 1963, and on 12 July 1963 Mona Mona became an electrical works reserve under the trusteeship of the co-ordinator general of public works in order to provide land for the proposed dam. The dam was never built. Mona Mona residents began a protracted bureaucratic battle for both access and title to the land. When the reserve was advertised for public auction as a five year lease in 1968, a past resident of Mona Mona, Clarrie Grogan, wrote a letter (dated 16 October 1968) to Pat Killoran, director of the Department of Aboriginal and Islander affairs, on behalf of the Mona Mona people in protest of the public auction of the lease, noting that Aboriginal people had already applied to lease the land and had been refused.[48] At least thirty past residents of Mona Mona then held a meeting at Mantaka and resolved to form a co-operative to collect the money that would enable them to bid for the lease. The lease was successfully bought for A$350 annual rent by Clarrie Grogan, Enoch Tranby and Joe McGuiness on behalf of the Mona Mona people and with money collected from the same. The lease was then transferred to the Mona Mona Co-operative Society, which was later incorporated on 13 January 1969 under the Co-operative and Other Societies Act of 1967. However, after some years the lease was lost and the land was handed into the trust of the Department of Communities as a state government Aboriginal reserve.

The Aboriginal people removed from the mission in 1962, as well as their descendants, still refer to themselves as 'Mona Mona people'. They express intense attachment to Mona Mona as a place. Perhaps it is because of this intensity of feeling that the spectre of native title has caused such angst. In spite of numerous studies and reports by consultant anthropologists and other experts, a dispute continues among some Mona Mona people as to the tribal identity of the traditional owners. Some argue it is Djabugay country, others that it is Muluridji. In particular, people whose ancestors were brought to the mission from other parts of Queensland fear that a native title determination will exclude them from the place they now call home.

Several families moved back to the mission site within a few years of its closure in 1962, and the site has been continuously occupied ever since. Currently, it is estimated that ninety people live permanently at Mona Mona, but many more dream of returning one day, and some families have established holiday camp sites that they visit on a regular basis. Some years ago, government contractors built four houses that were allocated to particular families, but for over forty years now there has been a continuing battle for adequate housing and secure title over the Mona Mona land. When I first began field work in Kuranda during the 1990s, the Aboriginal and Torres Strait Islander Commission allocated funds for a capital works programme to improve housing and infrastructure, but in spite of years of planning and community development workshops with the Mona Mona people, the money was redirected to increase Aboriginal housing stock elsewhere. As Glenis Grogan said in an interview with Jonathan Strauss for the *Green Left Weekly:*

> All of last year we've had weekly visits from State Housing offering the people living out there homes in Cairns and Mareeba … They're getting everyone to sign documents to move … But as they move out, other people are moving into the mission (Strauss 2009).

On 9 December 2008, the Department of Communities, as the trustee of the reserve, called a meeting to inform the Mona Mona people that within five years they would be forced to leave the reserve and that the 1,610 hectares of land would be turned into a national park, with only 100 hectares set aside for cultural and historical purposes for Mona Mona descendants. The issue quickly became a hot political football in the state elections, and an Action Group was formed to advocate for the rights of the Mona Mona descendants and residents. After a long, hard campaign, a thirty year lease was granted on 12 December 2010 to the Mona Mona people under the auspices of the newly formed Mona Mona Bulmba Aboriginal Corporation.

Australian Egalitarianism in Practice

The push for people to move off the mission meant a period of turmoil and uncertainty for those people who had not yet established themselves on the outside. In 1962, the population of Mona Mona was 338. According to the minister for health and home affairs, the majority of these people said, when asked where they would like to live after the mission closed, that they would prefer to remain in the Kuranda area. They feared that their families would be split up and that they would be removed to government reserves such as Yarrabah and Palm Island.[49]

The Seventh Day Adventist Church appointed a missionary/welfare officer not only for 'spiritual guidance', but to provide practical assistance to Aboriginal people in finding suitable accommodation and employment.[50] The church authorities proposed a 'unique home ownership plan' to the director of native affairs: Aboriginal families were to be given the houses in which they had already been living on the mission.[51] These were to be transported to blocks of land made available by the Lands Department. Families were given their houses for free, but they were expected to take out loans of 'fifty to sixty pounds' each to pay for the transport of the houses from the mission.[52] The Church authorities also proposed that a small weekly rental be paid by each householder into an account in their name, withdrawals from which were to be countersigned by the church welfare officer and could only be used for house repair and maintenance.[53] Aboriginal people would be given the opportunity to lease these blocks in their own names. This plan was seen to be in accordance with the government's assimilation policy. However, it catered only to married couples. Government bureaucrats decided that any people 'not competent to come within the foregoing scheme' – such as elderly people, orphans, widows with children, and single mothers – would be sent to Palm Island.[54] This decision led to protest and to the Aborigines and Torres Strait Islanders Advancement League rallying to the aid of the Mona Mona people, with particular attention paid to the proposed removal of nine young single women. The secretary of the League, Joe McGuiness, wrote to Mr O'Leary of the Department of Native Affairs on 16 July 1962:

> Much resentment has been expressed by the parents and relatives that these girls were to be sent away suddenly, at night time and by truck, with-

out opportunity for their people outside the Mission to say good bye to
them. They are asking – Why were the girls to be sent away in this manner?
And why to Palm Island which is regarded as a place of punishment?[55]

Nevertheless, a number of Mona Mona people were forcibly relocated to
Palm Island. One man remembers being loaded on to a boat with his grandparents as a seven year old boy. The family was able to leave the island after
1967, but not before his grandfather had died there of what he believes was
a 'broken heart', yearning for his home place, Mona Mona.

For those people who were allowed to stay in the Kuranda area, the land
commissioner initially made twelve building allotments available for lease.[56]
These were conveniently located along the Barron River and railway sidings
at Koah, Mantaka and Kowrowa (see Map I.1). The Seventh Day Adventist
Church also leased a larger block of land at Top Kowrowa from the Lands
Department for the use of Mona Mona people.[57] The government policy was
that the people should be split up as much as possible to avoid the formation
of Aboriginal 'ghettos', and that they should not be located 'on the outskirts
of any small town, thus avoiding the danger of creating a "fringe" area'.[58] An
application for four additional building sites within the limits of Kuranda
town met with opposition from residents, who approached their local
member of parliament over the issue. The local member, Mr T. V. Gilmore,
wrote to the minister of education that 'the town people do not want four
coloured families living in the immediate town surroundings'.[59] The deputy
director of native affairs visited Kuranda, and a special meeting was held
over the issue. As a result, only one housing allotment was made available
within the town precinct, and the Church authorities gave an assurance to
the Shire Council that 'an outstanding family would be selected to reside on
this block'.[60] It was later agreed that further housing blocks would be made
available, but that they would be scattered around the town.[61]

In spite of the efforts of the welfare officer appointed by the Seventh
Day Adventist Church, which continued its pastoral care of the Mona
Mona people after the closure of the mission and which took responsibility
for assisting families in relocating, there was never sufficient housing for
all the Mona Mona people. The legacy of this period of displacement is
evident in Kuranda today. There continues to be a severe housing shortage,
and Aboriginal people spend much time and energy in trying to secure
adequate accommodation (Henry and Daly 2001). Moreover, because the
church authorities were called upon to nominate suitable families for the
allocation of housing allotments, it was inevitable that the hierarchy that
had developed among families on the mission was perpetuated. Church
attendance and compliance with the rules and regulations of mission life
were rewarded in the allocation of house and land packages.

While they awaited housing allocation, some people resided temporarily with relatives who had earlier received exemptions. Others built their own shelters and camped on the Barron River at Oak Forest.[62] This was on land that had been used as a holiday camp by Mona Mona people during the life of the mission and that was known to be a meeting and camping place prior to European settlement. Since 1926, however, the land had been a camping and water reserve under the trusteeship of the Mareeba Shire Council.[63] In 1962, officers investigated the 'illegal' occupation of the reserve by Aboriginal people from Mona Mona. There were at that time 'three clusters of some thirteen huts' on the reserve, three of which were toilets, as well as a couple of dwellings still under construction. The total population of fifty comprised eight households. All the adult men, except for old age pensioners, were employed.[64] They were refused application to lease any part of the reserve – even a proposal that the newly formed Ngoonbi Co-operative Housing Society be granted the leasehold was rejected[65] – and so the people remained 'illegal occupiers' until they were eventually 'dispersed'.[66]

Many Mona Mona people are not sure what happened behind the scenes with regard to the closure of the mission and their relocation. They were simply pawns in a bureaucratic game. One woman recalled that people had no control over which particular leases they took up, and that she simply went where her house was 'put down'. A male householder, however, remembered pulling a straw out of a hat to see where his house would go and therefore which of the allocated blocks of land he would be leasing. Some people appear to have been able to exercise more choice than others with regard to where they were placed. A woman who was granted a lease at Mantaka complained to the church welfare officer about the poor facilities there and was allocated a house in Cairns instead. She argued that on the mission there had been electricity and running water and that she was not used to living in the conditions at Mantaka and the other settlements, where no such conveniences were provided. A man told me he had given up his house because he found living at one of the settlements too inconvenient with regard to transport and employment for his family. His house was promptly allocated to a different family. The old mission cottage was eventually replaced by a new government-built house, which the new resident leased from the Department. However, the original leaseholder, as the owner of the old mission cottage, felt that he still had a claim on the land. His understanding was that the money he paid for the transport of his house from the mission was payment for the house itself, and he felt cheated because he had, after all, paid for his mission house and had never been justly compensated for it. Both men sought tenure of the land and appealed to the Queensland Department of Lands for a resolution in their favour. In 1988, the resident tenant again applied to the District Lands Office for lease of the allotment, but his application failed. By this time, the allotment had been gazetted as a Departmental and Official Purposes Reserve and, as its trustees, the Department of Community Services and Ethnic Affairs argued that it wished to retain the block as part of its Aboriginal housing construction programme.[67] Thus, this man's effort to free himself from dependency on state welfare by leasing his own housing allotment was foiled.

Housing and Land Rights

It is difficult to distinguish housing from land rights issues in the Kuranda area. I suggest that land rights were – and indeed continue to be – phrased in terms of a discourse about home ownership. Aboriginal people in the Kuranda area have made repeated attempts over the years to independently 'own' land in the Kuranda area within the Western system of land tenure by applying for leases.[68] The Queensland state government, however, was determined to 'assimilate' Aboriginal people by scattering them physically into different towns and cities. The fear was that Kuranda would become 'a "coloured" town'.[69] The director of Aboriginal and Islander affairs wrote to the Lands Department noting that leases were not required for Aboriginal people in Kuranda because the Department's policy was to 'acquire land and erect homes for Aborigines in areas where employment is assured, and this does not apply to the Kuranda area'.[70] Yet a survey submitted by the church welfare officer showed that the majority of Aboriginal men in the Kuranda area were regularly employed with the forestry or the railways, or else in seasonal employment with local cane and tobacco farmers. The church welfare officer appealed to the commissioner for lands noting that Aboriginal people did not want to be forced to leave the Kuranda district to live in the larger towns and cities. The Department responded by writing a letter to the church authorities expressing concern about the welfare officer's activities in Kuranda and his 'attitudes to his work'. In particular, the church authorities were threatened with cancellation of their government subsidy for the current financial year if the welfare officer did not conform to departmental policies of assimilation by encouraging Aboriginal residents of the Kuranda area to move on to other centres 'where work opportunity presents'.[71]

It was not that there was no land available in the Kuranda area. In fact, in a number of cases Aboriginal people were disappointed to find that blocks of land for which they had specifically applied were subsequently put up for public auction by the Lands Department.[72] This was in accordance with the government's policy of assimilation and with Australian egalitarian ideology: It was considered that Aboriginal people should have to bid competitively for land just like any other Australian. Assimilation policy can be linked to the post war period, during which egalitarian individualism in Australia was consolidated (Kapferer 1988). Aboriginal people were encouraged to dream the great Australian home-ownership dream. The egalitarian ideology that lies at the basis of this dream generated the scheme for resettlement of the Mona Mona people. The idea was that, like other Australians, they would have the opportunity to purchase their own houses on their own quarter acre blocks. What was not taken into account was the fact that having spent their lives under the 'protection' of the mission, they were now effectively refugees in their own country without the financial resources and the knowledge base required to compete within 'mainstream Australia'. Any failure to be competitive on the part of Aboriginal people was explained as being their own fault as a group of individuals who shared innate qualities and was not recognised as being founded on a social situation which in the very process of making them the same actually constituted them as different.

Assimilation policy was about 'granting' access to the body politic and the public sphere only to those Aboriginal people whose 'difference' could be erased, or to those Aboriginal people who were willing and able to display capacities that settler society deemed valuable. The legislative regime provided a process whereby Aboriginal people could escape the provisions of the special legislation that regulated every aspect of their lives if they were able to demonstrate those qualities that marked their difference from the 'primitive' (other Aboriginal people) and their identity with the 'civilised' (Europeans). Aboriginal people who qualified were issued exemption cards as proof of their new status. The process of 'letting in' through the issue of exemption cards, however, insidiously operated to confirm these very people's categorical difference to the society into which they were allowed. Aboriginal people today produce their old exemption cards with mixed feelings of pride (that they were among the chosen few that qualified), shame (about their apparent complicity) and anger (that they were subject at all to such legislative and bureaucratic violence).

Assimilation policy, although not considered politically correct today, was originally supported by many Aboriginal people. This can be explained, I submit, by the fact that they actually shared the egalitarian 'logic of inclusion', as Kapferer (1988) puts it, out of which assimilation policy was born. The political platforms of many of the early Aboriginal political associations in Australia were openly assimilationist. In New South Wales, for example, the president of the Aborigines Progressive Association urged 'all Aborigines in Australia who want the privileges and benefits of civilisation

... to get behind this movement. We want to be absorbed into the Nation of Australia, and thus to survive in the land of our forefathers, on equal terms' (as cited in McGregor 1997: 251). Many Aboriginal people were eventually to learn from bitter experience that assimilation policy was in practice insidiously inequitable. There are, as Kapferer (1988: 180) argues, 'possibilities in egalitarianism that can cause great suffering when harnessed to the machinery of state'. Assimilation policy in Kuranda was effectively used to deny Aboriginal people the capacity to purchase land.[73]

Throughout the sixties and seventies, Aboriginal people in the Kuranda area lobbied the relevant government authorities for housing, mainly through their church welfare officer. Even those families lucky enough to have houses from the mission were inadequately accommodated, as these houses were mostly one bedroom cottages originally built for married couples whose children had been removed to the dormitories. For more than twenty years people lived in these old cottages, building extensions out of scrap materials to accommodate growing families and networks of extended kin. Eventually, during the 1980s, these old mission houses were replaced with new government-built houses for which people were required to pay rent.

Within twenty years of the closure of the mission, the status of Aboriginal people as independent leaseholders was erased, and they became once again clients of the state welfare bureaucracy. How did this happen? In 1975, the Seventh Day Adventist Church applied to the government to have its leasehold block at Top Kowrowa[74] converted to freehold and transferred to the Ngoonbi Co-operative Housing Society. The application was denied, and the church was informed that 'it would not be in the best public interest to allow conversion of the lease to freehold tenure in view of the developments proposed by the Department of Aboriginal and Islanders Advancement'.[75] The Church thereupon surrendered the lease to the Lands Department. This incident marks the beginning of what was to be an eventual total state government takeover of all the original blocks of land that had been leased to Aboriginal people.

In 1979, people were asked to surrender their separate leases to the Lands Department, and the Department of Aboriginal and Islander Affairs (DAIA) was made trustee of the land. People were convinced to give up their leases by the promise that their rates arrears would be paid by the DAIA and that they would no longer be required to pay the rates owed on their blocks of land. The actual signing over of the leases occurred at a meeting in the Church Hall. One man told me that it was the pastor who had 'got everyone to sign back their leases'. He said that people were bitter about this and that they believed that they were 'tricked', as they did not understand what it meant to sign 'that piece of paper'. The forfeiture of the

leases was gazetted in January and April 1980,[76] and the leases were declared Aboriginal reserves under the control of the DAIA.[77] The DAIA was
responsible for providing adequate housing for Aboriginal people. According to Andrews (1982: 1), 'it was not until 1981, when rumours started to
the effect that housing would be built and people moved to it from their ex-
leasehold blocks, that people discovered that they no longer legally owned
their land and houses'.

In response to the concerns of Aboriginal people regarding their status as house and land owners, the Department called a meeting in January 1982 at the Seventh Day Adventist Hall. At this meeting, people were
promised that they would not be moved and that they would be consulted
regarding the plans of any new houses that the Department planned to
build for them. Yet it was not until after an article was published in the
Cairns Post (8 July 1982), and the builder had already been contracted, that
some people became aware of what proved to be a fait accompli. The DAIA
had decided to begin its building program by constructing several blocks
of single story apartments at Top Kowrowa. This further fuelled people's
fears that they would be removed from their blocks of land at Mantaka,
Koah and Bottom Kowrowa to be 'herded' together with the people at Top
Kowrowa. They mobilised in protest against their treatment and were assisted in their struggle by settlers sympathetic to their cause. In addition, a
number of settlers who were fearful that the construction program would
result in an Aboriginal 'ghetto' on their doorstep or who were against the
clearing of the land that went with the development joined the protest. I
have selected the following two speeches from recordings of the meetings
held on 19 and 21 July 1982 as representative of the different views of the
non-Aboriginal protesters:[78]

> They invested a lot of money levelling out this beautiful countryside ... so
> we have to get somebody responsible up here to stop all this destruction
> what's going on. ... As a resident of Kuranda I hope to live here for many
> years and I hope to live here peacefully and happily in this community and
> I'd like to say that for the last two years that ... I *have* been living here hap-
> pily and peacefully. It seems to me that black people, white people have
> lived together with one another happily and peacefully ... Now things can
> continue to be peaceful if the Abos are allowed to live like they are liv-
> ing ... They are spaced out in other words. They are not concentrated
> like rats ... If we do get concentration camps going on here ... well what
> I anticipate is simply this: there will be more incidents like we see down
> in Cairns and Yarrabah. People will be consuming more liquor. There will
> be more stabbings. There will be more murders. Kuranda is not going to

be what it used to be. So for the sake of the black people, and for the sake of the white people, I hope this bloody nonsense over here will be taken care of swiftly.

These people were promised homes, not units ... No one was notified, no one heard any more from the DAIA until we saw it in the paper the other day, and that's what these people are extremely angry about. Not only are they not getting homes, they're not getting homes that are suitable for their style of living. They're just bloody units! That's a slum of the 1990s. That's a ghetto. That's Soweto in South Africa. ... They talk about refugees from overseas, and we got genuine Australian refugees in our own country, being refugeed from here, and refugeed from there and they're put in not much better than an encampment, another settlement, and I think, I agree with these people. It's just not on. They've been cheated and lied to and they can't take much more of it. It's just ridiculous.

The building contractor was sympathetic to Aboriginal people's concerns and attended the meeting to explain the plans to them. After seeing the plans, some people from other settlements expressed fear that they would be moved to Top Kowrowa. Particular families had, after twenty years, developed close attachments and identifications with the settlements at Mantaka, Bottom Kowrowa and Koah, and each of the settlements had developed its own identity. Some of the responses of Aboriginal people to the plans at the meeting of 21 July 1982 were recorded as follows:[79]

Woman: As far as I'm concerned I don't trust DAIA one bit ... They can move us, put all the damn houses up here, like a mob of cattle ... but they got another thing comin' ... As far as I'm concerned, I think they trying to get us all away from Mantaka so they can sell Mantaka off because that's good land there.

Man: I left Mona Mona mission when I was five years old, and I was sad to leave it, most of you knew that. I think all of youse probably be sad, you loved it. But I'm talking for Bottom Kowrowa. I think most of youse like where you stayin' now ... I mean most of you don't wanna leave there. Like ... was saying, she don't wanna move from Mantaka, because the government probably want it for real estate or something like that.

A key concern of people was the architectural design of the buildings. As the comments below evidence, people were angry that DAIA was building apartments and not separate houses. Their dream – which I stress is well accepted as 'the great Australian dream', and not culturally particular to them – was to own their own houses on their own quarter acre blocks.

Not only that, they wanted the traditional Queensland settler-style wooden house on high stumps.

> Woman 1: We don't like that … We want this to be separate, quarter of an acre … It's all shut in!
>
> Woman 2: If they cannot allow black people to live in places like Cairns and Mareeba in home units, then why put them put here? They should be having decent homes, a decent fence, not homes built by walls.
>
> Man: They too close. That fella there he gonna know all these fella's business eh?
>
> Man: This like a bullock yard, living in a yard. They must think we bullocks.
>
> Woman: Or like a prison camp.
>
> Man: They're more homes for people that come and go, but these people here they're not comin' and goin'. They're comin' and stayin'!
>
> Woman: They can't put us on high-block house? It's all muddy when it's wet, mucky.
>
> Man: They told us they gonna build high blocks, but it's not. And the families … will be squabbling all around. Let's say drunks come home, waking up the children from their sleep, maybe one of you. If someone gets sick over there in one house, it'll spread like wildfire.
>
> Woman: You don't like to hear the next door neighbours having their own row. And coming from my heart, I'm sure a lot of you people don't want to live near our people who drink. There're a lot of our people who like to live on their own without any disturbance of drunkards. Now isn't that true? We love our people, but we like to live peaceably.

There was much resentment expressed at the protest meeting against the treatment that Aboriginal people have had to endure and have continued to suffer at the hands of the state. People focused on the state government – and in particular the Department of Aboriginal and Islander Affairs – as the villains in the piece. Some people also wondered how big a part the missionaries had played in their oppression. They spoke about their lives at Mona Mona, partly with nostalgic fondness, partly with anger at their unjust treatment on the mission. In particular, they raised the issue of what had happened to the wages that had been kept in trust accounts for them under the Aboriginals Preservation and Protection Act of 1939–1946. This was twenty years before the officially recognised campaign for government reparation of Aboriginal 'stolen wages' (Kidd 2002). One man who had worked in the mission sawmill for all his adult life said:

> I always think this when we come out of the mission, we come out with nothing. The only receipt we get out when we working there was only a tithe receipt, and where the receipt that we got from banking? We get nothin'. Now that's under cover ... I came out mission just only with the house that we bought, no receipt from the house, no receipt from the bank that we put in. We came out penniless, only just with the house. So, where that money go?

After someone at the meeting called for people to forget about the past and concentrate on the current issue and on fighting for the future, a woman responded that they needed to remember the past in order to be able to deal with the present and the future. As she put it:

> We all gotta stand for the same thing, and that thing is: Don't let a white person put it over us. Don't say yes and say no. Don't forget about the past, because the past is right just stickin' up again! It's gonna be here again! It's gonna be like another reserve, another mission! Now we wanna wipe that right out. We wanna be free! Don't listen to what white people say ... I never like a white person telling me what to do and I want youse to be like that too, because you gonna be living the same life like at Mona Mona, and nobody's gonna tell me you won't because that's gonna be another reserve ... So stand up and fight for your rights ... Fight for free home because the government owe us that. They owe us a free home; I don't care what anyone say; because our men worked for government.

The references to the past and to fears that the system of imprisonment, or reserve confinement, is being reproduced in the present are significant. They constitute a critique of the disciplinary practices which kept Aboriginal people under domination in the past, and a recognition that such strategies of power continue to operate, albeit in newly disguised forms. The development went ahead as planned at Top Kowrowa, but people were not moved from Mantaka, Koah or Bottom Kowrowa as they had feared. Additional protest meetings and a sit-in at the office of the local Member of Parliament secured more appropriate houses for the people at Mantaka and Koah (although they were not high-set as was preferred). However, once their own mission houses were demolished, householders were expected to pay rent to the Department for their new houses.

The social situation regarding Aboriginal housing demonstrates the destructive possibilities of Australian egalitarianism in practice. Egalitarian ideology in an unholy alliance with state paternalism insidiously provided the rationale for denying to Aboriginal peoples both communal and individual land ownership, as well as for locking them into a situation of welfare dependency. Issues concerning Aboriginal rights to land in Kuranda have been thoroughly consumed by a welfare discourse focused on the government provision of adequate housing. This is an example of what Collmann (1988: 16) described as the 'predatory and expansive' nature of the Aboriginal welfare apparatus in Australia, practices which have more recently been referred to by Noel Pearson (2000) as 'welfare poison' (see also Sutton 2009).

The Incorporation of Self-Determination

In 1972, the election of a federal Labor government heralded a new government policy of Aboriginal 'self-determination'. Yet in practice, state governments, through their welfare apparatuses, maintained a firm control of Aboriginal affairs. While people were no longer institutionalised, the tentacles of welfare bureaucracy, in particular with regard to housing, reached into the very heart of Aboriginal social relations and continued to keep Aboriginal people under administrative surveillance. During the 1970s, the Aboriginal communities of Aurukun and Mornington Island were granted local government status under the Local Government (Aboriginal Lands) Act of 1978 (Qld). All the remaining Aboriginal communities in Queensland were granted deeds of grant in trust (DOGIT) and the various community councils were granted self-governance. However, this was not the case with the Aboriginal people of Mona Mona who had been dispersed around the Kuranda area in 1962. They had no access to the resources available to DOGIT communities. In cases such as that of Kuranda, where Aboriginal people do not have their own community councils, the policy of self-determination has been implemented through the establishment and proliferation of Aboriginal organisations or representative bodies. Aboriginal difference is accommodated within the Australian nation, but only through state approved structures of governance.

During the 1970s and 1980s, one of the ways that Aboriginal people responded positively to the policy was by forming housing associations under the Co-operatives and Other Societies Act of 1967 (Qld). This was a structure of governance that was acceptable within the state definition of self-determination. In the Kuranda area, several housing associations were formed. Later their interests expanded to encompass other welfare issues such as employment, health, alcoholism, youth suicide and land rights issues. For example, the Ngoonbi Co-operative Housing Society was formed and incorporated in the mid-1970s in response to the appalling housing circumstances of Aboriginal people in the Kuranda area. Most people lived in poor and overcrowded conditions. There was no electricity or running water in the old mission houses.[80] People were forced to carry water from and bathe in the river. Most households relied on candles and kerosene lamps for lighting and wood fuel for cooking and for keeping warm on the cold, foggy nights that are typical during the winter months. Ngoonbi was formed to address this situation. However, it soon became the focal organisation through which both government and non-government agencies dealt with Aboriginal people in the area. Access to social security benefits were handled through the organisation, as were various recreational, educational and employment programs. Today, Ngoonbi is recognised as encompassing and representing the interests of all Aboriginal people resident in the Kuranda area, whatever their tribal affiliation. During my fieldwork, I was advised by an executive member of the Djabugay Tribal Aboriginal Corporation to contact Ngoonbi as the more far reaching organisation with regard to consultation over issues encompassing the wider population.

Ngoonbi owns a building on the main street of Kuranda, which houses its office, as well as a number of houses for which it collects rents. The corporation also owns a farm on the edge of the town with a manager's residence and a large shed that is used for recreational purposes and for workshops and meetings. Ngoonbi, however, has never been able to keep abreast of the housing requirements in Kuranda, and two other housing corporations, the Mantaka Shanty Association and the Kowrowa Community Association, were formed to service the more localised needs of people who lived in the settlements along the Barron River. The proliferation of Aboriginal organisations is not merely a reflection of the inability of these organisations to be representative in the context of the 'Aboriginal domain' (see Martin and Finlayson 1996: 4–8)[81] but is also related to the wider phenomenon of governmental devolution and thus to general strategies of disciplinary power. Such organisations are spawned by the particular material conditions of Aboriginal people's lives that draw them into welfare dependency and bureaucratic bondage.

Bureaucratic Bondage

Aboriginal community-based associations in Kuranda, like many elsewhere in Australia, are incorporated under the Aboriginal Councils and Associations Act of 1976 (Cwlth). The provisions of this act set the constraints and bureaucratic process according to which the lives of Aboriginal people in Kuranda are organised and, I suggest, operates as one of the strategies through which they are maintained as 'docile bodies' (Foucault 1977: 135).

However, practices of resistance are also apparent in this area, and often the requirements of the act are not followed. It could be argued that this is not so much an expression of resistance as an outcome of the impossible demands of the legislation: that is, complying with the provisions of the act is just too onerous a task. This argument, however, is based on the assumption that resistance depends on the existence of a given subject who self-consciously *intends* to resist. Yet as Foucault (1979: 55) notes, 'There are no relations of power without resistances'. In, his exemplary Foucauldian analysis of the social history of the Dhan-gadi Aboriginal people of New South Wales, Morris has demonstrated how the forms that the struggle by Aboriginal people take 'are not necessarily expressed in terms of an overt political consciousness or actions but more specifically as a culture of resistance: that is as cultural practices which develop as a "way of life" in opposition to the specific structures of domination' (Morris 1989: 4).

In Kuranda, there were in 1997 six different incorporated bodies servicing an Aboriginal population of less than 420. These were the Djabugay Tribal Aboriginal Corporation, Buda:dji Aboriginal Development Association Aboriginal Corporation, Ngoonbi Co-operative Housing Society Ltd, Mona Mona Aboriginal Corporation, the Mantaka Shanty Association Aboriginal Corporation, and the Kowrowa Aboriginal Corporation. Under the requirements of the Aboriginal Councils and Associations Act of 1976 (Cwlth), such incorporated bodies are obliged to keep current registers of members (s. 58) which must be given each year after 30 June, or any time upon request within fourteen days, to the government appointed registrar of Aboriginal corporations (s. 4). Associations are contractually obliged to call and conduct annual general meetings and special general meetings (s. 58B) as provided in the rules of each association (s. 47). Except when exempted under section 59A, incorporated associations are required to keep 'proper accounts and records' (s. 59), and the governing committee of the Association must cause a report to be prepared each financial year including a statement of income and expenditure. The existence of so many incorporated bodies presents an onerous amount of work for the few Aboriginal people who have the skills, energy and dedication to ensure that these legislative requirements are met. During my field work, people regularly complained to me about the number of meetings that they had to attend. They were expected to attend not only meetings of these associations, but also meetings called by the Native Title Representative Body on the subject of native title claims and meetings regarding claims under the Aboriginal Land Act of 1991 (Qld). In addition, they were called upon to attend numerous other special working group meetings, such as the community taskforce meetings in connection with the development planning of the old Mona Mona mission land and management of the Barron Gorge National Park.

In 1997, some Aboriginal people in Kuranda attempted to free them-selves from the bondage of these legal and bureaucratic requirements by amalgamating all their associations 'under one umbrella'. First, however, a committee had to be formed: the Dagil Nyiya Nyiya Regional Steering Committee.[82] The committee managed to secure funds to hire a consul-tant to 'develop a new operational system and structure that will bring all the organisations together, as one organisation, under the one community owned and operated structure'.[83] But this only led to the formation of yet another incorporated organisation: KMKM (Kuranda, Mantaka, Kowrowa, Mona Mona).

The incorporation of Aboriginal organisations serves to mask an in-sidious process of 'bureaucratic erasure' of Aboriginal people (Kapferer 1995b). Self-determination, although ostensibly a radical departure from the policy of assimilation, stems from the same ideological foundation of egalitarian individualism. The Australian government policy of self-deter-mination was introduced in concert with its new multicultural policies. As Kapferer (1988: 205–6) has argued, although the multiculturalist ostensibly values difference while the assimilationist values sameness, they are both 'grounded in the one egalitarian individualist logic'.

Accountability through Planning and Management

A discourse of strategic planning, management and 'accountability' has penetrated Aboriginal organisations in Kuranda. Planning is recognised as necessary for bureaucratic recognition and for legitimate access to govern-ment grants and other resources, including land. For example, as a means of achieving government recognition of native title to the Barron Gorge National Park, the Djabugay Tribal Aboriginal Corporation engaged con-sultants to help them prepare a land use and management strategy for the park. Yet planning is also a disciplinary practice, an apparatus of state con-trol (Lefebvre 2009). In his case study of Majd el Krum, an Arab village in Israel, Yiftachel (1995: 221) argues that planning can 'facilitate domination and control of three key societal resources: space, power and wealth'. He notes that the 'very same planning tools usually introduced to assist social reform and improvement in people's quality of life can be used as a means of controlling and repressing minority groups' (Yiftachel 1995: 219).

The devolution of governmental power to community organisations and the transfer of bureaucratic responsibility that this devolution entails is an example of what Foucault (1977: 211) describes as the tendency of disci-plinary mechanisms to become 'de-institutionalized', or 'to emerge from the closed fortress in which they once functioned and to circulate in a "free" state'. This is particularly evident with regard to Aboriginal organisations.

The 'discipline-blockade', the enclosed institution and the Mona Mona mission may no longer be operative today, but they have been replaced by the 'disciplinary-mechanisms' of bureaucracy. National concern with 'accountability' in Aboriginal organisations is an expression of this disciplinary regime (Martin & Finlayson 1996). 'Accountability' was a key factor in the federal government's justification for dissolving the national Indigenous representative body, the Aboriginal and Torres Strait Islander Commission (ATSIC) and transferring its programs to mainstream agencies.

What is particularly insidious about the bureaucratic regime, as Kidd (1997) has observed, is its ability to camouflage the incompetency of civil servants and the failure of government policies and administrative programs through a system of continuous transformation. Policies and processes are constantly changed, fostering a situation of uncertainty. Aboriginal people have to deal with the incessant modification of bureaucratic requirements and the continual mutation of the government departments authorised to manage them. The regime disguises the failure of its government, and the social situation of Aboriginal people is interpreted as a natural outcome of those racial and cultural traits peculiar to them. As Kidd (1997: 347) writes: 'Diverse objectives, incompatible funding priorities and conflicting power strategies underwrite endemic ineffectuality and default ... Poverty, derelict housing, low education and employment levels, alcoholism and domestic violence, individual despair and community upheaval are still – conveniently – interpreted as aspects of an Aboriginal, rather than a governmental problem'.

Re-empowering Place

I have highlighted the practices which operated to erase the Aboriginality of the places settlers colonised from their memory. These processes also resulted in a mutilation of Aboriginal memory, one which left wounds that Aboriginal people are still actively seeking to heal in ways that I discuss in the following chapters. Removal from their home places and hearth lands into reserves meant that they were denied access to the mnemonic experiences[84] that operated as a means of transmitting a way of being in the world to the next generation. Moreover, because places are only empowered for memory by the people that occupy them, their removal meant that many of these places lost the agency that they would otherwise have accrued as sources of the experience of being-in-place and thus of emplacement (Casey 1997: 201).

Between 1916 and 1962, most Aboriginal people of the Kuranda area were confined on the Mona Mona Mission. Since the mission closed, they have engaged in a continuing struggle against projects of the state that deny them the security of connection to their home places. Ironically, as Austin-Broos (2009: 5) has similarly noted in relation to the Arrernte of Central Australia, state-managed withdrawal of the mission 'entailed radical marginalization'. They were abruptly drawn entirely into a cash economy where they were '*marginalized* and not simply peripheral because the forms of value they brought from the past could no longer redefine their circumstance'.

Thus, Aboriginal people have had a long experience of the state's power to reorganise social space through the erasure of place. Today, they increasingly face the encroachment of private real estate developers. A potent means for the reproduction of power relations is the control of space. As Harvey (1985: 23) writes: 'The state, or some other social grouping such as financiers, developers, or landlords, can thus often hide their power to shape social reproduction behind the seeming neutrality of their power to organise space'. In this chapter, I have explored some of the responses of Kuranda Aboriginal people to the state's spatial strategies, particularly in relation to housing. In the following chapters, I explore further aspects of Aboriginal people's struggle to re-emplace themselves in the face of a continuing history of colonisation, including the arrival of new waves of settlers during the late twentieth century.

NOTES

1. Woolston and Colliver (1967: 30) note that he did not actually reach the Barron Falls.
2. The explorers and early settlers did not use the term 'rainforest', but 'scrub'. Many of the old settlers in Kuranda and other locals in the region still use this term, and in fact some deride the use of the term 'rainforest' as an expression of New Age romanticism.
3. Tindale (1976: 21) corroborates: 'In 1938 Tjapukai men told me that they had created some areas of grassland in their time, as was also done in their father's time. They took advantage of very dry days at the end of the dry season, to set fire to the margins of the rainforest, thereby making for better camping and hunting opportunities. It was also their custom to fire glades [pockets] before rain time'.
4. Tindale (1976: 22) was told by the son of one of the original settlers of Atherton that 'Atherton was a natural open wet forested glade ... this being the reason it came into being as the first settlement'.
5. During the Mission days, some of the Mona Mona residents were allowed to camp on the river at Oak Forest for the holidays. The Bannings, a Djabugay family who had escaped the mission system and who lived on a settler farm at Redlynch, would sometimes join them. Oak Forest continues today to be a

favourite holiday camping place for many Aboriginal people who remember having camped there regularly since childhood. There was much resentment during the 1990s when the Mareeba Shire Council erected 'No Camping' signs in response to complaints from residents who had bought newly subdivided land allotments along the Barron River.

6. According to Bottoms (1992: 10), 'the first relatively detailed report of a private beche-de-mer expedition occurred in mid-December 1857', on Green Island off Cairns.

7. Chris Anderson (1983) includes an account of this contact era in his PhD thesis. See also Anderson (1979).

8. Walter Hill Veivers (1848–1912) and Georgina Veivers, whose many descendants still live in the Kuranda area, were among those who took up selections in 1893. They purchased 407 acres in the Speewah area, apparently anticipating (wrongly) that the railway line would take that direction (Veivers 1988: 63).

9. I emphasise this passage because it is an early recognition of the existence of Aboriginal customary law with regard to land.

10. This story of a massacre in the Davies Creek-Speewah area was also told to Cassells (1977) and Patz (1978) during their linguistic studies among the Banning family at Redlynch. The story, which today features in a film shown at the Tjapukai Aboriginal Cultural Park (with a script written by historian Timothy Bottoms), was passed on to the descendants of Granny Buttercup Banning, who had witnessed the event first hand.

11. Hughes (1982: 3) notes that 'All the descendants of Thron and Elizabeth Matthisen who remember these two adopted members of the family speak highly of their integrity and loyalty and the influence they had on them as young children. They taught them Aboriginal words and their meanings, the tribal corroboree, how to spear fish ...' This is a common theme. Children of other settler families also have fond memories of learning to fish and hunt from Aboriginal people who worked off the mission.

12. Alfred Street's plantation was called 'Fernhill'. Today the property is a cultural tourism and wildlife park called the Kuranda Rainforestation, featuring the Pamagirri Aboriginal dance troupe.

13. On his list of pioneer families of the Kuranda district, Crothers (n.d.) lists Hobler as a railway engineer and the Newbury family as having lived in the first house on the Cairns side of Collins Bridge, over the Barron River. A member of the Newbury family worked on the construction of the range railway and was killed with six others in a cave-in at No. 15 tunnel in April 1889 (Broughton 1991: 32). George Hobson, who had a selection at Myola, was 'gashed to death with scrub knives' there on 20 July 1890. An Aboriginal man, referred to in the *Cairns Post* as 'Darkie', was sentenced to death for his murder. His sentence was commuted to life imprisonment, and he was sent to Fraser Island. He escaped and was eventually recaptured in Kuranda in 1902 (Jones 1976: 314).

14. The people living in this camp at Port Douglas were removed by the police to the Mona Mona mission in the late 1930s. According to oral accounts re-

corded by Wood (1990: 6), they were removed 'some say because of their as-
sertiveness, others because it was feared that they might be recruited by the
Japanese military (the luggers on which many of them had worked were largely
owned and/or skippered by Japanese)'.

15. Finlayson (1991: 49) has recorded similar experiences with regard to the problem of names and the difficulties people face in trying to find relatives.

16. Section 4 of the Act read as follows:

    '4. Every person who is –
    (a) An aboriginal inhabitant of Queensland; or
    (b) A half-caste who, at the commencement of this Act, is living with an
    aboriginal as wife, husband, or child; or
    (c) A half-caste who, otherwise than as wife, husband, or child, habitually
    lives or associates with aboriginals;
    shall be deemed to be an aboriginal within the meaning of this Act'.

17. Kidd (1997: 346) also points out that 'until the 1950s, Aboriginal administration was largely run as a personal fiefdom'. Only three men held the position
of chief administrator between 1914 and 1986.

18. Mona Mona was proclaimed a 'Reserve for the Use of the Aboriginal Inhabitants of the State, Kuranda' on 29 August 1913. According to Collins (1981:
19), the first Aboriginal people to be brought to Mona Mona were a party
of seven from Barambah (now Cherbourg) in southeast Queensland. Taking
his figures from the original Aboriginal rolls in the Seventh Day Adventist archives, he notes that other early arrivals were brought from Cairns (twenty-
four), Yarrabah (twelve), Redlynch (two) and Mt Carbine (twelve). In 1914,
two more people were removed from Cairns, three people were transferred
from Yarrabah, and thirty-eight people were brought from Mareeba. Among
this Mareeba group were fourteen unnamed children. According to the Chief
Protector's annual report for the year 1914, there were ninety-three Aboriginal
people at Mona Mona by the end of that year. Their ranks soon swelled, however, as police brought in more groups from the Mareeba area. Removal Order
correspondence names a total of fifty-five men, women and children removed
by police from Mareeba to Mona Mona during 1915. The annual report of
the Chief Protector of Aboriginals for the year 1915 lists a total of 128 people
removed to Mona Mona (fifty-nine men, fifty-nine women, and ten children)
by the end of 1915 (Mackett 1989).

19. Correspondence files, 1901–1944, Mona Mona, 1913–1933., SA A/58784. See
also Kidd 1997: 71–72.

20. Ironically, a drought during 1914–1915 meant that the Mission was not immediately able to accept sixty extra mouths to feed, so the removal order was
delayed until March 1916.

21. Letter from E. Hunter of Hunter's Barron Falls Hotel to Hon E. Theodore, 6
March 1916. In Correspondence Files, 1901–1944, Removals – removal of
Kuranda Tribe to Mona Mona, 1916, QSA A/69429 (16/3998/16). The same
file includes a telegram from M. Fitzpatrick, another local publican, to Hon
McCormack voicing similar concerns. He complained that two of the Aborigi-

nal people had been taken in handcuffs and that no notice was given their employers of the intention to remove them.

22. Memorandum from Chief Protector of Aboriginals to Protector of Aboriginals, Brisbane, 18 February, 1916. In Correspondence Files, 1901–1944, Removals – removal of Kuranda Tribe to Mona Mona, 1916, QSA A/69429 (16/3998/16).

23. Memorandum from Senior Sergeant Henry Butler Kenny, District Inspector's Office, Cairns to Commissioner of Police, Brisbane, 14 June 1916. In Correspondence Files, 1901–1944, Removals – removal of Kuranda Tribe to Mona Mona, 1916 QSA A/69429 (16/3998/16).

24. According to Finlayson (1991: 48), as well as people from the Kuranda area, the Barron Falls depot attracted people from Speewah and Redlynch, both of whom camped together. She notes that the Mareeba camps had greater regional diversity than the camps at Kuranda, as the three camps at Mareeba had people 'from territories ranging from the southern reaches of the Atherton Tablelands, including Ravenshoe, west to Mt Surprise and Chillagoe'.

25. According to the removal records, people were brought to Mona Mona from Mt Garnet, Herberton, Mt Molloy, Mt Carbine, Meadowbank Station, Almaden, Ashmore Station, Malanda, Cairns, Redlynch, Port Douglas, Mowbray Vale, and as far afield as Georgetown.

26. See Tindale (1938–1939), Harvard and Adelaide Universities Anthropological Expedition, Australia, 1938–1939, contents of Vol. II, unpublished notes on contents for cards N.332–N.945 of the Expedition series, photocopy held at the Australian Institutes of Aboriginal and Torres Strait Islander Studies.

27. Names are spelt according to their currently recognised spelling, which is not necessarily the way Tindale spelt them.

28. As extracted by P. J. Mackett (1989).

29. The watchhouse charge book from the police station at Mt Molloy records four people as 'unlawfully leaving Mona Mona' in 1915. Among these are a married couple who were taken, as punishment, to the Hull River Mission.

30. See Finlayson (1991: 50–52) for an account of the economic hardships of the mission. The mission was not a profit-making venture but was run as a mixed subsistence farm to feed its population. It was not always able to provide sufficient food, and the inmates were expected to work to feed themselves.

31. According to Roberts (1986: 147), the first baptisms at Mona Mona took place on 23 July 1916 and were conducted by H. E. Piper.

32. This code changed over the years and depended also on the leniency of the incumbent supervisor. At one stage, parents were only allowed contact with their children across a wire fence barrier. They used to be able to talk to them and pass them morsels of food, but they could not hug or cuddle them. Policy eventually changed, and children and parents were allowed to go on day excursions together on the weekends, as well as have closer contact during the annual holiday camp at Oak Forest. It was during these times that people remember being taught about bush foods and how to fish and hunt by their parents and grandparents.

33. Finlayson (1991: 116) records the following account by an ex-Mona Mona resident. There is no date given as to when the strike occurred, but I suggest it

would have been during the late 1950s: 'Everybody used to have their meal all in one, in a dining room until all the men had a strike. They wanted everybody to have their own meal. You know, cook at home. The men used to have one slice and a half [of bread] in the dining room, and a cup of coffee and the ladies only had one slice. We used to get hungry and then the men had a strike. The superintendent said, "If you want your own meals like that then you have to do away with all the dogs". Poor dogs, they had to shoot all the dogs. They think that you are going to waste your food on the dogs. We felt sorry for all our dogs that got shot you know, poor things, and then we started to have our own meals then'.

34. The term 'language' in the singular is used widely among Aboriginal Australians to refer not only to a language in its entirety, but also to special words, phrases, songs and so on that are considered spiritually powerful.

35. This belief in the power of words is widespread among Aboriginal Australians. In his autobiography, the Yolngu leader Wandjuk Marika wrote that what he and his people most objected to in the work of anthropologists who had written about them was the publishing in written form, not the detailed description of the ritual practices themselves but 'language': the actual secret and powerful words associated with the rituals (Marika and Isaacs 1995).

36. The practice of standing over a fire as a means of spiritual cleansing.

37. See Briscoe (2003) for an excellent analysis of ideologies and responses to disease and health among Indigenous people in Western Australia and Queensland from 1900 to 1940.

38. Visit of Inspection to Palm Island, Yarrabah and Mona Mona: Report by Sir Raphael Cilento, Director General of Health and Medical Services, February–March 1937, QSA A/58861 (37/5698).

39. Report by P. Graham Croll, 28 April 1939. In QSA QS501/1 (6J/9).

40. Memo from the Medical Officer to the Deputy Director General of Health and Medical Services, 2 September 1940, QSA QS 505/1 (6J/9).

41. Letter from A. W. Waddell, Clerk, Woothakata [Mareeba] Shire Council, to the Director General of Health and Medical Services, Mareeba, 30 September 1940, QSA QS505/1 (6J/9).

42. Memo from Chief Protector of Aboriginals to the Superintendent of Mona Mona Mission, Brisbane, 31 August 1938, QSA QS505/1 (SJ/9).

43. Memo/Letter from the Deputy Director of Native Affairs to the director of Native Affairs, 30 May 1955. In General Correspondence (Torres Strait Region), 1936–1985, Missions – Mona Mona reserve, 1953–1955, QSA A/59487 (6H/2).

44. See memos to the Minister, to the Under Secretary and the Sub-Department of Native Affairs, from Public Service Inspector (22 September 1941, 8 October, 1941, 28 August 1942). In Health and Home Affairs Department Batch files, Welfare fund 1941–1947, QSA A/69634.

45. In a submission presented in 1963 to the Select Committee Appointed to Examine the Aboriginals Preservation and Protection Acts of 1939–1946, the Queensland Council for the Advancement of Aborigines and Torres Islanders discusses the many limitations of the trust fund system of forced saving and

lists first hand accounts of abuses of the system. Aboriginal people were not issued with passbooks. They were not free to withdraw their money at will, and the Department often forced them to justify their need for their own money. Some people claim never to have had access to their accounts and are not sure what happened to their money. Currently there is an active campaign in Queensland to deal with what has come to be known as the 'stolen wages' issue. See Kidd 1997 and 2002.

46. From 1930–31, it became the practice to use money from the various Aboriginal trust funds for the purpose of 'supplementing the Vote'. This included interest from the savings accounts of Aboriginal people not living on reserves. For many years during this period, employers also followed the practice of deducting 10 per cent of the wages of married men and 5 per cent of the wages of single men who were inmates of reserves but employed outside on work agreements for the purpose of maintaining their dependants who lived on the reserves. In practice, the money obtained this way between 1931 and 1943 was credited to the Standing Account. The state used the money to provide 'relief for sick and indigent natives' and to provide maintenance for relatives on reserves, as well as to defray the costs of removals.

47. *Government Gazette,* 26 November 1955, 1426.

48. QSA QS505/1, SJ/38.

49. Submission to Cabinet on closure of Mona Mona Mission and disposal of Native Cottages, by H. W. Noble, Minister for Health and Home Affairs, Brisbane, 8 March, 1962, QSA A/58934 (6J/35).

50. The Queensland Council for the Advancement of Aborigines and Torres Islanders wrote in 1963 of the closure of Mona Mona: 'This Seventh Day Adventist mission (4000+ acres with farming, timber, cattle) was closed down in late 1962 for an irrigation scheme. One might have expected compensation similar to that provided for the township of Adaminaby (moved for the Snowy Mountains Project). A "unique home ownership scheme" was officially announced, but reports from the North only mention – so far – 3 groups of 4 huts each, in 3 different localities, housing in all 60–70 of the 280+ population. The rest? – Mr Adair, Member for Cook, referred in debate (1/11/62) to people from Mona Mona "camped on the banks of the Barron ..." in gunyahs and shacks'. See also Kidd 1997: 212–14 regarding issues leading to the closure of the Mona Mona mission.

51. There was also a large auction held at which people were allowed to place bids for other buildings and chattels on the mission. However, these were mostly bought by settler farmers, with Aboriginal people bidding only for small items.

52. Memorandum Re: Re-erection of Homes for Coloured People ex Mona Mona, from Director of Native Affairs to Deputy Director of Native Affairs, 11 April 1963, QSA A/59487 (6H/4).

53. Letter from Deputy Director of Native Affairs to Pastor Townsend, North Queensland Conference of Seventh Day Adventists, Brisbane, 26 April 1963, QSA A/59487 (6H/4).

54. Memo from the Director of Native Affairs to the Under-Secretary, Department of Health and Home Affairs, Brisbane, 6 September 1962, QSA A/58934 (6J/35).
55. QSA A/58933 (6J/35).
56. Letter from the Director of Native Affairs to the Secretary, Land Administration Commission, Brisbane, 2 May 1963, QSA A/59487 (6H/4)
57. Three of the old Mona Mona houses were relocated to this block. Because the lease was held by the church, unlike the housing allotments at Mantaka, Koah and elsewhere, people whose houses were located on this block were not able to have individual title to their respective allotments. The church later requested that the government convert the lease to freehold to be held by Ngoonbi Cooperative Housing Society, incorporated under the Co-operatives and Other Societies Act of 1967 (QLD) to meet the accommodation needs of all ex-Mona Mona people in the Kuranda area.
58. Submission to Cabinet on closure of Mona Mona Mission and disposal of Native Cottages, by H. W. Noble, Minister for Health and Home Affairs, Brisbane, 8 March, 1962, QSA A/58934 (6J/35).
59. Letter from Mr T. V. Gilmore to Hon J. C. A. Pizzey, Mareeba, 4 March 1963, QSA A/59487 (6H/4).
60. Memo from the Deputy Director of Native Affairs to the Director of Native Affairs, Brisbane, 26 April 1963, QSA A/59487 (6H/4).
61. A freehold housing allotment for sale on Meroo Street was purchased and set aside as a 'reserve' under the control of the director of native affairs as trustee for subsequent lease to an Aboriginal person. Other blocks were made available on land that had been 'reserved for electrical purposes', but that was transferred to the trusteeship of the director of native affairs. On 25 October 1965, the Cabinet decided (Decision No. 8289) that particular building sites could be set aside as reserves. Such areas could then be leased by the director of native affairs, who would remain in control over the area. QSA TRI 1855 (1A/698).
62. Some people had lived at Oak Forest since the 1930s after receiving their exemption papers, and others joined them during the 1950s.
63. Queensland, Department of Lands, Regional Director, Far North Region, Memorandum to the Cabinet Legislation and Liaison Unit, Brisbane on R 158 Reserve for Camping and Water, Parish of Mona Mona, 30 October 1992, File: CNS/009735.
64. Queensland, Department of Lands, Report to the Lands Commissioner Regarding Camping and Water Reserve, R158, Parish of Mona Mona (HO. Ref: 10/298; DO. Ref: R149 CNS/009735); see also QSA A/69475.
65. See letter from the Under Secretary, Department of Community Services and Ethnic Affairs to the Secretary, Land Administration Commission, 2 March 1988, Department of Natural Resources (Res 22144), Department of Natural Resources File: CNS/009735.
66. At least one of these families was subsequently offered an allotment and an ex-mission house at Mantaka.
67. See Application in Department of Lands File CNS/009363.

68. See various documents in Department of Lands Files CNS/005035, CNS/005248, and CNS/005030.
69. Letter from the Director of Aboriginal and Island Affairs to Pastor W. A. Townsend, North Queensland Conference of Seventh-Day Adventists, Brisbane 19 December, 1969, QSA TRI 1855 (1A/698).
70. Letter from the Director of Aboriginal and Islander Affairs to the Secretary, Land Administration Commission, Department of Lands, Brisbane, 15 October 1970, QSA TRI 1855 (1A/698).
71. Letter from the Director of Aboriginal and Island Affairs to Pastor W. A. Townsend, North Queensland Conference of Seventh-Day Adventists, Brisbane 19 December 1969, QSA TR 1855 (1A/698). See also Confidential Cabinet Minute, Brisbane, 1 December 1969. Decision No. 13818, QSA TRI 1855 (1A/698).
72. In one case, an ex-mission house had already been relocated to the site on the understanding that the lease would be given to a particular Aboriginal householder. The householder was dismayed to find that the land where his house was standing had been put up for public auction.
73. A better known case, simply because it was taken to the courts, is that of *Koowarta v Bjelke-Petersen* (1982) 153 CLR 168. In 1976, the Aboriginal Development Commission had contracted with the lessees of a pastoral station in Queensland to purchase the station on behalf of a group of Aboriginal people, the Winychinam people. The Queensland minister for lands refused to approve the transfer of the lease, explaining that his refusal was based on 'declared government policy' which was opposed to 'proposals to acquire large areas of additional freehold or leasehold land for development by Aborigines or Aboriginal groups in isolation'.
74. Special Lease No 28128 over portion 360 (11 acres), Parish of Formantine (Kowrowa).
75. Letter from the Acting Secretary, Department of Lands to Mr R. E. Eager, Secretary-Treasurer, Seventh Day Adventist Church, Brisbane, 14 September 1976, Department of Natural Resources File: CNS/006353.
76. Qld Govt. Gazette, No. 5, 19 January 1980: 119; Qld Govt. Gazette, No. 66, 5 April 1980: 1173.
77. In total seven special leases in the name of Aboriginal people were forfeited at Mantaka, four at Koah, two at Kowrowa and two at Kuranda. In 1994 the Aboriginal Land Amendment Regulation (No 1) declared the Reserves at Mantaka and Kowrowa to be Aboriginal reserve land under section 2.08 of the *Aboriginal Land Act* 1991. Since then, in accordance with the Act, these reserves have been transferred to the Aboriginal community, to be held in trust.
78. I thank Judy Andrews for providing me with copies of the tape recordings she made of the protest meetings.
79. I have taken some literary licence here, as these selections are not necessarily arranged according to the order in which they were said at the meeting. I have left all individuals unidentified except for gender.

80. Taylor (1988: 105–125) includes excellent photographs of the old houses; see also Collins (1981: 84).
81. According to Martin and Finlayson (1996: 5): 'The Aboriginal domain is typically highly factionalised, and characterised by the complex and often cross-cutting allegiances which people have to groupings based on families, clans, ancestral lands and so forth, as well as to contemporary forms such as Aboriginal organisations. A defining characteristic of this domain lies in its localism … Localism is characterised by such features as a strong emphasis on individual autonomy, and priority being accorded to values and issues which are grounded in the particular and local, rather than in the general and regional or national.'
82. Dagil Nyiya means 'All Together Strong'.
83. This is taken from an advertisement for the consultancy in the *Cairns Post*, 25 June 1997: 64.
84. An example of such a mnemonic experience from my own family history is associated with a mountain south of Cairns known as the Pyramid. Almost thirty years ago, as a child, my brother entered a race up this mountain, descended the wrong way, and became lost and disoriented in the sugar cane field below. My parents found him hours later, distraught and in shock, walking down the highway in the opposite direction to home. Several times a year, I drive past the Pyramid, and each time it triggers in me the memory of this tale and an impulse to retell it to my children.

⊰ Chapter 2 ⊱

Countering Place

Hippies, Hairies and 'Enacted Utopia'

There are also, probably in every culture, in every civilisation, real places – places that do exist and that are formed in the very founding of society – which are something like counter-sites, a kind of effectively enacted utopia in which the real sites, all the other real sites that can be found within the culture, are simultaneously represented, contested, and inverted.
—Michel Foucault, 'Of Other Spaces'

During the 1970s, just ten years after they were 'evicted' from the Mona Mona mission, Aboriginal people in the Kuranda area were confronted by a sudden influx of new settlers. In this chapter, I examine the history of arrival of the so-called 'hippies' and 'alternative lifestylers' in the Kuranda area, their practices of place making and their desire to recreate Kuranda as 'a kind of effectively enacted utopia' (Foucault 1986: 24). I refer to Foucault's concept of heterotopia not simply because it captures the image of Kuranda as a polysemous place of contested identities – an image held by Kuranda people themselves – but also because it recognises the dialectical relationship between resistance and power that drives people's spatial practices.

In the concept of heterotopia, Foucault acknowledges not only the possibility of resistance, but also its impossibility (Genocchio 1995: 42). The concept of heterotopia highlights how practices of resistance – such as the attempt by the new Kuranda settlers to 'escape the system' and to create another order, or a counterculture – actually operate to reproduce structures of power. What follows is a history of settlement of Kuranda as told mainly from the perspective of these new settlers, who came to Kuranda to find an alternative way of life. Many members of this group have now lived in the Kuranda area for over thirty years, and much of their time is spent in the village coffee shops, nostalgically reminiscing about the past. For these people, Kuranda 'began' in the early 1970s when they started to make it their place. In this chapter, I examine some of the origin stories and settlement activities of these new arrivals. I discuss the rise and decline of communes and 'tenancies-in-common' in the Kuranda area during the 1970s and 1980s, as well as the responses of Aboriginal people and established settlers to the newcomers. I conclude the chapter with an examination of the significance of land and home ownership to both settlers and Aboriginal people. I analyse the settlers' practices of emplacement in detail in the following chapters.

First Stop: Holloways Beach

The destination of many of the people who travelled north – mainly from the southern states of Australia, but also from other countries such as the United States, Germany and Great Britain – was not at first Kuranda, but rather Holloways Beach, near Cairns. The following arrival accounts establish the connection between Holloways Beach and this new wave of Kuranda settlers:

> I arrived and there were about three or four camps on the beach. And as time went by other people just kept arriving. It must have been a response to something far greater than individually we could recognise at the time. The camaraderie that built because we were all in similar circumstances, and the beautiful freedoms that were available here in those days, were just unparalleled; like, to be able to just live on a beach and go fishing for your food and go eat seasonal foods. Primarily we were all city people. You know, we were brought up, well I was anyway, western suburbs Sydney (Brian Clarke, pers. comm. 5 July 1994).

> Well I was a sixteen year old working girl in Perth and I met four guys who spent time on Holloways Beach and they told me tales of beaches and palm trees which from a Perth city-scape sounded good and I kinda got drawn here from that story (Dawn Glass, pers. comm. 12 April 1995).

> Yeah, well I was escaping from the stigma of a war [Vietnam], hurt, very hurt. I mean I didn't like where I'd been but to come home and to be ostracised and absolutely dumped on for having done it! I was looking for an environment that I could survive in because I could not have survived in the other one. I'd have gone mad and shot myself, you know. So I ended up on the beach at Holloways Beach, which was every kid's fantasy, to go to a tropical beach somewhere, with palm trees and, you know. Anyway, this is what I was looking for. I was looking for a total escape, out of Melbourne, out of the whole movie (Lee Bones, pers. comm. 10 January 1996).

During the late 1950s and through most of the 1960s, Holloways Beach was made up of only a camping ground and a few old houses mainly occupied by Torres Strait Islander people, as well as others working in seasonal jobs in the fishing industry or as crocodile-shooters. The first people to arrive from 'down south'[1] were in their mid-twenties or older. Some of these people were artists and others were professionals who had worked in the cities. They knew how to support themselves, and they were literally looking for 'sea change'. They did not call themselves hippies. Rather, they saw themselves as the 'cultural heirs' of the bohemians of the Beat generation, part of that expressive social movement 'derived from post-World War II French existentialism and from various *avant garde* artists and performers of the early post war period' (Munro-Clark 1986: 59). As Munro-Clark (1986: 60) describes them, 'the beats stressed the "existentialist" goals of self-definition, spontaneity, creativity and innovativeness in lifestyle as in art. Their antagonism to the work ethic was expressed in voluntary poverty, disaffiliation from family and future "prospects", and effective withdrawal (in bohemian ghettos) from the mainstream society'. Before the so called 'hippie invasion', Holloways Beach was in the process of becoming a bohemian ghetto of this type.

Many of these 'bohemians' joined their Torres Strait Islander neighbours in making a living on the side through seasonal labour: diving for coral and trochus shell, fishing, and crocodile shooting. This form of labour allowed them the freedom to pursue their various artistic endeavours. However, their idyllic beach lifestyle was soon swamped by a new wave of people:

> As the population of Holloways increased we were starting to get travellers coming in from various parts of the world. That was eventually known as the 'Hash Trail' which started in Europe, made its way through Pakistan, Afghanistan, across country India, down through Thailand, down through Malaysia, through to Bali. Bali, there was a cheap flight to Darwin, and then overland from Darwin to Cairns on the milk trucks. The drivers would carry passengers because it was a long drive for them and they were carrying fresh milk from Malanda through to Darwin. So Holloways was part of a global overland trekking network and it became known for that. Over those couple of years I was at Holloways Beach, it went from being a matter of like eight or ten people to being up to about two to three hundred people living in tents, caravans, kombi vans, under the stars. There were some houses there that were being rented and multiply occupied. There were some real crash pads amongst the couple of houses that worked like that (Brian Clarke, pers. comm. 5 July 1994).

People say they heard of Holloways Beach through networks of friends and acquaintances, through word of mouth, and through the increasing media reports on the 'hippies of Holloways'. They heard tales of beautiful northern beaches fringed by rainforest with palm trees and balmy tropical weather, beaches where they could live freely off of the sea and the abundance of coconuts and mangoes growing wild. They heard of a place where all kinds of mind-altering substances were readily available, and where you could meet and socialise with like-minded people who were also looking to escape the system. By 1968, people began to arrive in such droves that the bohemians there before them began to feel utterly invaded in their little piece of paradise:

> We had a really charmed lifestyle there; we were paying no rent or anything you know so people were turning up. Eventually the hippie thing really happened in the cities and suddenly we were inundated by kids who had run away from home and who couldn't wipe their bums basically. And they were all trying to live off us in a sense. I mean we had them living under our tent ropes they wanted to be that close, because they were basically insecure. We were alternate but they were *more* alternate. There was some tension between us because we were regarded as not straight by that time, so that we didn't belong to society, but we also didn't feel like they and us were a totally homogeneous group, particularly in terms of their youth and their lack of skills. I mean, basically we all had some kind of professional background, or we had all worked for a living and knew how to feed and clothe ourselves and manage ourselves (Eve Stafford, pers. comm. 4 January 1994).

The influx of so many newcomers to the scene created tensions and threatened the peaceful existence of the Holloways bohemians. In an article that appeared in *Pix* magazine, entitled 'Get Out, Hippies! – You're Not Wanted in the North', D. K. Wheatley wrote:

> For years, genuine artists have been living a carefree existence on the beaches. They have developed their talents and made new industries for the tourist trade. But the hippies, with their drugs and naked parties, have threatened the bohemian life. Local authorities, unfortunately, too often see the artists and the hippies in the same shade of black. Forgotten by-laws are suddenly remembered. Everyone is asked to "move on" and resentment has built up (Wheatley 1969: 2–3).

As the hippie population of Holloways Beach expanded, there were more and more complaints from rate-payers and from representatives of the real estate industry, as well as increasing attention from the Cairns City Council health inspectors, and the police eventually drove the people from Holloways to Kuranda. Kuranda residents who had lived at Holloways Beach described the situation to me as follows:

> We started to be targeted as a group of people that came under a lot of social pressure from the police force, from the conservative red neck type attitudes that were very prevalent in these parochial, more regional areas. We were seen as invading the space. I just wanted to live my life, but unfortunately we were not allowed to do that under the social order of the day. Therefore, we were isolated as a radical fringe group of undesirables worthy of write-ups in not only our *Cairns Post*, but in the *Pix* and *Post* magazines of the day. Photographers would come and drive along the beach in cars with their windows wound up taking photographs through the glass. It was like a damned game park. We were being victimised by the police, everyday violating basic human rights. There was needless violence involved. It was a peaceful resistance; in that no one was really resisting the police, but they wanted to be resisted so that they could then take you into court for whatever they could get (Brian Clarke, pers. comm. 5 July, 1994).

> I didn't like this, you know, running down the beach with the coppers for fun having shots at you, with a spotlight, trying to pick you up. As soon as I became a marked person, I moved [from Holloways Beach] (Lee Bones, pers. comm. 10 January 1996).

> I mean we used to have some people drive out from Cairns in their cars with their windows wound up because they had read about hippies and that we eat our babies! They wanted to sell the real estate so they sent the police out to harass us (Eve Stafford, pers. comm. 4 January 1994).

The media reports in the *Cairns Post* of the time testify to the fact that people were regularly being arrested and convicted on a range of offences, from vagrancy to possession of drugs. The police would attempt to 'get them' on any charge they could. In one case, a man had to appear in court on a complaint that he had 'affixed an indecent picture so that it was visible to a person in a public place' (*Cairns Post*, 21 May 1970: 7). The police had gone to the beach 'on another matter' and had glanced inside a boat used as a dwelling by the defendant and had seen a painting of 'two naked female bodies'. The witnesses called to testify for the defence said it was simply a 'nude study', and that they thought of it as 'art'.

Eventually, the Cairns City Council directed a special committee to compile a report on the camping situation at Holloways Beach. On the basis of this report, the Council decided that people camping illegally on the Esplanade and private property at Holloways Beach would be required to move immediately, and the health inspector was authorised to inform all campers of this Council decision. Some moved voluntarily while others were forcibly evicted. The next stop for many of the Holloways Beach campers was a caravan park on the outskirts of Cairns:

> So we went to the Caravan Park and there was 'straights' down one side and there was all of us down this side and everyone who went to Cairns then said, 'Where's the scene man?' And we ended up with about 200 people out there and it was only four months; it only lasted four months. Everyone was going down daily to the mushroom fields you know; it was a scene (Eve Stafford, pers. comm. 4 January 1994).

Participating in practices related to the use of drugs was one of the key forces creating community identity among the group of people that chose to live together at Holloways Beach, at Kamerunga, and later in Kuranda. Such practices operated as a boundary marker, creating the sense of an in-group versus an out-group.

The Global in the Local: The Psychedelic Movement

The Holloways Beach campers saw themselves as part of a global movement – which found its expression in music, art and literature, as well as in the use of particular mind-altering substances which could enhance one's experiences of human creativity and therefore of life itself – termed 'the psychedelic era':

> We were starting to identify ourselves with this global movement. We were starting to hear it in the music. We were starting to see it in the magazines. We were part of it and we could clearly identify ourselves with that global movement, so we didn't feel as if we were on our own and this was significant (Brian Clarke, pers. comm. 5 July 1994).

People began to experiment with different varieties of fungi that they found growing in cow paddocks in the area, and the collection and consumption of psychedelic mushrooms became a focal activity of the group:

> It was about that time that somebody read about these funny mushrooms in the US, and there was all that stuff was coming in the press, although we weren't very connected to the press. So they went out as human experiments and tried a few things in the fields and came back with the

goods and so we all got into the mushrooms, but we never regarded it as drugs in those days. It never occurred to us that we were taking drugs, it was just like something we did, and we did that for six months before the thought occurred to us that we were taking drugs (1970s Kuranda settler, pers. comm. 4 January 1994).

We were the first group of people to discover that there were psychedelic mushrooms growing in this area. We picked everything, every fungi that we came across was collected and brought back with us, and they were divided into what people knew as being edible or toxic types. Volunteers offered themselves and a couple of people were violently ill, others thought they were quite tasty, and some people obviously experienced the psychedelic effects of that variety. So it was just through trial and error that it got down to this one variety (1970s Kuranda settler, pers. comm. 5 July 1994).

The discovery of these mushrooms enabled the Holloways Beach people to connect to a global movement:

Once this discovery [of psychedelic mushrooms] was made, that was quite significant, because all of a sudden we could understand some aspects of this other influence that we identified with, this whole era which we now know as this psychedelic era. And the people went through that process with *organic* psychedelic substances rather than *chemical*, manufactured substances, which gave it a completely different point of focus (1970s settler, pers. comm. 5 July 1974; original emphasis).

In terms of identity and difference, the group felt that in eating these mushrooms, they had become part of what they thought of as a global movement. At the same time, they celebrated their difference, their local identity, by emphasising the fact that as opposed to LSD and other drugs, the mind-altering substances they consumed were totally organic, natural, *local* products. Consumption of mushrooms and the shared practices associated with drug use in general provided a common bond for the group. These practices, however, also brought increased conflict with police, which in turn reinforced the beachgoers' counter-cultural identity. The continual harassment by police drew them into an even more tightly knit group.

Moving 'Out of It'

Eventually 'the scene' at the caravan park became too much for some members of the group, particularly the older people. They realised that in order to stop being hounded by police and local government, in order to achieve the freedom as individuals that they desired, they had to become landowners. A number of people started to look for suitable land. Prices along the northern coast were already prohibitive. Eventually word got around that land was much cheaper inland, and up the range, in Kuranda:

> We started looking along the coast initially; looking into places like Cape Tribulation, the Daintree; something that was similar to what we had already experienced, this beach culture, which is all barefoot and sand and out in the sun, printing and making your own clothes and very simplistic; lots of boats, lots of orientation towards the sea. So looking for land along the coast, even in those days land prices were relatively expensive; and then it was Roger Quinn that came to Kuranda and found land was quite cheap here (Brian Clarke, pers. comm. 5 January 1994).

> A lot of us had been living on the beaches, Holloways Beach, and a chap called Roger Quinn brought us all up. He'd got to know a farmer up here, a cattle farmer. He owned all of this, but for him that was just regarded as rubbish land and he sold this land four hundred dollars an acre. I bought this with three people as tenants-in-common (Mark Weaver, pers. comm.15 April 1995).

What attracted people to the Kuranda area was not only the price of land there, but also the fact that Kuranda was mushroom country. Psychedelic mushrooms grew prolifically in the country cleared for cattle:

> Yeah, there was a group of people that moved up here. Basically what it was, was down there was sugar cane and up here was mushrooms. That brought me to Kuranda because everyone went wow! I was experimenting with lots of drugs. Yeah but the gig was tripping on mushrooms which I found were the most amazing things (1970s settler, pers. comm. 10 January 1996).

The arrival of these ex-Holloways Beach people triggered a new wave of settlers that arrived in the Kuranda area throughout the 1970s and 1980s. Established Kuranda residents thus began to experience an invasion of people who were searching for a haven from the complexities of urban industrialised society.[2]

Settlement Practices

The new arrivals in Kuranda were not a homogeneous group. The Holloways Beach people came to Kuranda with the intention of buying land and burrowing in. Those that could not afford to purchase individual title to land pooled their resources and bought land in common. They had already developed a common identity through their shared experiences at Holloways Beach:

> We were a community already; already the basis of the Kuranda community was that we all stuck together. As soon as a policeman arrived [at Holloways Beach and at the Caravan Park at Kamerunga] we would all stand around like that. We had our own legal fighting fund, you know, to deal with them. When they put a charge on someone we all went to court to fight it and we sort of did it like that (Eve Stafford, pers. comm. 4 January 1994).

Shared experiences of police harassment and the creation of an in-group identity through practices associated with the counterculture and the psychedelic movement created the communal bonds necessary for a successful shared tenancy in land.

This first group of new settlers should not be confused with the wave of young hippies that arrived after them. Most of the latter were young people who had neither the wherewithal nor the intention to purchase land. They simply built themselves temporary shelters and squatted in the rainforest, or they rented old farmhouses and sheds from the locals. A number of communes were established during this period, but they did not last very long. Many of these hippies stayed for less than a year in Kuranda. They soon realised that what seemed like a tropical paradise in the dry season was 'hell on earth' in the wet.

Communes

I use the term commune very loosely here to refer to 'a group of people who are not all from the one family or kinship group and who have come together voluntarily in order to share a deliberately chosen pattern of living' (Munro-Clark 1986: 11). Such a group organisation may or may not involve the pooling of income and may range in size from smaller households to hundreds of people. Whatever their size and composition, in the Kuranda area communes were all built on a rationale which demanded the rejection of or withdrawal from those features of urban industrialised society that the builders considered destructive to both nature and culture. Communes are thus heterotopias *par excellence*. According to Foucault (1986: 24), unlike utopias, which are 'sites with no real place' representing 'society in its perfected form', heterotopias are real places, 'counter-sites ... in which the real sites, all the other real sites that can be found within a culture, are simultaneously represented, contested and inverted'. In their attempts to actualise utopia, the new settlers would generate a continuous contestation of place, not just in relation to their communes and tenancies-in-common, but eventually in Kuranda town itself.

The sorts of places that Foucault classes as heterotopias include prisons, hospitals, retirement homes, cemeteries, museums, libraries, fairgrounds, theatres, gardens, brothels and colonies. What these places have in common is firstly that they are 'capable of juxtaposing in a single real place several spaces, several sites that are in themselves incompatible' (Foucault 1986: 25). Secondly, they are 'linked to slices in time', whether 'oriented towards the eternal' as with museums and cemeteries or to time 'in its most fleeting, transitory, precarious aspect' as with fairgrounds and vacation villages (Foucault 1986: 26). Thirdly, they have boundaries and systems of 'opening and closing' which makes them not freely accessible. Entry may be compulsory, as in the case of a prison, or it may require a rite of passage or some other qualification. In some cases, entry may appear to be completely free and open to all, but this openness actually hides exclusions. As Foucault (1986: 26) puts it, 'Everyone can enter into these heterotopic sites, but in fact that is only an illusion: we think we enter where we are, by the very fact that we enter, excluded'. The most well remembered commune in the Kuranda area was such a place, a place that in its very openness operated to exclude. It was located on Weir Road and was simply called 'the Commune' or 'the Kuranda Commune'.

The Kuranda Commune

The Kuranda Commune was established in 1971 and lasted only a year. It was on land owned by an Englishman, one of the people who had started at Holloways Beach. He had bought the four acre block for A$400 an acre with three people as tenants-in-common, and he allowed in anyone who wanted to live there. A woman who came to Kuranda to participate in the commune remembers:

> There were a few people there with babies and young children, but not very many. It was mostly everything from about fourteen, fifteen up to about twenty-one. [When I arrived there were] I would think about forty or fifty [people]. We used to make up big huge pots of rice and vegetables and that sort of stuff. At that point in time I used to get up every morning and I would walk over to what's now Mason Road and pick mushrooms and start off every day by eating mushrooms. Yeah and then sort of trip.

> It was very much like *Alice in Wonderland*. Sometimes it was scary, you
> know, I went through a lot of hallucinations, not all of them were all that
> fantastic (1970s Kuranda settler pers. comm. 16 April 1995).

The Kuranda Commune was known as an 'open commune'. In other words,
the landowner placed no restrictions on who could come and live there. In
order to join, you had to be willing to live in the existing conditions or create your own living space (a platform, a tree house, or just a hammock), and
if you were going to share in it, you had to contribute occasionally to the
communal meal. Yet although it was defined as open, people were excluded
from the Kuranda Commune. This happened neither by force nor regulation, but by their own inability to fit into that particular 'scene':

> There were too many people. I mean, there must have been seventy peo-
> ple living on the commune then. For one thing I didn't know any of them,
> and for another thing, I've always been very independent. I don't know,
> they were a bit wild and woolly as far as I was concerned. I don't know
> why, but it didn't really interest me. Crowds have always worried me. It
> was fascinating really that all these people could be living down there and
> you'd hear pots sometimes crashing but you'd never hear people yelling at
> each other. It was all very quiet unless they were singing, you know, and
> sometimes they'd all just sit around and play drums so it was quite wild.
> It sounded very, kind of, tribal. I never went down there because it was all
> too much for me, all those people, but I would sit and listen to them (Suzie
> Creamcheese, pers. comm. 10 January 1994).

Gender also played a significant role in the membership of, and acceptance
into, the various communes:

> Being a girl, being a woman, I was quite quickly absorbed into the com-
> mune. I found that the two guys I was with were not really accepted you
> know. Because I could cook and sew and do all those sorts of things, I was
> quickly taken in as being, I guess, another woman to help, because it was
> exactly that way, and the women did all that stuff you know (Gayle Han-
> nah, pers. comm. 16 April 1995).

Although some people who entered the commune had communitarian visions of working 'for the common union', for most of the young city people
who hitchhiked north the commune was simply a 'crash pad'. Some only
stayed for a night, others for a few weeks or months. Once a week, someone would collect a dollar from those who could afford it to buy foodstuffs,
mainly cereals, rice and vegetables. This was supplemented with surplus

or damaged produce that farmers were willing to give away and discarded bread collected from the local bakery. Some people would supplement this diet with takeaway food from the cafe attached to the petrol station. A few had allowances from their parents, while others were on unemployment benefits. There was also seasonal work available, such as stringing tobacco and picking fruit on nearby farms.

Eventually, the owner of the land was forced to close the commune because it was attracting too many people and raising the ire not only of the established settlers in the area but also of some new settlers. These settlers did not like the attention that was being drawn to them by the activities of the residents on the commune:

> The young hippies were wild. I mean they used to go up, they were tripping on mushrooms in town and going into the pubs on mushrooms and driving around and one time they drove through town, about ten or twelve of them in one car, on the bonnet and on the roof. They were pretty wild times. [The Holloways Beach people,] they'd bought land up here and they'd got into their houses and they wanted to fit into town. They were going to live here for twenty years, and most of them have, so they didn't want young yahoos creating a bad name or partying all the time. They just became conservative landholders. These young people were like pretty high profile you know, sitting around outside the post-office in their raggedy clothes playing guitars (Mark Weaver, pers. comm. 15 April 1995).

As more and more people arrived over the course of the year, the composition of the commune altered:

> It was really getting very bad, in terms of hygiene and all that kind of stuff you know. It was becoming a real sort of dropout centre you know. There were people starting to turn up, like ex-bikers and their wives with kids, with guns and knives and all that kind of thing. The whole picture started to change and also up until then there hadn't been a lot of alcohol and then all of a sudden there was a lot of alcohol, and it became a very different sort of scene then. And those people who came, people called them the 'scrub ticks', because basically they clung on and sucked everything out you know (Gayle Hannah, pers. comm. 16 April 1995).

The land on which the Kuranda Commune was located is very steep rainforest with a creek running through the middle. There was one large long house at the top of the block, but most people just lived under tarpaulins on little platforms they had built for themselves between the trees on the slopes, or simply in hammocks strung between the trees. It was idyllic in the dry season but miserable in the wet. Once the rains started, many of the people who had come to Kuranda to 'drop out' were quite happy to 'drop in' again, or to move back to city squats 'down south'. Those people who decided to stay on longer in Kuranda or who wished to settle permanently found that it was necessary to buy land and to build more substantial shelter. This need for shelter was eventually to draw them into conflict with the Shire Council, an issue I discuss in more detail below.

The Titanic

There were other, smaller communes that people remember as having existed in the 1970s in the Kuranda region. Perhaps one of the most notorious of the communal households was 'the Titanic'. This was a wooden platform covered by a tarpaulin on which lived a group of men, mostly university students from Sydney. The absentee owner of the land had originally given permission for two women to live there, and the male students had offered to help them build a house. They got as far as the floor, but when the rains started the men moved on to the platform, much to the chagrin of the women:

> We got the floor in and it started raining. The boys went down and bought a tarp and put the tarp over the top of this platform and moved into it! We kept saying we were supposed to move in there and they said, 'But you have the kombi van'. So the boys got the platform and that turned into the Titanic, which you probably have heard about. Anyway so the Titanic was infamous in its own right because it was this group of guys ... And it was a big wet season, and that wet season actually started on Christmas day of 1971 (Suzie Creamcheese, pers. comm. 10 January 1994).

Her friend left Kuranda, but Suzie continued to sleep in her Kombi van. She eventually managed, however, to secure a position 'cooking for two guys and doing all their house stuff', giving her the use of part of their house during the day. In comparing the Kuranda Commune with the Titanic, an ex-member of the Kuranda Commune, Gayle Hannah, noted:

> Well they were a little bit older, that was the main thing, just a few years older, but it made a difference, yeah. You'd go there and they'd be reading James Joyce or something like that and everyone over here [in the Kuranda Commune] was reading Hermann Hesse you know. This was all the hippy trippy sort of stuff and that kind of thing. These guys were much

more into, a bit more intellectual, I suppose (Gayle Hannah, pers. comm. 16 April 1995).

Gayle and a friend eventually moved from the Kuranda Commune to a small 'shack' on a block of land next door to the Titanic. To distinguish themselves from the Titanic, the two women called their place 'the Good Ship Lollipop'. Nearby was a dwelling named 'the Lighthouse'.

There were also many other less notorious communally organised households and 'crash pads' that either had no particular names, or else the names have disappeared from memory. However, it appears that the people who came to the rainforest of Kuranda as refugees from the 'urban jungles' in which they grew up made a symbolic connection between their living spaces and ships or boats. What possible connection, one might ask, could there be between mountain top communes and boats? One explanation might be that many of the commune dwellers had come to Kuranda via Holloways Beach, and boats had been part of their beachcomber existence. Another might be that the constant rain and floods made it seem that the only way one could last the wet season in this rainforest waterscape was in a boat. My interpretation, however is inspired by Foucault:

> If we think, after all, that the boat is a floating piece of space, a place without a place, that exists by itself, that is closed in on itself and is at the same time given over to the infinity of the sea and that, from port to port, from tack to tack, from brothel to brothel, it goes as far as the colonies in search of the most precious treasures they conceal in their gardens, you will understand why the boat has not only been for our civilisation, from the sixteenth century until the present, the great instrument of economic development ... but has been simultaneously the greatest reserve of the imagination. The ship is the heterotopia *par excellence*. In civilisations without boats, dreams dry up, espionage takes the place of adventure, and the police take the place of pirates (Foucault 1986: 27).

That boats and communes come together in the imagination is not only evidenced by the names that were given to the communes, but also by the fact that the members of one commune in Kuranda, which I discuss in detail below, spent many years actually building a large boat. I am not suggesting that making a connection between communes and boats is particularly distinctive of Kuranda hippies; rather, it is a general cultural association that some of them made. Boats and the sea represented a means of escape from the system, both for the bohemians of Holloways and for the wave of hippies that followed them north.

Communitarian Ideologies

The various communes tended to differ markedly from one another in structure and composition. Even in retrospect, people do not articulate any coherent system of beliefs that drew them together at that time. Because of this, some people may dispute my use of the term 'commune' to cover the diversity of the groups that established themselves in Kuranda during the 1970s. As Munro-Clark (1986: 11–12) points out, in the sociological literature such groups are variously referred to as 'intentional communities', 'alternative lifestyle groups', 'rural co-operatives', 'multiple-occupancy settlements', 'land-sharing communities', and 'sustainable communities'. Some social scientists wish to restrict the use of the term commune to groups that actually form and maintain a single collective or common household in the economic sense (see Zablocki 1980: 7). I prefer a more inclusive and holistic definition that takes into account the insider view and the fact that Kuranda communards think of themselves as having come together communally, whether intentionally or otherwise. What is significant about their communitarian discourse is its grounding in libertarian individualism. The attraction of people to Holloways Beach was not just palm trees and golden sands, but the idea of freedom from social constraint that a life connected with the sea and boats conjured up for them. They brought this idea of the freedom of the individual with them to Kuranda when they came in search of cheap land and mushrooms. They and the hippies that followed them may or may not have shared household income and other resources. They certainly, however, shared an ideology of individualism that ironically drew them into communal living arrangements. They also shared a desire to link themselves to a global movement defined by such practices as the consumption of mind-altering substances and the music, literature and art – or 'cultural capital' – that went with such consumption, as well as an experience of growing marginality as they became the targets of state agencies: first the police and then the Shire Council.

Some communes in the Kuranda area developed a more consciously articulated ideological foundation either at the outset or later in their lifespan. Perhaps these could be more legitimately referred to as 'intentional communities' of the type that Munro-Clark (1986) surveyed as part of her research into 'rural communitarianism' in Australia. One of these is the Christian community of Arona, also known locally as 'the Indonesian Commune' in reference to the common past of its core members, who had migrated to Australia from Indonesia.

There were other communes, more short lived than Arona, that also could be considered intentional communities. These included a Buddhist *ashram*, as well as a number of communities founded upon aspirations and principles that the communards did not attribute to any particular world religion. For example, there was a commune of 'fruitarians' on the Clohesey River near Koah (see Map I.2). A woman, who visited in 1973 seeking a commune to join, described it as follows:

> I was greeted by a naked woman who was a real streak, like she was very, very thin, very, very thin, and she explained to me that they were all fruitarians. She took me on a tour of their farm and there was lovely fruit growing everywhere, organic fruit. She invited me to have a meal with them. There was nothing very earthy about it actually [the farmhouse]. It was actually a great big aluminium shed with bunks built around the sides of it that all the recruits lived in. The guy who owned the farm had a double bed in the middle of the shed with a huge mosquito net hanging down from the ceiling. I don't know who shared the double bed with him! There weren't many men there, there were mostly women. But everybody was very, very skinny. It didn't have a real wholesome feel about it, although it was a beautiful place. I must say I'm wary of these, you know, leader type people that seem to have this little group of followers who almost worship them (Wendy Russell, pers. comm. 13 January 1995).

During the 1970s, a number of communards in the Kuranda area were interviewed by Robin Williams for the ABC Radio program 'New Society and Alternative Australia' (1976). One woman he interviewed had this to say about the principles on which the particular commune that she joined was based:

> These principles are sobriety, purity, chastity, harmlessness, divine love, sincerity, fruit diet and conformity with the will, intension and consciousness of the infinite intelligence ... They're not exactly rules. They're laws of the infinite God. ... We don't eat meat, we don't eat vegetables, because we understand that to do these things is a parasitic action and we understand that parasitism is the cause of all the evil in the world, any sickness, any decay. To eat even a seed is to be parasitic on that life ... Any sexual orgasm which any human being has is like an atomic explosion which absolutely destroys the very substance of their life. It destroys the nerve fluid; because the whole life is based on love. It's based on the electrical magnetism which you generate when you love somebody or when you love something ... And when you have an orgasm ... it completely destroys that love which you have developed, so any orgasm is against love ... and it destroys the nerve structure and the nerve structure is the most important thing we have to receive intuitions through ('New Society and Alternative Australia' 1976).

This woman and other members of this commune claimed that they did not follow any particular established religious philosophies, but that they followed their own 'intuitions'. They argued that all knowledge 'comes from the voice within our hearts', from an 'inner voice' that can be heard by following dietary and other principles that nurture the body and keep it open to the reception of 'love, which is God'.

Rosebud Farm

One of the best known and most long lived of the communes was 'Rosebud Farm', also known as 'the American commune' because it was founded by a group of men from the United States of America in their early twenties who had dropped out of university. They had left the States because of their disenchantment with their country's involvement in the Vietnam War. The story begins with two friends who flew to Australia in 1970, bought a utility truck and camping gear and started touring the country in search of a place to settle for a while. In their travels through country Victoria, they befriended a young Australian. According to his own account, the youth was completely taken with the Americans. He was a working-class country boy who had never seen as much ready cash as the Americans appeared to have, much less the generosity of spirit with which they spent it. They opened his eyes to new possibilities, so he spontaneously decided at the age of seventeen to leave home and join them in their travels. On their way, they met and made friends with a couple of other young Australians, and eventually two more Americans also joined them.[3] About six months later, they arrived in Cairns and camped at Holloways Beach before meeting a real-estate agent who took them to see a farm for sale in the Kuranda area. The Americans loved the farm, and one of them decided to buy it then and there with money he had inherited. They did not initially intend it to be a commune, but simply saw it as a beautiful place to live for a while. They were not really thinking of the future and thought it would be fun to build up the farm for subsistence purposes. It was their idea of a 'Boys Own adventure'. They called the farm 'Rosebud' and themselves 'the Rosebuddies', inspired by the movie 'Citizen Kane':

> The movie actually deals with that one word. Right before he died he wrote down the word 'Rosebud', and this reporter is going back to find out why in the whole movie and it's not till the end of the movie when they're cleaning out the cellar, they come across a child's snow-sled with the word 'Rosebud' printed on top. So obviously in his dying moments he's remembering his youth and innocence and joy and all that. And we used to have

a good friend, [who] said, 'This place is a real "Rosebud", let's call it "Rose-bud Farm"'. Rosebud was actually 160 acres and it cost $16,000 which for us, coming from the States, was like you know, too good to be true. In 1971, $16,000 was a lot of money but relative to the prices in the States it was, you know, nothing, because land over there, where we grew up, was about $10,000 an acre; so Kim actually bought the land. People would go out and get jobs and come back and donate the money and people would have day jobs in Kuranda and come back and bring food or whatever, beer and flagons of wine, and it was a real chip-in type of atmosphere. The major expenditures on the farm, like building sheds and buying tractors and all that, was pretty much dealt with by Kim and Jeb and myself. You know, Kim and Jeb had some money from the States, whereas I didn't have a lot of money, but I had a little bit and I worked as well and the Australian guys worked and chipped in. It was good (Ritchie Trapnell, pers. comm. 13 October 1993).

After the first six months they began to receive a constant stream of young friends, mainly women, who were visiting from the States to have their hip-pie commune experience. A number of Australian women also made the commune their home. One of them had lived in the Kuranda Commune and after it was closed down was invited to join the Rosebuddies. Another young woman had travelled alone from Melbourne and had hitchhiked around the Kuranda area in search of a farming commune where she could learn organic farming:

I was on this search. I knew that I wanted to find a farm. I knew that I wanted to have a communal type of lifestyle and be with lots of people. I didn't really find a lot [of communes] around but one day this guy stopped on the highway at Speewah Road and said: 'See that boat down there, there's a whole farm full of people who live up that road there, building that boat. They sound like the kind of people you'd like to meet'. So off I trotted down this winding walk all the way to the farm. And a little man with a red beard and fluffy hair popped out of the cornfield and said, 'Hello'. I said, 'I'm looking for somewhere like this to live and learn more about organic gardening', and he said, 'Well you're quite welcome to stay here for a few days and just feel the place out'. So the next time I arrived I had my rucksack on my back and found myself a bunk in the bunkroom and more or less made myself at home (Wendy Russell, pers. comm. 13 January 1995).

At its peak, approximately twenty-five people were living on Rosebud, but of these only about twelve ever considered it their permanent home. They were all young, mostly in their early twenties. One of the Australian men remembered that they 'worked very hard but partied every night'. He recollected that there was always plenty to eat and drink and smoke and that one or other of the Americans would go home each year and bring back Levi jeans for them all, so they were always 'well fed and clothed'. No one was visibly in charge, he said, but there was an unspoken awareness of the existence of a hierarchy based on the fact of land ownership, and if a decision had to be made, the American landowner had the last say. Day to day, however, people worked according to their own interests and abilities. Some focused on planting, watering and weeding the vegetable patch, and some looked after the farm animals: the cow, some goats, chickens and ducks. Others worked in the fields, planting and tending the corn and the soy beans or fixing the tractor and other machinery. In addition, almost everyone took a turn at one time or another in helping the landowner to fulfil his dream of building a sailing boat. The large ferrous cement boat was called 'Big Mama' and was parked on a block of land along the highway. It became a popular tourist attraction. According to one of the members of Rosebud, tour bus operators used to stop and say, 'Well, there they are, the hippies building the Ark, just waiting for the flood so they can take it down the mountain'.[4]

Entering Excluded: Gender, Work and Class

As there were many more men than women among the hippies who came to Kuranda during the early 1970s, women found that they were readily accepted into already established communes. The system of gender hierarchy was actually reinforced rather than challenged, and women were expected to adopt traditional gender roles:

> So as the sun went down, the truck would load up and all the boys would climb on and go to the pub and drink and carry on and then they'd sort of head home and the women would be keeping the [home fires burning], stopping the meal from burning, all the things my mother used to do (Gayle Hannah, pers. comm. 16 April 1995).

The impression of some of the women who lived on Rosebud, looking back, is that the farm was just a 'boy's club' with the women there simply to do the traditional chores of cooking and cleaning. As one woman put it, 'there was always a lot of male bonding going on'. A comment by one of the men corroborates her assessment:

[The arrival of women,] ah well it definitely broke up the group of males and then, and also in the kitchen, I mean, it's you know, night after night after night. It's easy for one woman or even two women but as soon as you get three or four women you get so many conflicting ideas about how to run a kitchen (pers. comm. 13 October 1993).

There appears to have been very little conflict in the early years among the group of men who established Rosebud. However, as more people joined, some tension developed among the men over their relative workloads, and there was also some gender conflict as women began to object to the gendered division of labour on the farm. As Wendy Russell recollected:

Corn, you know we used to grow huge amounts. That was our cow feed, our goat feed. We used to have a big corn mulling thing, you know, and you'd have to feed the corn cobs through it for the chooks, to get the corn off the cobs, and we used to do that. Things like that we used to do manually every day; heaps of manual work. Sometimes it was disheartening because you'd be criticised by someone who hadn't seen what you'd done and you'd feel really hurt because you'd been working so hard and you were tired and yet they didn't realise it. That did happen a bit with the genders. A lot of the men didn't realise that we women spent so much time looking after the kitchen, the pantry, you know, all those type of things, you know, and we really did work hard, especially when we had babies and had to carry them up the hill (Wendy Russell, pers. comm. 28 November 1994).

One woman in particular refused to be, as she put it, 'pigeonholed' by the men on the commune, but she was told by another woman that in challenging the system she only made it harder for the rest of them. Not many of the women associated with the Kuranda communes pursued feminist ideals. An absence of feminist ideology has, in fact, been noted as being typical of communes in Australia during this period: 'The struggle against gender discrimination was not pursued or advanced by the counter-culture of the 1960s and 1970s' (Munro-Clark 1986: 106).

Apart from disputes over work on the commune, women remember the difficulties they experienced in having to conform to the expectations of other commune members – both men and women – with regard to such issues as nudity, sexual freedom, and personal hygiene:

All the things that were sort of taboo, like shaving your legs, or make-up, or deodorant, or being on the pill, that was like modern medicine. I mean, you know, you were supposed to really be drawing on the wisdom of ages. Same with birth really; I mean, it was 'Well this is the way it should be because peasant women have been doing it squatting in the fields'. And things like period pain, I mean it was like, 'Forget it, it doesn't exist, peasant women don't have problems like that you know'. I know there was one woman there who had a real body odour problem, and she used to have her deodorant hidden because she didn't want anyone to know she used a deodorant. Anything that you did that brought the modern world in was considered bad news. I was just thinking how difficult it must have been for them [the other women] to be, to feel, loose sexually without being worried about it. I'm sure they were all on the pill. I mean I was very lucky. I never took any contraception at all. I had this whole theory that it was all in the mind. I didn't want to be pregnant; therefore I wasn't pregnant (1970s communard, pers. comm. 16 April 1995).

Such defining features of communal ideology as an opposition to technocracy, the celebration of the idea of sexual freedom, emphasis on naturalness with regard to bodily practices, and withdrawal from products associated with modernity meant that certain people – and in particular many of the women – entered the commune already excluded.

Class issues also played a part in who was welcome on the commune and who was not:

> There were little patches of people living in tree-houses and things in the National Park and the surrounding areas. I never really associated with them much. To me they actually, they were more feral than what I felt that I was, and we did have a lot of visits from those kind of people, and of course they were always in for the parties and all that. Like I say, we socialised in those scenes but they weren't part of what we were doing as a whole (Member of the Rosebud commune, pers. comm. 28 November 1994).

Because the word had spread that the original Kuranda Commune was open to anyone, people thought that the same applied to Rosebud Farm. The Rosebuddies thus constantly had to deal with people who would turn up and expect to be allowed to stay and live off the products of their labour. A key factor determining whether one could become a member of Rosebud was one's demonstrated willingness and ability to contribute to the labour pool. 'Hangers on' were not welcome. Eventually, the Rosebuddies posted a sign in Kuranda announcing that Rosebud was not an open commune and that only invited people were welcome. More and more communes in the Kuranda area began to fold and the situation came to a head. Rosebud experienced an influx of refugees from the folded communes, as well as from the remote settlement at Cedar Bay after it was raided and destroyed by heavily armed police who turned up in helicopters and four-wheel drive vehicles:

> You know, the whole Cedar Bay thing, well a lot of people from Cedar Bay had moved to Cape Tribulation and the people who owned Cape Tribulation property had thrown everybody out and they had moved *en masse* to the commune [Rosebud]. There were probably twenty-five, something like that. Yeah, they just sort of arrived. It was becoming outrageous because people who had been going to the Kuranda Commune were now coming to Rosebud and you'd wake up in the morning and you'd get up and there'd be like people in sleeping bags on the kitchen floor who'd arrived in the night and just squatted. Just couldn't handle it (Member of the Rosebud commune, pers. comm. 16 April 1995).

In a sense, history was repeating itself, and the Kuranda scene became the Holloways Beach situation all over again. An established group of people who were largely of middle class origin, found themselves challenged by an influx of mainly homeless urban runaways who expected to be welcomed into the communitarian fold. That they did not receive such a welcome was due to the same problems of social class that denied them a place in the system from which they were attempting to escape: 'lack of skills, inarticulateness and no capital' (Munro-Clark 1986: 63).

Responses of the Old Settlers

People who had the capital to buy land were initially welcomed with open arms by the old settler families of Kuranda. There were only a handful of such families, and they owned a lot of what they thought of at the time as unproductive land that they were keen to sell. Joan Dods, who bought eighty acres in Kuranda in 1964 with her husband, noted:

> [There was] lots of land for sale. Yes we were inundated with people saying, 'Wouldn't you like to buy our land?' Everyone was very interested in what new people were doing here because there were very few new people moving into the area. Everybody was related. You had to be very careful about what you said because you were bound to be talking to someone's auntie or something like that. We were probably the first people who were not locals to move into the area and then about five years down the track from then, sixty four you know, just before 1970, alternative lifestylers started to move in (Joan Dods, pers. comm. 8 July 1994).

According to Eion Hunter (pers. comm. 13 January 1994), a member of one of the original settler families in Kuranda, responses to the arrival of these newcomers were varied among the established Kuranda townspeople: 'Some people looked on them as wasters. See this is when Whitlam [the Australian Labor Party Prime Minister] brought in all the social service business [unemployment benefits] and they wouldn't work; they didn't want a job. A lot of them were half educated and they gave themselves a bad name by not working'.

Newspaper reports at the time tended to feature the negative. '"Hippies" paradise is locals' hell' read one headline (*Sunday Mail* 19 September, 1971). Another article, headed 'Hippie "families" invade north', reports on local farmers' concerns about the activities of the newcomers, in particular the fears of a pastoralist who 'found clusters of toadstools had been disturbed in a paddock that "hippies" had been through' (*Sunday Mail* 5 July 1970). Today, some of the older Kuranda residents remember the hippies as having been 'a menace', 'a terrible problem', or 'awful people' whose main reason to be in Kuranda was to 'get stoned'. One elderly Kuranda resident responded to my question about hippies as follows:

> I don't think the hippy era should be highlighted. It was an unfortunate effort. I never had hippies working here. I always refused to have anyone that took drugs because you tell them something and they do something else. No, the hippies, no fear. I'm very much against drugs. They were all on dope. I don't know what kind of dope. The gold mushrooms, I don't think they're all that plentiful. There's another plant here that they also imbibed. I've taken all of mine out now because I did have a person here that got completely stoned on it and wandered off to Kuranda and they picked him up and dehydrated him, apparently. It's quite dangerous. It's got the most beautiful perfume, *datura* (Marjory Spear, pers. comm. 11 January 1997).

Local Kuranda shopkeepers were ambivalent, but mostly positive about the influx of young people. According to one shopkeeper:

> Some of them were exotic looking. Others were just, you know, pretty dirty actually. I didn't find them difficult to get on with. But the village, you see it had been a pretty small village up until then and most of the families were intermarried. Nobody minded them buying land. The old-timers were not using it for anything. Well they might have had a bit of cattle on it, but not really that much. Some of course were on quite bad drugs. You know, I mean *heavily* into drugs. The sort of system of life was a bit of a shaker to, you know, the ordinary people living here because no one had met anything like them, and certain people found it a bit difficult to ac-

cept, at first anyway. And of course they used to have these full moon parties and things and one or two of the babies were born out in the camps too with everybody helping by singing and everything else. I don't think I would have liked something like that, but it was their choice and they were happy about it and the children appeared to me to grow alright, you know, to be healthy. But of course obviously there was a certain amount of growing and selling of marihuana. Not, I think, here on a big scale, but it was grown on a much bigger scale you know further up the coast and people here were involved in it, and sometimes got caught, obviously (Kuranda shopkeeper, pers. comm. 2 July 1994).

In spite of the economic benefits that the hippies and new settlers brought to established shops in the town, as discussed in later chapters, many the townspeople felt themselves increasingly displaced by the practices of the newcomers. One of the residents of the main street of Kuranda complained to me:

Well then they got to the stage where they thought, 'Oh we can take this town over'. One time they even conned the Council into closing the main street; never told anyone. They just stood there, all their raggedy clothes on. 'You can't come through here. This is our street'. Well they wanted to dance on the street and they had all these bloody guitars. I said to one bloke, 'Christ, I'd like to have enough money to buy the biggest guitar in the world and, see that bloke dancing over there? I'd smash it over his bloody head'. Then eventually I just tossed the barricades away and I had to go over this way for something and they wouldn't let me through that end and so I just sat on the horn and blew it. I mean, they can't just stop you from going to your own home; but they tried to (Eion Hunter, pers. comm. 13 January 1994).

Responses of Aboriginal People

In contrast to the established white population, Aboriginal responses to the arrival of the hippies appear to have been in general very positive: 'We saw all these people coming with long hair and long beards and all that. They dressed differently, all raggedy clothes, and we'd never seen things like that before, but we made friends with them; some of them come to our place here and we made them welcome' (Lyn Hobbler, pers.comm 4 January 1995). Marita Hobbler went with her husband to the Kuranda Commune in order to find the son of a white friend of theirs who had gone missing, and had this to say about their experience:

They had a house, but not properly a house, walls, roof, just like a big dormitory, commune; all the beds in a row. They make homemade beds with logs and things. It was clean and all those girls sit down and do patchwork. Patchwork quilts on all the beds, and yet they dress anyhow. They offer us coffee and ricebread. They welcomed us. They wanted to give us coffee. We frightened to take it 'cos we thought they might put drug in it. 'You want drugs?' they asked us. We said, 'No' [laughter] (Marita Hobbler, pers. comm. 4 January 1995).

Other Aboriginal people were, however, shocked by the lifestyle of the hippies:

We used to see these hippies, you know. We were once like that, but coming into town see, we used to have clothes, but [not] their children. It was shocking. We didn't like it. So did the white elders from in town there, the Veivers and that, because they said, 'Dark people don't strip their children off like that'. But police probably talked to some of them. They dressed properly then. It was shocking to see them. We knew we used to strip off when we were small, but not in town, in public (Ester Snider, pers. comm. 18 June 1995).

In general, Aboriginal women avoided the communes, although some did attend parties at Rosebud with their partners and friends:

We used to go out to Rosebud Farm, oh yeah. And we used to go up there and I can remember they used to have this big table made of timber from the bush and all the fruits on this table, eh! And we used to sit with them there and we used to feed with them after the pub closed. Or on the Sunday we'd go there for dinner, for lunch. Oh we used to have fun with them (Flo Brim, pers. comm. 11 January 1995).

A number of Aboriginal men remembered spending time at Kuranda Commune, trying out mushrooms and marijuana for the first time. However, most socialising between hippies and Aboriginal people went on in public places such as outside the post office, the grocery store, the service station, the pub and, later, the amphitheatre (Chapter 3). In general, Aboriginal people say that their relationship with the people who came to Kuranda during the 1970s was a harmonious one:

The thing is, Rosita, they didn't interfere. They did their thing. We did our thing and there wasn't no fuss about, you know, who own this place or what you had to do in this corner, or this is my corner you keep away, no, and everybody was happy. There weren't any break-ins. There weren't any stealing around the place, nothing. Everybody lived a contented life, peaceful. You could just sit anywhere and not get hassled by anybody, you know (Flo Brim, pers. comm. 11 January 1995).

Yet not all Kuranda people have such fond, happy memories of life in the town. A key uniting factor among hippies and Aboriginal people was the

Figure 2.1. Dancing at the Amphitheatre, c. 1982.
Photographer: Mark Williams.

conflict that the new settlers had with the police and the Shire Council bureaucrats. The newcomers were regularly subjected to police harassment
of the kind with which Aboriginal people were very familiar. Moreover,
the living conditions of the newcomers were more like those of Aboriginal
people than other white people. As Marita Hobbler (pers. comm. 4 January
1995) put it, 'They were just like us, like Aboriginal', and her husband, Lyn
Hobbler, added: 'They were living just like us. The way they lived, they were
living just like us in the bush, and they were one of us'.

The arrival of the people from Holloways Beach and of the hippies that
followed them meant that Aboriginal people were able to mix with non-
Aboriginal people in a way that they had never been able to before. They
drank with them, partied and danced with them (Figure 2.1). They played
music together and they visited one another's homes and ate together: 'All
the Aboriginals and the hippies we used to mix. Oh, everybody just mix
together. It was just really happy, happy times' (Flo Brim, pers. comm. 11
January 1995). Thus Kuranda developed an image as a relatively non-racist
place when compared with other rural towns in Australia. Relationships
with non-Aboriginal people had previously been confined to the 'white
boss' variety where Aboriginal people 'attempt[ed] to set up dependency
relationships with a European who can channel goods and services to
them, as their boss' (Finlayson 1991: 291). The relationships between Aboriginal people and hippies, however, were often the reverse, with some of
the young hippies in fact becoming dependent on their Aboriginal friends.
After the Kuranda Commune folded, a number of Aboriginal households
took in the homeless hippies. In one case, an Aboriginal couple appealed
to the Kuranda Caravan Park owner on behalf of two young women who
had been living with them for a few weeks. The women were given an old
house at the caravan park to rent, and the Aboriginal couple bought them
some groceries. In my field experience over the past fifteen years, I have
noticed several Aboriginal families in Kuranda providing food and shelter
for young non-Aboriginal people in need.

With regard to race relations in Kuranda, Aboriginal and non-Aboriginal people particularly mention the 'scene' on Friday nights at the 'bottom pub'. People fondly remember the atmosphere of camaraderie and the
breakdown of social barriers at the hotel. These, however, did not necessarily translate into deeper friendships. People freely use the expression
'we were all in the same boat' to account for the bonding they experienced
at that time. To be 'in the same boat' meant that they held the experience
of marginality in common. On one occasion, the arrest of a member of the
Kuranda Commune for drunkenness resulted in a demonstration outside
the police station by other Commune members. Aboriginal youths are reported to have kept the peace by helping the police disperse the crowd,

and afterwards they roamed the streets together with hippie youths, yelling 'peace brother' and 'black is beautiful'.

The comments of a Mareeba Shire Council member attest to the shared marginal position hippies and Aboriginal people occupied relative to the established non-Aboriginal population of the area. The councillor is reported in the *Sunday Mail* (19 September 1971: 3) as saying that people in the town had applied for 'police protection' because there was only one policeman assigned to Kuranda and 'he couldn't be expected to cope with 200 hippies and 500 aboriginals as well as look after the permanent population of 300'. Apparently the councillor did not consider the Aboriginal people part of the 'permanent population'! The councillor claimed that the hippies were causing 'a terrific lot of trouble', the most recent being that six of them had been found lying on the garden beds at the Kuranda railway station, for which he 'ran them in'. Because the town had not been allocated additional police, the councillor is reported to have said, 'I think the only solution to our problem is the old-fashioned one of running them out of town'.

Other locals, however – in particular the shopkeepers and publicans – were sympathetic to the mostly young people who flocked to the town. One local publican is reported in a national newspaper as saying:

> I suppose I am talking through my pocket but they seem to be well connected and well educated although the odd one or two admit to being mixed up with drugs. They're easygoing and clean, they're always in the river, but their clothes look a bit worse for wear. And they're very honest. I mean apart from nabbing the occasional paw paw and who didn't pinch a few pieces of fruit when they were young? About the only trouble I have is trying to pick which ones are the females (*The Australian* 21 September 1971).

Many of these young people eventually left Kuranda. However, those who stayed on and bought land confronted escalating conflict with the local shire council, which I discuss in more detail in the following chapters. The conflict was partly generated by the alternative forms of land tenure adopted by the new settlers.

It is clear that the group of people who came as part of the global counter-culture movement to Kuranda was not homogeneous. A key criterion that people used as a marker of distinction was ownership of land. Ownership of land legitimised one's status as a permanent Kuranda resident, as opposed to the itinerants who just came up for the season:

> I guess there was a class thing as much as there was the landed people who had bought land up here, people who owned land, and what would now be

called ferals, who were just up for the season, as the ferals are now. I mean there's hardly any ferals in town now, because it's supposed to be the wet season so they're down at Nimbin or wherever they go, and come winter they'll come back, and the season used to be like that back then (Mark Weaver, pers. comm. 15 April 1995).

Thus the next step for people who wanted to stay on in Kuranda was to follow the example of the Holloways Beach people and purchase land. As one of the members of the Kuranda Commune told a reporter who had visited the commune for an article published in *The Bulletin* (Wynhausen 1971: 39): 'Quite a lot of the people from the commune leave to get land. ... They're starting to see that of all material things land is the most important – the only one you can do something with'.

Hairies and Hippies

A commonly recognised distinction that was made in Kuranda during the 1970s was between 'hairies' and 'hippies'. According to one source, these names were first used by one of the shopkeepers in town to distinguish those who actually could afford to spend money in her shop from the 'down and outs':

> We were hairies. Hippies were dead-shit, nowhere, useless bums, and hair-
> ies were people that paid their own bills, very polite, shopped, had long
> hair but didn't dress in op-shop leftovers, which none of us did. We wore
> exactly the same almost as everyone else was wearing. We just happened
> to have hair down to our arse. So we were hairies. The other ones were get-
> ting their six dollars a week dole [unemployment benefit]. See none of us
> did any of that. We were not hippies. We were hairies and hairies actually
> owned land up the road (Lee Bones, pers. comm. 10 January 1996).

Some of these so-called 'hairies' were indeed extremely wealthy, in particular the Americans from Rosebud. They were known to hail from old
moneyed stock in the United States and a local mythology soon developed
about the actual extent of their wealth:

> [They called us] all hippies [but] they didn't understand that the collective
> value of those people was probably thirty million dollars at the time. The
> coppers would turn up and shopkeepers would say, 'Don't hassle them',
> because you'd be spending forty grand a year there. Big money these guys
> were (Lee Bones, pers.comm. 10 January 1996).

According to John Bax, who owned a café in Kuranda during the 1970s:

> Rosebud, all the boys from Rosebud used to come to Sunshine's [café] then. I don't know whose father or mother it was, they were extremely well off. They came and gave me, I think it was five hundred, or a thousand [dollars], at the time it was a hell of a lot of money, because [the boys from Rosebud] didn't want to accept any money from the parents. So they said, 'John, here is so much', you know, 'and whenever they come in for takeaways and everything else, it's paid for' (John Bax, pers. comm. 14 January 1994).

Several of the Australians, who lived and worked at Rosebud, suggested that it was the idea of land ownership that eventually tore the commune apart. After the partying was over and the initial *communitas* had started to wane, they began to realise that there was a pecking order on the farm based on who owned the land. They realised that they would never get any more than their food and lodging in return for the labour they put into the commune. A few of them, therefore, started to look around for their own blocks of land. Unfortunately, by that time the price of land in the Kuranda area had already begun to escalate dramatically. Like the settlers from Holloways Beach, many people seeking land could only afford it if they joined forces with others and bought it in common.

Tenancies-in-common

The response of the Shire Council to the purchase of land in common by the new settlers was to subject them to a high level of surveillance and policing by enforcing its by-laws and building regulations.[5] The comments of Kuranda's only representative on the Mareeba Shire Council at the time is indicative of the attitude to the new land owners: 'Unfortunately, some have bought land here ... A few have built their own homes, but they are not fit habitations and we have served notices on them to bring the places up to standard' (*The Sunday Mail*, 19 September 1971: 3).

Even if people were able to realise their dreams and purchase land, many did not have the finance needed to build houses to the standard required under the shire building regulations:

> You had to submit building plans, so in the long run that's what I did. It's a bit tricky because I still live below the poverty line. I haven't borrowed money from the bank. I can't because it's tenants-in-common and because I've always worked for myself so it's not like a bank will approve a loan. So

I can't build; you're supposed to have it done in a year, but I could never do that. So if they [the building inspectors] come out now, I have done a lot and I have followed the building plans but it's not done [finished]. Personally I think we're over governed. I think I should have the right to build the house as I so desire. I mean it is strong. I'm not going to build it so it's going to blow away! (1970s settler, pers. comm. 10 January 1994)

There was much resistance amongst the new settlers against government regulations that they considered to be stifling to individual creativity, and today people take pride in the unique houses they built:

We can see now even in our architecture, the places that we live in, some of these places were allowed to evolve and, because of that mechanism, they are very individual. They have a lot of character, something that is devoid from processes that aren't allowed to evolve. They have to be set on a plan prior to the starting point, which really is stifling individual talents, stifling creativity. And we suffer greatly from a bureaucratic regime which has a tendency to over regulate. This burgeoning bureaucracy seems to want to keep swelling its ranks to the detriment of individuals who are outside of it (Brian Clarke, pers. comm. 5 July 1994).

Some people simply ignored the building regulations and constructed whatever they could afford. Others tried to comply with regulations as best they could by registering their house plans and living for as long as was permitted in caravans or sheds or other shelters officially classified as 'temporary dwellings'. For many people it was not just a matter of finance but a matter of freedom from a regulatory system: 'Yeah, well you learn a few tricks too; you learn the way they think; you get a bit clever. So I knew that by building this [pointing to her new council approved house that she rents out] I could continue to live like this [hidden in the rainforest in the shelter of her choice]' (1970s Kuranda settler, pers. comm. 22 April 1994).

Whether or not they were council approved, the houses that people created came to be celebrated as an art form. Although in most cases it was economic constraint that spawned these constructions, there was also much social pressure among the new landowners not to build a suburban-style concrete-block house. While concrete-blocks were the most economical material under the building code, to use them meant selling out to conformity. The unique houses of the new settlers, thus, became a celebration of individual creativity:

The house cost about a hundred and fifty dollars to build, this original house, this part. Most of the timber was new. It all come from up at Tolga

Mill. I think Roger Quinn found all that, this cheap timber up there, and we all went up and got truck load after truck load of it in borrowed trucks; everything was borrowed. I had the frame of the house up and I had the floor out of a second hand house; really good floor. I had a couple of friends help me. I did a lot of it myself, most of it. I didn't have money for the roof but a friend of mine I hadn't seen from years ago in Sydney arrived and he'd just won some money in the lottery, you know, and he gave me a hundred and fifty dollars or something to buy the iron for the roof (Ronnie Bruce, pers. comm. 8 January 1997).

Some of the members of tenancy-in-common were women. It was the only chance they had of becoming independent landowners:

I came up with a partner and we split and then I decided I'd go and buy some land [tenancy-in-common]. It's for poor people, you know, women especially. You don't want a mortgage. You can't *get* a mortgage with tenants-in-common. You can't borrow money, although you can get a personal loan, which I did at one stage (June Rees, pers. comm. 25 August 1997).

Some tenancies-in-common worked very well, while others became horrendously complicated, with deep enmities and feuds developing among the co-owners. Such situations proved particularly difficult for women who, on top of everything else, had to struggle against entrenched gender inequities. The following account reveals the situation faced by one woman with regard to her membership in a tenancy-in-common:

Because I ended up being the one that was actually on my own, like a lone girl, everybody else got their first choice [of land on the common block] and I kept going along with everybody because I didn't want to cause any trouble, and I ended up with nine acres here and nine acres up the back. And then, when it came down to it, there were two people that weren't going to give me access to my back block. So one of them wanted me to sell it to them, and I said, 'Ok, this is my price'. Well, for six months they tried to break my price. I'm pretty tough and I just stuck to my guns and it was really hard because I can remember one of the fellows leaving one day [after pressuring her to sell] and the kids were sitting there and they said, 'What does tenants-in-common mean anyway'? And I burst into tears. And then I went to the pub and I'm sitting there having a beer and [a man] sat down next to me and he said, 'Oh, the hippy bitch. They're going to break you; they're going to get you to give them the land for a cheaper price because they know that you're just going to give up because you are, you know, the soft little hippie girl that lives out there' (Suzie Creamcheese, pers. comm. 10 January 1994).

Gender also became an issue when women wanted to build their own houses:

> Yeah, I mean I went to get my building permit. They weren't going to give it to me. They said, 'Oh, and what's your husband's name'? And I said, 'No, it's just for me. I want it in *my* name. *I'm* going to do the building'. They said, 'I'm sorry but we can't give you that', and I said, 'What do you mean you can't give it to me?' and they said, 'No, no, no, we've only ever issued building permits to men and we can't give you one'. Luckily there was a solicitor standing behind me and he said, 'I think you'd better give it to her. You can't discriminate against her according to the law' (Suzie Creamcheese, pers. comm. 10 January 1994).

Some of the people who bought into tenancies-in-common were indeed inspired by communitarian ideals. Countering these, however, was a strong ideology of egalitarian individualism. Many of the tenancies-in-common were on rainforest blocks of land where members lived separately and privately as individual land owners on the sections they had surveyed according to goodwill agreement among themselves. What most people said they had in common was a commitment to maintaining the rainforest in as undisturbed a state as possible. People mostly avoided fences:

> No, we haven't put fences up. In the front there people have put fences up because they have horses; otherwise not. There are only fences built to keep animals in or out, but not at boundaries (Uli Seidel, pers. comm. 22 April 1994).

The settlers wanted the best of both worlds, individual freedom within a communal situation. Today people comment with nostalgia about the naiveté of their communal ideals:

> It was still the era of this hippie movement, all sharing and love and peace and nature ideas, and I was just riding on that wave and never mistrusted anyone because I had no experience either, Rosita. I never owned any land, or anything, so just the idea to have my own piece of dirt, you know, really lifted me on cloud nine. So, of course, in the next fifteen years, which means up until now, we all learnt. We have not much in common with anyone at all, funny that, common huh, nothing in common. Very few people have anything in common (Uli Seidel, pers. comm. 22 April 1994).

The idea of buying land in common was soon taken up by land speculators: people who were not really purchasing land in order to live on it, but in order to make a profit when the land prices went up. In one case, two of the members of a tenancy-in-common sought to force all the other members to sell the property by auction, at which point they planned to buy it back so as to subdivide it. The different visions of the people who bought into tenancies-in-common, particularly some of the larger ones, meant that conflict inevitably arose among the co-owners. Moreover, as their life circumstances changed, many co-owners, even some of those who had originally intended to live on their land permanently, chose to sell.

Counter-Culture Contradictions

The Kuranda settlers of the 1970s and 1980s brought with them communitarian ideologies and settlement practices that generated conflict with the established white population and local government agents. Yet they were generally sympathetically received by Aboriginal people, who saw them as sharing a similar style and standard of living and who appreciated their willingness to socially engage in ways that the early settlers had not. Aboriginal people and the new counter-culture settlers began to form bonds in a mutual struggle against the disempowering effects of state bureaucracy they experienced on a regular basis in their dealings with local government agents. The new settlers also introduced the drug-taking practices, music and dance styles of the global counter-culture movement to Aboriginal people. Marijuana smoking was widely adopted among young Aboriginal people, and drinking and dancing with the hippies, especially at the 'Bottom Pub' on a Friday night, was a popular social activity throughout the 1970s and 1980s. However, my fieldwork in Kuranda – begun twenty after the first influx of these new settlers – reveals that while some long-term friendships developed between particular settlers and Aboriginal individuals, such relationships are actually few and far between. That there were numerous intimate sexual relationships is evident in the number of children of mixed parentage among the population of the Kuranda area, but only a handful of these unions resulted in marriage or in long-term committed relationships of any kind.

Members of the counter-culture movement placed a high value on individual autonomy at the same time as they sought a utopian world in communal harmony with nature, in the way they believed Aboriginal people had once lived. In this chapter, I have argued that while gender and class were key factors, it was also a contradiction between the egalitarian individualism of the new settlers and the communitarian ideology underlying their communal living arrangements that eventually led to the demise of many of the communes and tenancies-in-common. As I show in the following chapters, contradictions between autonomy and relatedness – between individualism and communalism – continued to generate much social conflict during the 1980s and 1990s and into the early 2000s in Kuranda. Contested concepts of community and ways of relating to place underlie many of the social dramas that that continue to erupt in the village.

NOTES

1. In North Queensland, people talk of the rest of Australia as being 'down south'.
2. 'Hippies Invade Kuranda' reads the title of a contribution by resident Joan Dods to a history book commemorating the 1988 centenary of the town (Humston 1988: 118).
3. They were John C. (Jeb) Buck, and Christopher Patterson. An American newspaper article (*The Sunday Bulletin*, 9 February, 1975) represents the communes four 'founding fathers' as follows: 'There is Kim Haskell, whose grandfather was a DuPont Co. vice president and director and whose father, a former Delaware congressman, is now chairman and controlling stockholder of Abercrombie & Fitch, the New York-based chain for sporty outdoorsmen. There is John C. (Jeb) Buck, whose mother was formerly secretary of the Republican National Committee and whose father, an architect, once headed the New Castle County, Delaware, Council. There also are Christopher Patterson, a 1974 graduate of the University of Pennsylvania, and bearded Richard Trapnell, both members of prominent Wilmington families'.
4. The boat was started in June 1972 and was taken on the back of a semi-trailer down the range and launched in Cairns harbour in August 1978.
5. People who had built houses before new building regulations were passed in 1975 were not subject to the same level of surveillance as those who built later.

ᖍ Chapter 3 ᖘ

Performing Place

Amphitheatre Dramas

> *What began as a community building a stage became a stage moulding the very life of a community.*
> —Eve Stafford, 'The Multiplier Effect in the Arts: the Kuranda Amphitheatre Example'

Social conflict in Kuranda tends to focus around particular places that are classed as common property by the townspeople. Several of these places were created by the new settlers. In this chapter, I focus on the Kuranda Amphitheatre and the performances staged therein.[1] This is the first of five chapters that analyse the conflicts associated with particular public places in Kuranda and that uncover the politics of the relationships between people and place. From its initial conception to its ongoing construction and use, the Kuranda Amphitheatre can be best understood, I suggest, not merely as a venue for performances but as a total social situation. In this performance place, collective identity is actively constituted through *experience.* Through performances *on* the amphitheatre stage, Kuranda people generate 'experiential situations' (Kapferer 1986: 191) that work to contain 'the difference within' (Chauduri 1991: 192) so as to produce their concept of community. However, the amphitheatre project also generates experiential situations *off* the stage. Following Turner (1974, 1996), these may be called 'social dramas'. Turner (1974: 43) explicitly compares the 'temporal structure of certain types of social processes with that of dramas on the stage'. He defines 'social dramas' as 'units of aharmonic or disharmonic process, arising in conflict situations' (Turner 1974: 33). Disputes connected with the amphitheatre are born of contradictions between individual autonomy and communal relatedness, I argue, and as such they allow people to interrogate the notion of community. Such performances throw issues of social conflict into the limelight of people's experience, demanding of them an active role 'in the fashioning and refashioning of their own existential realities' (B. Kapferer 1996: xiii).

Bachelard illuminates the link between people and place through the study of poetic 'images of intimacy' and what he calls 'felicitous space' (Bachelard 1969: ix). He begins with the intimate poetics of the house and moves on to such images as the nest and the shell, noting, for example, that to live in a shell is associated with the ability to 'curl up comfortably'. 'To curl up', he suggests, 'belongs to the phenomenology of the verb to inhabit and only those who have learned to do so can inhabit with intensity' (Bachelard 1969: xxxiv). These remarks are particularly relevant to my theme because the Kuranda Amphitheatre was originally known as the 'sound shell' or 'music shell'. Although this is a reference to the acoustic dimensions of the space, the image of the shell generates other meanings that associate the space with a protective home. In building their 'shell', the new settlers of Kuranda saw themselves as marking their identity and belonging as local inhabitants.

People place themselves and constitute places through 'dwelling', which Heidegger (1971: 160) regards as '*the basic character* of Being' (original emphasis). According to Heidegger (1971: 147), dwelling is inescapably linked to 'building', which encompasses both building as cultivation (Latin *colere*, *cultura* – from which comes the term 'culture') and building as the raising up of edifices (Latin *aedificare*). The essence of dwelling is the care one takes in the practical creation of an environment; it is the building and cultivation of space into familiar scapes (landscapes, soundscapes, smellscapes) that in turn give us emplacement and a sense of belonging. Cultivation, I argue, also encompasses the cosmological tending of place. Australian Aboriginal Dreaming narratives and rituals, for example, are a form of such cultivation.

Similarly, Casey (1993: 175) argues that 'We get back into place – dwelling place – by the cultivation of built places. Such cultivation *localizes caring*' (original emphasis). Yet my examination of conflicts associated with the Kuranda Amphitheatre reveals that dwelling is not simply a sheltering, caring process. An emphasis on cultivation, nurture and care obscures the fact that emplacement often occurs within – and indeed generates – situations of conflict and violence. 'Being in place' often occurs in tense situations of contested space and surveillance. I contend that in building the Kuranda Amphitheatre, people were not just 'localizing caring' or, to play on Bachelard's formulation, 'curling up comfortably' to protect themselves from the raging storm outside. They were at the same time opening up – as indeed some shells do – and actually bringing the storm into the shelter. Dwelling, as I reveal it through the Kuranda example, in its very practice creates *discomfort*.

Related to these concerns is the view of symbolism that I adopt in preference to an overly cognitive formulation of human communication. Here

I follow Schieffelin (1985: 707), who writes: 'Symbols are effective less because they communicate meaning (though this is also important) than because, through performance, meanings are formulated in social rather than cognitive space, and the participants are engaged with the symbols in the interactional creation of a performance reality, rather than merely being informed by them as knowers'. It is my contention that in the context of the Kuranda Amphitheatre, people experience and participate in symbolic performances that actualise community through the containment of difference. These performances, however, end up reproducing difference. They are neither a mere reflection nor a representation of structurally given and/ or cognitively encoded categorical identities; rather, they are generative phenomena that constitute such particularities through experience.

Making a Performance Place

In July 1979, a group of twenty-one Kuranda residents met on a piece of Shire Council land within the town of Kuranda. The land was to be the site of a community performing arts venue, the Kuranda Amphitheatre.

Before the influx of the 1970s settlers, Kuranda township had a population of less than 350, a number that excluded Aboriginal people who would then have numbered about twenty.[2] Along the main street there were two hotels, a news agency, a post office, a grocery store, the Returned Serviceman's League (RSL) Hall and a bakery. To the newcomers, Kuranda was a village, and they were determined to preserve this image. Their concept of village expressed a 'rural nostalgia' that Newton (1988: 55) has identified as being a distinctive feature of the global counterculture movement of the day. Yet as cosy and collective as the term 'village' sounds, from the very beginning it marked the divergent interests in the community. The first edition of the *Kuranda Village News* was introduced as follows:

> To us Kuranda is a village.
> It has the heart, the charm and the personality that the word implies.
> And now it has a voice. A tiny one, but watch it ... At times we feel like 'Ma Reeba's' illegitimate child. (Poor little bastard, no doubt, 'Pa Reeba' shot through long ago, skipping maintenance!) (*Kuranda Village News* April 1979: 1).

The statement refers to the history of conflict between the new settlers and the Mareeba Shire Council. There was a feeling among some of the settlers that Kuranda was 'out of place' in the shire. Until the 1960s, its identity as a rural town appears to have been relatively unproblematic. Apart from the handful of people who had settled in the town specifically to run tourist related businesses, Kuranda was mainly populated by descendants of early settler families who worked in the timber industry and/or who owned cattle or small farming properties. As discussed in earlier chapters, the Aboriginal population had until 1962 mostly been confined at the Mona Mona mission, and when the mission closed down only a few families were resettled within the Kuranda town precinct. With the sudden influx of people from urban areas into the Kuranda region in the 1970s – an influx that during the 1980s and 1990s included entrepreneurs eager to take advantage of the tourist boom – the Mareeba Shire Council was suddenly forced to deal with newcomers who posed a threat to its conservative rural identity.[3] Many of the new settlers were artists, crafts people, musicians, and performers, and they thought of themselves as being the enlightened ones in a region of rednecks and bigots:

> At that time it was pretty obvious the town sort of broke up into three blocs. So there were the old timber-getters, the old settlers who were all aging and very fixed in their ways, far more fixed than Cairns people, and Cairns people were very fixed way back then, you know, sixty-nine-seventy. These people were the same as Ravenshoe[4] kind of people. I mean, they were very red-necky some of them. And then there were the hippies from all over the world who were pretty wild and alternative, and then there were the murris[5] (Mark Weaver, pers. comm. 15 April 1995).

The new settlers thought of themselves as bringing an alternative way of life to a rigidly conservative rural community. They also represented themselves as being in opposition to a state (Queensland) that was still in the hands of the highly conservative Country Party government of Joh Bjelke-Petersen. This political opposition is captured in the following anonymous poem about the then local Member of Parliament, entitled *The Barron River Bigot* and published in the *Kuranda Village News:*

> He's the Barron River Bigot with a store of oral tripe,
> And a fair amount of offal which is mostly over-ripe.
> He's a hostile hippie hater, and he hates the natives too;
> He's the mouth-almighty member, and his term is overdue.
>
> He's a cowboy from the country, sworn to set the jungle free
> Of hippie men and women-folk wherever they may be.
> He will take his dog and stockwhip, and his good old 45,
> And one by one he'll bring them in, if any's left alive.
>
> They will learn to fear his Yodel, and his mighty cowboy yell,
> And he'll burn their ammunition, and their forts and guns as well,

And if someone should escape him, they will never long be free,
For he'll fall upon the jungle and destroy it tree by tree.

So gather round you outlaws of the jungles of the north
And make a deep obeisance when your member travels forth.
Now let us charge our glasses for a toast if you're inclined –
'To mouth-almighty Marty and his microscopic mind!' (*Kuranda Village News* October 1981: 4)

The drug issue was one that united many of the new settlers. It was not so much a common ideology as the actual experience of constant police raids and the intense legal gaze of the state that provided a unifying force. The situation came to a head in 1980 when police shot and killed a fleeing man during a dawn drug raid, later claiming that foggy conditions had made for poor visibility. Numerous items in the local newspaper attest to the strength of feeling among Kuranda residents against this violent expression of state power. These include letters of outrage at the actions of the police, as well as such humorous items as:

Kuranda Foggerick
When it's foggy up here in Kuranda
You better hide under the verandah
For some boys in blue
Will without much ado
make you look like some kind of colanda.
(*Kuranda Village News* July/August 1980: 5)

T-shirts printed with a target on the back, accompanied by the words 'Don't Jog in the Fog', were a popular item for sale in the Kuranda market that year.

As discussed in the previous chapter, the antipathy between the Mareeba Shire Council and the new wave of settlers expressed itself particularly in terms of the enforcement of building regulations. After they arrived in the area, the settlers began to recreate Kuranda in their own image. The Shire zoning laws rendered many of the houses they built illegal, and some of these houses were also rated as substandard according to the building regulations. People remember experiencing extreme harassment from the Shire Council's inspectors and from the police:

We painted our outhouse green so that it would blend into the rainforest. The council threatened to bulldoze it down and told us that we had to paint it white. I said 'What's the difference what colour it is? It's only a shit-house!' (Ramona Rusch, pers. comm. 6 March 2005)

The following narrative by a 1970s settler is illustrative of the extreme antagonism of the council towards the new settlers, particularly those on tenancies-in-common:

> They [the engineer and the building inspector] came in on me with armed police, and they tried to force entry into my house. I knew they were there illegally. Well it ended up the policeman told them to enter and I was blocking the way like this, and the policeman grabbed me and pulled my arms up my back and dragged me back, split my shirt open and my boobs all hung out in front of them. He grabbed me round here and strung me up in the air and all the way to the paddy wagon kneed me in the back. Fifty metres to the paddy wagon he belted me forward like that, he propelled me and threw me head first into the paddy wagon. I lost my glasses and a thong [slipper]. When he dragged my arms up like that his watch caught in my hair clips and broke the strap and it fell to the ground. Well, he charged me with assault for that. He charged me with assault for struggling, I guess, I don't know. I was in agony because I've got terrible arthritis and he was treating me like a dead duck. So I had five assault charges against me. That was a three-day trial. I was put in gaol. I had never been in gaol and nor did I ever think I would, because I'm a law abiding citizen, you know. Anyway I won the case (June Rees, pers. comm. 25 August 1997).

The settlers took great pride in the creative individuality of their houses, and in defiance of the Shire Council, the *Kuranda Village News* featured a different house each month under the heading 'Stately Estates'. No addresses were given as most of these structures were not approved by the council. In general, the homes were constructed of recycled timber and/or natural rock to make them blend in with the rainforest environment or 'float on a green sea of fronds' (*Kuranda Village News* April 1979: 11). The newcomers saw themselves as escaping the 'blight of the concrete shoe box' (*Kuranda Village News* January 1980: 11) that had hit the cities and larger towns in Australia. Concrete bricks – locally known as 'Besser blocks' after the company that produced them – symbolised conformity, conservatism and control.

The new settlers did not confine themselves to moulding domestic space, but also set about transfiguring public space in Kuranda. They wanted a town hall and their own performance place. The only suitable performance venue was at the bottom pub. Otherwise, there was the Returned Serviceman's League (RSL) Hall and the Country Women's Association (CWA) Hall. A man who settled in Kuranda during the 1970s recalls the tension between the town establishment and the newcomers during a meeting of a ratepayer's association known as the 'Progress Association':

There was this thing called a Progress Association in Kuranda, and all the hippies went along one night and voted to close it, which was a crazy thing to do really in retrospect. But that was the power they had, the voting power. They suddenly found out they had the power by number of votes. So this ratepayer's group, or the Progress Association, which was always run by the town folk, the old timber-getter type people, was closed down for them (Mark Weaver, pers. comm. 15 April 1995).

One of the so-called hippies who had voted at this meeting explained to me (after having read an early draft of this chapter) that his attendance and his vote had been inspired by egalitarian principles. Because he had managed to buy some land as part of a tenancy-in-common arrangement, he happened to qualify, as a ratepayer, for membership of the association. He wanted to replace the association with one that was open to all residents, not just landowners.

The concept of the amphitheatre was born out of this democratic displacement of the older settlers. By creating their own performance venue, the new settlers could also satisfy their desire as newcomers for a connection to – and control of – place. This desire was couched in terms of the concept of 'community'. The newcomers saw themselves as building a new community by creating a space where experiences could be shared through performance. They would emplace themselves by placing themselves on stage. Joan Dods – who had been living in Kuranda longer that most of the other new settlers, having moved to Kuranda in 1964 – was approached to investigate the possibility of making a 'community performance space' in Kuranda. She promptly wrote to the Mareeba Shire Council and managed to secure a ten-year lease on six acres of land, part of a forty-acre site that had been gazetted for recreational purposes.[6] A group of four trustees was then appointed to manage the project and liaise with the Council.

It was decided to call for community volunteers to create a structure symbolic of democracy: an amphitheatre. There were also grand plans eventually to construct a much bigger community complex, with funds for the construction to be raised from future performances in the amphitheatre. These plans called for a town hall, a library and a botanical garden. Large and well-supported working bees were held. The Shire Council assisted with the water connection and contributed funds toward the fencing, but the creation of the amphitheatre was mostly done by enthusiastic volunteer labour:

I should think the whole community over the years has had some input. In the early days of course it was clearing the land and burning it and doing all that. We just called for volunteers. Every Saturday we worked, and I provided cooked chicken legs and beer out of my pocket, and that was lunch. And we just worked all day doing whatever it was, sowing the grass seeds, and then planting all the trees around, making the road. The construction was all voluntary. At that time it was called the music shell (Joan Dods, pers. comm. 11 January 1996).

People viewed the project as a labour of love. Through the moulding and planting of the earth into an enclosed womb-like space the newcomers saw themselves as creating a place for the birthing and nurturing of 'community' and for experiencing, through touch, smell and taste, the very earth they were making their own:

> It's a *community* venue. We built it *for* the community. It was built by locals. It was built by *local* performers. That's who built it, and their groupies, like me. Because there was nowhere in Kuranda and we wanted somewhere for us as a *community*. I was there the day the bulldozer was there making the terraces, and taking the trees out and walking around. I've got a sixpence I found that day, and a plant in my garden that had to be moved from that site. And a lot of stuff in the gardens there, all that green and white pandanus came from my garden, *babies* from my plants, you know like. So it's been in all areas I've worked, digging holes, and killing my lawn mowers there (Rhonda Young, pers. comm. 24 January 1996; original emphasis).

The amphitheatre was not only seen as a place built by and for the community but was also seen as a place which actually *made* community. This was expressed insightfully by Eve Stafford, a 1970s settler who was involved in the amphitheatre as a volunteer for many years, who wrote in a community arts publication: 'What began as a community building a stage became a stage moulding the very life of a community' (Stafford 1984: 4).

In their creation of a 'mimetic organ',[7] this womb-like pocket in the rainforest, the new settlers saw themselves as giving birth to community. They saw themselves as 'localizing caring', as nurturing their environment and, in the process, as becoming emplaced. They expressed this to me in the pleasure they took in pointing out particular trees they had lovingly planted,[8] rock walls they had constructed, pathways they had cleared, or the particular terraces on which they had laboured. Some people linked themselves to the amphitheatre directly through the plants they brought from their own gardens. Others claimed that they had played a role in constructing one or more of several performance stages, or had given a hand in building the 'top shed' and kitchen, the gatehouse, or the children's playground. Many Kuranda residents can claim to have served at one time or another on the amphitheatre committee, in the kitchen, behind the bar, at the gate. Others have performed in productions, worked as stagehands, sewed costumes, or operated the lighting. Being able to claim involvement at some time or another in the creation and continuing operation of the amphitheatre has become a marker of belonging, of being a true Kurandan. Today, one of the ways that new residents attempt to find acceptance in the town is by volunteering their skills and labour in the amphitheatre, or by participating in one way or another in a staged performance there.

Constructing 'Community'

The amphitheatre was envisaged and built as a 'community place'. As evidenced above, the word 'community' arises again and again in connection with the amphitheatre, and it is interesting to explore what it means. If we accept that community does not come to us fully constituted but as 'an attempt to dominate the field of discursivity, to arrest the flow of differences, to construct a centre' (Laclau & Mouffe 1985: 112), then what kind of community does the Kuranda amphitheatre construct? Eve Stafford has likened the amphitheatre to a 'village green'. She was quoted in a community arts publication as saying that 'this people's place, akin to the village green, is as egalitarian as the beach' (Kuranda Amphitheatre 1989: 28). As she explained to me eight years later:

> I did see it as the village green because there was a stage there in the mid-eighties where it was in daily use. It had kids kindie in the morning and it had classes in the afternoon and it had rehearsals at night. When we first came here in the seventies [at the movie theatre] you had Europeans on one side and Murris on the other, and hippies down the back; like hippies weren't either European or Aboriginal! They were the three categories of person in the town at that time. And so there were defined areas that we went, defined areas where others went. I felt that one of the reasons that Aboriginal people were welcomed into the amphitheatre was that we were alternatives and we were outside of the mainstream ourselves. So when the amphitheatre was built, we opened it up and they were welcome. That's why I said it was like the village green; they had a green light (Eve Stafford, pers. comm. 24 January 1996).

The creators of the amphitheatre saw themselves as constructing a community founded on solid egalitarian and democratic ideals. Their notion of community was, and still is, founded on a tradition of egalitarian individualism:

I see it as a place which has kept our community together as a *community*. I think if we didn't have the amphitheatre as a focus, I mean we might have a hall somewhere, or a theatre building somewhere, it would never be such a good focus as that type of an outdoor situation that we have, which allows an enormously broad spectrum of people to be catered to, and also the fact that *anybody* can use it. It's not restricted in *any way* at all (Joan Dods, pers. comm. 11 January 1996; original emphasis).

Although the new settlers were apparently espousing communal ideals and a commitment to collective values by emphasizing community, their notion of community was actually founded on a classical liberal conception of the individual and of individual freedom. For them, freedom meant the absence of the constraints imposed by the old guard in Kuranda and by local agents of the state. This explains the great pride people took (and still take) in the amphitheatre as a place that belonged to the people rather than a place conceived and imposed from outside or above (e.g. by the Shire Council). It also explains their strenuous attempts over the years to avoid relying on government support for the construction and maintenance of the amphitheatre:

We didn't apply for grants. We rather had the feeling we wanted to do things on our own, that we didn't want to be beholden to the government. And so we tended to have local things to raise money. It was started by the community and completely built by the community (Joan Dods, pers. comm. 11 January 1996).

Although the amphitheatre was compared to a village green, Kuranda was certainly not a peaceful pastoral scene. As stated above, the amphitheatre was created in a context of political conflict with the village establishment. The key political organisations within the town were the various service clubs (the Lions Club, the Returned Soldiers League and the Country Women's Association), and a proposal by the Lions Club to apply for a grant to build a community hall that would compete with the amphitheatre project drew much resentment from the amphitheatre supporters.

A letter to the editor of the *Kuranda Village News* (July 1980: 14) referred to the conflict in terms of competing soundscapes: 'For heaven's sake, a Sound Shell! More musical delights to be inflicted on the unfortunate residents ... the Service Clubs go about their business *quietly* doing good for the community' (original emphasis).[9] Other townspeople complained about the amphitheatre being nothing but a hippie hangout:

A lot of people said very rude things about, 'Oh yes we all know what people at the amphitheatre are doing. They're growing and smoking dope all day long. That's all they ever do. All the hippies gather there. That's all they're doing. It's a hippie place. Don't go near it'. There was a terrible lot of that stuff around, you know. It was very ugly (Joan Dods, pers. comm. 11 January 1996).

A small number of residents actually performed their community service orders for drug-related and other offences by working at the amphitheatre. One person's order consisted of sewing the costumes for a particular play that happened to be under production at the time. Another spent time painting the top shed. Others did work maintaining the lawns and building retaining walls:

> Oh hell, shit yeah, God Almighty, thousands of hours. When I had to go and do community service I went, 'Excuse me your Worship, can I just knock off a few of the hours from the thousands of hours I've *already* done in Kuranda community-wise'. You're kidding me; everything from acting, theatre, security, to being on stage, rock `n roll, the whole movie; oh yeah, cool you know, everything, yes (Lee Bones, pers. comm. 10 January 1996).

Much of the volunteer labour at the amphitheatre was possible because there was a population that was not in paid employment or that worked only part-time or informally and, therefore, was ready, willing and able to provide such support to the project. As one volunteer noted: 'I actually had some philosophy that, if I was on the dole [social security], I was happy to be around there pushing a mower, and mulching and planting'.

In spite of the tension between the new settlers and the Kuranda establishment, the amphitheatre volunteers saw themselves as building the amphitheatre not just for themselves but for everybody. For them, the amphitheatre was not merely a matter of defining boundaries of exclusion but of creating the conditions of encompassment. This idea of community extends Cohen's (1985: 13) argument that a people's 'consciousness of community is ... encapsulated in perception of its boundaries, boundaries which are themselves largely constituted by people in interaction'. Although the new Kuranda settlers were, in fact, invaders who were displacing another way of life, they did not see themselves as such. Rather, they saw themselves as liberators who were creating the democratic space to *contain* diversity. In making the amphitheatre, they were attempting to build community by providing a space in which differences could be encompassed. Community, for the new settlers, was not about constructing boundaries, but about the envelopment of difference by similarity, and the encompassment of diversity through the creation of a 'melting pot'.

A Place on Stage

The amphitheatre provided the new residents of Kuranda with opportunities for emplacement through participation in performances of place, performances that played out, tested, and contested the idea of community and that made it possible to experience differences within that community. Such performances articulate the universalising idea of community with the particularising differences within.[10] As with a park, the amphitheatre is public space. Non-profit community groups use the venue free of charge. Activities that have taken place in the amphitheatre, for example, include dance classes, aerobics sessions, *a capella* singing, children's gymnastics, group play for children, yoga, *tai chi* and self-awareness classes. Other uses have included charity fund-raising concerts,[11] pantomimes,[12] plays,[13] full moon dances and a number of large community theatre productions. The amphitheatre volunteers instituted the yearly Kuranda Spring Festival, which included a street parade, garden competitions and the like, in an attempt to extend the boundaries of what the amphitheatre represented to them into the main street and to encompass the village as a whole.[14] In 1990, the amphitheatre volunteers hosted the twenty-fourth Australian National Folk Festival (Figure 3.1).[15]

Figure 3.1. The Australian National Folk Festival, Kuranda Amphitheatre, 1990.

Photographer: Mark Williams.

The amphitheatre has also provided an outlet for much local Aboriginal talent. Aboriginal people were particularly influenced by the success of a band formed by some of the hippie settlers called 'The Rainbow Country House Band'. The band developed a wide following in North Queensland, and its popularity gave impetus to some Aboriginal youths to form a reggae band that they called 'Mantaka' after the settlement along the Barron River where they had grown up and to which their families had been moved when the mission was closed in 1962. One of the original members of Mantaka commented about the influence of the Rainbow Country House Band as follows:

That's another band I must say that inspired us to continue because they were winning the 'Battle of the Bands' and all that stuff at the time. And they were Kuranda and we supported them well, because we used to go to their gigs. And looking at what they've done, who were actually mates of ours, even though we were a lot younger than them guys. But we were taking on what they were doing because we had no employment in Kuranda, we had nothing in Kuranda. So music was the escape, you know, just to get rid of the boredom. So we used to sit down and start writing songs. And the songs that we wrote, we started feeling good about them songs because we were delivering a message as well. And it make us feel good to play that, to sing it for other people to enjoy what they're listening to so they go away singing this rhyme, like:

Living in Kuranda is fine,
Living in Kuranda is mine,
Look all around, what do you see,
No concrete jungle, but green trees.
Everybody is feeling fine, because the feeling of Kuranda is in our mind. (Willie Brim, pers. comm. 13 August 1997)

Mantaka's efforts were rewarded when it was given the opportunity to perform first at the bottom pub and then at the inauguration of the Kuranda Amphitheatre on 30 May 1982. The band came to be viewed by some people as *the* amphitheatre band, and there was an expectation that the group would become the official support band for all visiting bands. There was much hometown loyalty evident in the audience's response to Mantaka, who often got a better reception than visiting bands with a greater national reputation. I was present at a 1995 Yothu Yindi concert in the amphitheatre where people chanted for Mantaka when the band was not even billed for the night. Mantaka became a regular performer at the amphitheatre because the band could be relied upon to draw in the locals, and particularly Aboriginal people. The amphitheatre was home ground for the band, which adopted reggae as its trademark style:

> We didn't get much chance [before] to hear this music, reggae music. And Peter Tosh, but mainly Bob Marley, had a big influence on the style of music because of his lyrics. And he was singing about *real* things, you know, not just love, love, love, and all that stuff. He was singing about human pain and suffering, which we could really relate to, so we sort of adopted that. And we said, well this brand of music, you know, is meaningful, so easy to play and it's a *feel* music, you know, not every band can play reggae music (Willie Brim, pers. comm. 13 Aug 1997; original emphasis).

Mantaka tried to make it bigger by doing a number of tours 'down south'. The band stayed in Sydney for a while, but the members soon returned, feeling more comfortable playing for a home audience. According to Brim (pers. comm. 13 August 1997), 'Even at Townsville, we've been offered work all around Townsville with the band but we refused it because Townsville's *not our place*' (my emphasis). Mantaka was about place and connection to place. Performances by the band were an assertion of belonging, an expression of *inhabited* place.

Another less well known Aboriginal band that formed in Kuranda not long after Mantaka was Koah Konnections, led by Maxi Snider and also named after a place where Aboriginal people had been resettled after they were removed from the mission. The band's theme song was entitled 'Koah', and they also sang about their home places to a reggae beat:

> Chorus: Koah,
>   Mona Mona Mission is another place
>   Kuranda too
> Verse: We play our music
>   No one can compete
>   We do our music
>   Stompin' dancin' feet
>   Koah
>   Mona Mona Mission is another place
>   Kuranda too
>   Koah
>   We can do it too.

Reggae music has continued to be popular among Aboriginal people in Kuranda, and today a new generation of bands has taken over from Mantaka and Koah Konnections. There is now a recognised Kuranda reggae heritage that is celebrated each year with a festival. The festival website for 2004 advertised the event as follows:

> Since the early 80's Kuranda has nurtured a reggae culture of its own with bands such as Mantaka pioneering a distinctive Aboriginal reggae sound unique to Northern Australia. Kuranda Reggae Festival is proud to have the Pad Boys and the Yubbaz representing Kuranda's Djabugay reggae heritage.[16]

Another second generation Kuranda band is Zenith, led by Willie Brim from the original Mantaka and featuring his son Aiden Brim. The band's song 'Kuranda Reggae' won a spot in the 2009 Q Song Music Awards in Brisbane, nominated in both the Indigenous and the Blues and Roots categories. But in addition to providing a home for the local brand of reggae, during the past twenty years the amphitheatre has featured a wide variety of other bands and performers, including bush, folk, and rock performers.[17] There have also been performances from most of Australia's well-known Aboriginal bands – including Yothu Yindi, Coloured Stone, No Fixed Address and the Warumpi Band – all of whom have over the years provided inspiration to the Aboriginal youth of Kuranda.

Community Theatre

The amphitheatre is one of the places in Kuranda where Aboriginal people say they feel comfortably able to mix with white people. Aboriginal people take the term community to include them when it is used in connection with the amphitheatre and have taken part in many of the community theatrical performances staged at the venue. Indeed the now world famous Tjapukai Dance Theatre was born out of a community theatre production: *The Odyssey You'll Ever See,* produced and directed by Don Freeman, based on the history of the Palmer River gold rush, and featuring Aboriginal performer David Hudson. After the success of *The Odyssey,* the producers joined forces with David Hudson to open an Aboriginal dance theatre in the main street of Kuranda where performances by local Aboriginal people could be staged daily for tourists.

The exposure of Kuranda Aboriginal people to performances such as *The Odyssey* may have fostered the ready acceptance of the dance theatre concept among Aboriginal people in Kuranda. However, the amphitheatre also brought a number of different Indigenous dance groups to the attention of the local Aboriginal people. For example, The Saibai Island Dancers performed at the amphitheatre in 1981, the Yarrabah Aboriginal Dancers in 1982, and the Lockhart River Aboriginal Dance Group (winners of that year's Cape York Dance Festival) in 1985. Dancers from the Pacific Islands and Papua New Guinea featured along with the Yarrabah Aboriginal Dancers during a cultural day on 7 August 1983, and the Air Niugini Dance Troupe performed together with the Saibai Island Dancers and Mantaka on 6 October 1985. The amphitheatre has certainly been instrumental in fostering a heightened awareness of the political potential of dance and music as self-conscious practices of identity among Kuranda Aboriginal people.[18] For both the new settlers and the Aboriginal people, the amphitheatre became a space that provided opportunities to reach out and harness global cultural flows while at the same time attempting to produce a sense of local community identity. The way senses or experiences of community are produced can best be illustrated with a more detailed look at three of the larger theatre productions performed at the amphitheatre: *Babble on Babylon*, *Timewarp* and *The Multicoloured Dreamboat*.

Babble on Babylon

Babble on Babylon, showpiece of the 1984 Spring Festival, was the first big theatre production to be staged in the amphitheatre. *Babble on Babylon*, which played three times (7–9 September 1984), was advertised at the time as an example of 'improvisational community theatre'.[19] The idea behind such community productions was that the participants had the freedom to create their own parts and dialogue within broad parameters and a central theme. Over sixty Kuranda residents contributed to the production either as performers or behind the scenes, but except for one young rap dancer, no Aboriginal people performed in this 'musical extravaganza'.

The production consisted of three main acts followed by a series of brief sketches. The first act featured the prince and princess of a primitive tribe untouched by modern civilisation on the eve of their sacrifice to the idol of the tribe. In answer to the question of why the prince and princess should be sacrificed, the primitive tribe chants to the beat of drums:

> Idol moves me
> That's the way it's always been
> Crazy Idol
> That's the way it's meant to be
> Idol rules me
> That's the way it's always been

The prince and princess escape and are rescued in the second act by the passengers and crew of a cruise ship, the SS Babylon, who represent all the corrupting evils of modern civilisation. After facing this threat, the prince and princess eventually find themselves abandoned at the captain's table, where they turn back to their tribal chant. The chant is quickly taken up by the other passengers and turned into a new dance sensation, the Idol Motion. However, the ship sinks and, in the third act, the prince and princess find themselves in Kuranda in the year 1970. There they meet other people trying to escape from Babylon.

The play concluded with a number of sketches, attached in the manner of a postscript. One of them featured a group of new Kuranda settlers complaining about their marijuana going mouldy in the wet season and deciding to build a house which subsequently gets condemned by the council building inspector. Another skit featured a couple of hippies farming a crop with a billboard advertising 'Sunshine Marijuana' in the background, while a third skit alluded to the 1980 police drug raid and shooting of the Kuranda man with the presentation of a huge target that warned people not to 'jog in the fog'. The production ended with everyone singing:

I see you on the street
But you're so out of reach
Let's start relations
Open up communications
Don't put up resistance
We all need assistance
We have something to say
You are all in this play in Kuranda
Of one mind and one heart
We all play a part in Kuranda
We have something to say
We are all in this play
You are all in this play
We are all in this play in Kuranda

Babble on Babylon is an example of the kind of practice through which experiences of place are produced. People attempted to define their social space by performing Kuranda as a particular kind of place, a place from which one can escape the corruption of 'Babylon' and the wreck of civilisation. Such performances enable a fusion of place and community into one entity, one construct. Kuranda is presented as a place in which otherness finds a haven and the primitive a home.

One might be tempted to interpret this play as an expression of a primitivist discourse that informs the production of a certain kind of Australian national identity (Lattas 1997). Yet the play is not a celebration of primitive

otherness or of the redemptive unity of a primordial world. It is not a communitarian fantasy of *Gemeinshaft*. The narrative structure of the play is
threefold. The first act presents the original primitive environment as one
that must be escaped. It is an environment of regulation, control and submission of the individual to the will of the group. The first act thus calls for
a rejection of social constraint on the freedom of the individual. The second act comments on the corrupting forces of modern civilisation and, in
highlighting the development of the new dance sensation, the Idol Motion,
recognises primitivism itself as one of these corruptive forces. Kuranda is
celebrated in the third act as the place of escape from *both* of these worlds,
the primitive and the modern. I suggest that the tribal culture of the primitive in this play is simply a metaphor for social constraint on individual autonomy, and Kuranda is represented as a place of 'live and let live' in which
such constraint can be transcended.

Timewarp

The 1988 bicentennial production of *Timewarp* was staged from the 8–10
September 1988 at the amphitheatre by Kuranda's Junction Theatre Company with a cast and crew of about one hundred local people. This production was one of many celebratory events that occurred all over the country
during Australia's bicentennial year. Understandably, many Aboriginal people boycotted these events that marked two hundred years of their colonial
oppression. It is therefore remarkable that *Timewarp* had the support and
active participation of Kuranda Aboriginal people. The story – written by
one of the new settlers, Dave Harris, with assistance from others[20] – centres
around a teenager named Tim who lives with his mother in a rented house
in Kuranda. Tim escapes the tensions of his mother's affair with their landlord and her pressure on him to 'make something of himself' by hanging
out with his Aboriginal mate Baz and working for a mad scientist who has
invented a time machine. Tim's carelessness with the time machine eventually lands him and Baz in Port Jackson at the time of the arrival of the first
fleet in 1788, where they witness the tragic confrontation between the British colonisers and the local Aboriginal tribe, played by Kuranda Aboriginal
people who spoke their parts in Djabugay.

Sent by Tim's mother and the scientist to rescue the boys and bring them
back, the landlord eventually becomes trapped with them in a series of
travels through space and time. One of these trips lands them in Kuranda in
1888 on the date of the first survey of the town, where they meet some early
settlers and a group of Aboriginal people. Here the boys witness the first
Kuranda 'real-estate land grab' and have to prevent the greedy speculation
of the landlord who, with his foreknowledge of the inflation of land prices,

attempts to buy as much land as he can. Baz also tries to warn his Djabugay ancestors that the settlers are going to 'take away' their land. They respond with incredulity, 'Where are they going to take it?' and are told that 'Guns are nothing; these white people's weapons are them bits of paper'.

The time-travellers then move on through time and space and encounter two alternative futures. The first is an underwater world free of technology in which humans have evolved gills and fins and move in perfect harmony with one another and with their environment. The time travellers are told by the inhabitants of this world that humans returned to the sea to 'hide from poisonous rain' after ruining their planet by building 'machines of hate'. With the help of the dolphins, they adapted until their 'brains and souls became as one'. The Aboriginal boy Baz is tempted to stay behind but is dragged away by his fellow travellers.

The time machine then takes them to a world populated only by robots and androids that are continuously at war. Extinct humans had programmed them long ago. The time-travellers help to end the war using Tim's computer programming skills. This time it is Tim who is tempted to stay on as 'the most important person on the planet, in fact, the *only* person'. He is eventually persuaded that 'people and love mean more than all this'. A robot, played by an Aboriginal man, fixes their time machine. The robot installs 'a self-guiding return device', a boomerang, in their time machine, enabling them to finally return home to 1988 Kuranda. The play ends with the stage filled with all the performers dancing to a reggae beat until a group of about twenty-five children in different national costumes enters in the foreground, singing 'it's no good looking to the past to find your fate' or 'to worry for the future' but that 'we just want to be happy and be free'.

It is clear that *Timewarp* plays with different possibilities of being as well as making a political statement about race relations in contemporary Australia, in particular the issue of Indigenous land rights. In fact, the Djabugay parts are translated and printed in the program for the audience to take home:

> This is our land. Our land lies wide, northwards, southwards, eastwards, westwards. The good God gave us this country, the trees of the mountains, game in the waters.
> *DO NOT FORGET OUR WAY.*
> We followed one track (one Law, one Spirit). Today the young follow other paths, carrying English in their heads.
> *DO NOT FORGET OUR WAY.*
> That's our waters, our Storywaters. That's Djabugay. I belong to the land. I am Djabugay. We are telling you. Give us our home-land. Give us Mona Mona. You do not listen today. Maybe tomorrow.
> *THIS COUNTRY IS DJABUGAY.* (emphasis as in the original text)

However, Aboriginal difference is represented in the play as something that can be accommodated only through its encompassment within 'community'. As Kapferer has pointed out, the 'multiculturalist valuation of difference' is actually based on a 'logic of similarity' (1988: 205). Unlike *Babble on Babylon,* which, I have argued, was an expression of liberal individualism, *Timewarp* apparently places a stronger emphasis on communitarian ideals. However, there is an ambivalence about these ideals because of their threat to individual autonomy and because, taken to their extreme, they require the negation of the cultural differences and historical events that the show intended to celebrate. *Timewarp* resolves the contradiction by presenting its audience with a multi-cultural Kuranda community that lives in the here and now, 'happy and free'. As in *Babble-on Babylon,* different possibilities are rejected in favour of a home in Kuranda. In the under-sea world, communitarianism is represented in the extreme and individual identity is no longer possible, while in the outer-space world we find the complete negation of human community. Here, individualism taken to its limit leaves the possibility of only one human being, 'prince of the planet', living by himself in a world full of machines. Kuranda is presented as a community that transcends these two extremes by enabling individual differences and cultural differences to flourish, but only within the encompassing limits of identity (sameness).

The Multicoloured Dreamboat

Multiculturalism was most obviously celebrated in the 1993 amphitheatre production *The Multicoloured Dreamboat,* which was staged to mark the International Year of Indigenous Peoples. The production was directed by one of the new settlers, Diana Moynahan, and was developed as a community training program. In the course of developing the stage performance, which included a one act play and a variety concert, participants were trained in various theatrical arts, including acting, makeup, set design, lighting and sound, as well as in video production. The community venture was supported with funding from the Australia Council of the Arts and the Queensland Arts Council. Of the four actors in the one act play, entitled *The Foreman,* three were Aboriginal people who had never before performed on the stage. The compere of the variety show was an Aboriginal woman from Mantaka, Rhonda Brim, and among the acts was an Aboriginal children's dance group under the tutelage of Aboriginal musician Maxi Snider, who had written the song that the children sang for their finale: 'Koah, Mona Mona is another place, Kuranda too'. Other acts included a Celtic song group accompanied by didjeridus, a Torres Strait dance group from Mareeba, and a group of Aboriginal women from Kuranda who sang in Djabugay. Several rock and reggae bands also performed. The grand finale of the show was a song entitled 'Melting Pot':

What we need is a great big melting pot
Big enough to take the world and all it's got
We've been stirring for a hundred years or more
Multicoloured people by the score

The Multicoloured Dreamboat celebrates community as a container of human diversity in which differences are respected but at the same time mixed and 'melted' together, so that racial colour categories of black, white, red or yellow are broken down to form a single 'multi-coloured' society. Thus, the community production throws tensions between the concepts and policies of assimilation and multiculturalism into the limelight. The Australian government policy of multiculturalism was derived from a Canadian policy of the same name and has been defined officially as 'a policy for managing the consequences of cultural diversity' (*National Agenda for a Multicultural Australia* 1989: vii). However, Australia's immigration program 'has actually been carefully controlled to minimise difference and placate a population historically suspicious of immigration. This is expressed in such images as "the Yellow Peril", the "threat from the North", the "Red Hordes", and more recently "the Asian Invasion"' (Bottomley 1994: 142). It is also evidenced by government policies regarding refugee detention centres. State agendas and policies actually spawn the very differences that undermine notions of community. In productions such as *The Multicoloured Dreamboat,* people play with contradictory visions of how differences may be encompassed within community. These differences are reproduced within local arenas, but they are also the product of national and international political agendas.

Such performances as *Timewarp, Babble on Babylon* and *The Multicoloured Dreamboat* are not just statements or representations; they are not simply about communicating meaning. Rather, they are constitutive practices that play with different possibilities of being and thus work to create community. They provide experiences of a particular vision of community, one that does not just embrace difference but also encompasses it.

Timewarp, Babble on Babylon and *The Multicoloured Dreamboat* were musical extravaganzas, each requiring massive commitment from performers and each in turn attracting large local audiences.[21] Family groups and groups of friends filled the banked lawns of the amphitheatre, laughing and clapping and thoroughly enjoying the shows, as is invariably the case at amphitheatre productions. For the participants, cast and audience alike, such productions are remembered as 'performance realities' (Schieffelin

1985: 707) that produce palpable experiences of a difference-encompassing community. Yet differences resist such containment, as is evidenced by the continuing situation of conflict that the amphitheatre project generated off-stage.

Dramas Off-Stage

As stated above, the amphitheatre project began under the trusteeship of four 'upstanding members of the community'. Within two years, however, conflict was brewing between the trustees, as 'the management', and the ordinary volunteers, as 'the workers', over the control of the amphitheatre:

> There was an ugly faction in the community who wanted confrontation and to kill people. Yeah they saw us as being straight and not really representing them. They felt it was some sort of elitist group who were running them, you know, telling them what to do, so maybe we were. We didn't see ourselves as that. He [the leader of the faction opposing the trustees] was a very angry difficult man. He had a meeting at the amphitheatre, a real rabble rousing thing. He said, 'Kill the trustees'! (Trustee, 11 January 1996).

Much of the dispute with the trustees focused on the construction of a stage for the 1982 Kuranda Spring Festival. According to one of the workers, the trustees were planning 'a concrete block monstrosity' for a stage 'with a bloody moat to keep the audience at bay'. One day, after arriving for a working bee only to find nobody there, this worker decided to begin to build a simple stage out of recycled railway sleepers and timber off-cuts 'of the scale that people could relate to and that did not separate audience from performers'. Other volunteers soon joined him, and the stage was finished ten days ahead of schedule. The stage served well for some years with various repairs, but it was seen as a temporary measure, and there continued to be conflict over what should eventually replace it. According to one informant, 'There was some ugly stuff down there, like hanging nooses on the stage; yeah, there was a noose on the stage at one stage. I mean it got pretty bitter. It was like the market wars'.[22]

The amphitheatre builders pushed for abolition of the trustee system and for the establishment of an officially constituted body with a democratically elected committee. They believed that this committee would be more representative of the local community and would give more people more say in the development and operation of the amphitheatre. Eventually, a new 'democratic society' was formed, and the trustees were replaced by the Kuranda Recreation Society. The Society's inaugural meeting was held on 15 December 1982. It was renamed the Kuranda Amphitheatre Society in 1984 and became an incorporated body in 1986. Nevertheless, as the minutes of the Amphitheatre Society committee meetings evidence, the dispute over the amphitheatre stage continued throughout the 1980s and 1990s. Should the Society bow to the demands of big touring bands, or should the focus be on a smaller stage and clubhouse for local community use only? The Amphitheatre Society managed to finance the upkeep and improvement of the venue through hiring it out for large rock concerts, a practice that caused the most conflict amongst Society members, as the temporary stage that was built for the Spring Festival in 1982 was not seen as suitable for large rock concerts. To construct the type of stage required for such concerts represented an opening up to and bringing in of the outside world. This was in tension with the vision of the amphitheatre as a place in which to 'curl up comfortably', to use Bachelard's (1969) phrase. Moreover, a permanent stage structure within the body of the amphitheatre challenged the image of it as an egalitarian place of freedom 'where magical transformations can occur' and a place which, like a garden, was 'cultivated but not fully constructed' (Casey 1993: 162). Numerous stage designs were submitted and discarded. One design was commissioned from the architect J. Hockings of the University of Queensland with a bicentennial grant of A$20,000. But consensus could not be reached over this stage either. While it was true that not everyone thought the design in keeping with their vision, it was the prohibitive cost of building Hocking's stage that delivered the telling blow: the size of the debt that the Society would have incurred threatened the Society's ability to maintain community control of the amphitheatre in the face of a possible take over by the Shire Council, and the plans were accordingly shelved.

Pressure for a larger and more permanent stage structure continued until the Amphitheatre Society eventually became utterly entangled in an apparently endless bureaucratic process of filing grant applications to replace the stage. Realising it was in crisis, the Amphitheatre Society held a 'future search' workshop in January 1994. In her keynote address to the workshop, Eve Stafford (1994: 2) said: 'We kept changing the Constitution to fit funding guidelines. This was the beginning of blurred vision, as to who we were and what was our purpose . ... As we tried to fit in with different funding opportunities, we lost some clarity in our idea of who we were'. In spite of the attempt by volunteers to avoid the tentacles of state power by refusing to become dependent on government funding, they eventually became insidiously entrapped. State power – now expressed in the form of the bureaucratic order rather than as the direct force of the police – appeared to have won out as one successful grant led to the partial construction of a concrete block stage that many people abhorred. This new stage remained unfinished behind the old stage for some years as various Amphitheatre Society committees looked for further grants to complete it. Morale was at an all-time low during the early nineties. However, the committees eventually achieved some success in this area, and under the auspices of the 1997 committee, the old stage was finally dismantled. Large working bees were held and ingenious ways to disguise the concrete block structure of the new stage were plotted. These ways included building a dance area at the base of the stage and bringing it closer to the level of the audience in an attempt to recapture the egalitarian unity that had been the spatial experience induced by the old stage. There was renewed hope among the more than two hundred Amphitheatre Society members in the future of their project (Figure 3.2).

However, the Society continued to face opposition from residents who objected to the noise generated by bands and other amplified musical performances. In order to address these complaints, the Shire Council imposed restrictions on the use of the venue. Without the big bands, the Amphitheatre Society was unable to afford its public liability insurance premiums and faced the unsavoury prospect of handing over control of the amphitheatre to the council. A number of public meetings were held to dis-

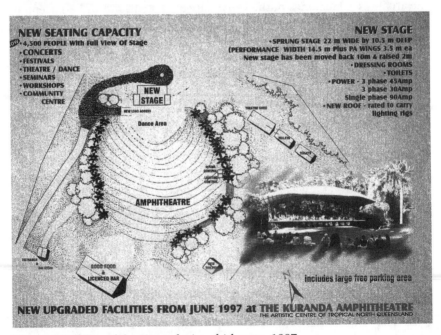

Figure 3.2. Plan of the Kuranda Amphitheatre, 1997.
Courtesy of the Kuranda Amphitheatre Society.

cuss how to deal with the crisis. Because it had no public liability insurance, the Society was obliged to close the venue to the public while dedicated members continued to work to find a solution. Eventually, they found affordable insurance, and on 3 August 2003 the Amphitheatre reopened with a special community variety concert and a welcome address by Aboriginal elder Milton Brim:

> I am a Djabugay elder of the Djabugay tribe that used to roam, hunt, collect bush foods throughout the Kuranda area. Even right here at this theatre where they once camped. So you see that this theatre plays an important role to the Indigenous people, the Djabugay.

His speech was a clear assertion on behalf of the Djabugay of the significance of the amphitheatre to them by virtue of their priority in place as traditional owners. The claim was made not merely in terms of a general association with the Kuranda area, but specifically in terms of the prior traditional use of the amphitheatre itself by the Djabugay as a *lived* place, a home camp or *bulmba*. During the opening concert, Willie Brim spoke in Djabugay, and his words were simultaneously translated as follows:

> Long ago there was a beautiful place where people came to sit, to listen, to sing and to dance. The place stayed with the people for many years. But bad spirits entered this land and took the beautiful place away from us. All the people became sad because there was no more singing, there was no more dancing, there was no more storytelling and just being together as one people. The spirit saw that this was no good for the people. The spirit then entered some of the people and gave them the strength and the sight to see the energy circle. The fire is in the energy that burns inside each and every one of us. So when we come together in circles, magic happens. The people's good energy drove the bad spirits away. Tonight we see the rebirth of our energy circle. So everyone, who comes here tonight, you can take your own share of this energy and you can take it and share it with your friends, and your sons and your daughters. Let the energy circle enclose Kuranda mob.

Following this, an Aboriginal dance group performed and made fire on stage by rubbing two pieces of wood together in the traditional method.

These performances at the re-opening of the amphitheatre were an important public statement of the significance of the place for Djabugay people, delivered in the context of native title politics. Yet there was no attempt to exclude the wider non-Aboriginal community. Djabugay people also have an inclusive vision of community, one that encompasses the various waves of settlers that have made Kuranda their home, but particularly those who arrived as heirs of the counter-culture movement. To date, while there have been numerous social dramas among the settlers, to my knowledge no conflict has erupted between Aboriginal and non-Aboriginal people regarding the amphitheatre.

A Performance Reality

Social dramas or 'public episodes of tensional irruption' (Turner 1974: 33) *off* the stage, whether in connection with the amphitheatre stage or with other issues, tend to spotlight political and other ideological differences among the townspeople. Yet performances *on* the stage attempt to envelop or encompass such differences. Nevertheless, like performances on the stage, dramas off-stage are eventually temporarily resolved in the name of community. Both on and off the stage, performances are productive practices in which people become active participants in the making of their own social realities. The amphitheatre was born out of a particular social situation – one in which there was resistance to the power of state agencies, including the Shire Council – and to the new settlers, it represented what they thought of as their rejection of social constraints on individual freedom and expression. At the public level, the amphitheatre paralleled the new settlers' private creation of felicitous places through which they sought emplacement.

To be emplaced means to inhabit space in the fullest sense of the word, that is, with belonging. Bachelard (1969) illuminates this sense of inhabiting in his study of poetic 'images of intimacy'. The amphitheatre, or sound shell, presents just such an image. In the building of the sound shell, the settlers tried to locate themselves as inhabitants of Kuranda. This is indeed 'dwelling', in its Heideggerian sense. However, as I have shown, dwelling occurs not merely through the sensual nurturing of place. The essence of dwelling is in its practice, and thus dwelling involves the exercise of power. The amphitheatre situation demonstrates that dwelling is not simply a sheltering process, a 'curling up' in place, but that it expresses itself in social conflict.

For Kuranda people, the amphitheatre is more than a mere venue for the performing arts. It is itself a 'performance reality'. What makes it such is the focus it provides for performances through which people emplace themselves and in which they play out, test and contest the idea of community. Such performances include not only theatrical productions for the stage like *Babble on Babylon*, *Timewarp*, and *The Multicoloured Dreamboat*, but also the social dramas generated by the very processes of dwelling. While *on*-stage performances provide the experience of *communitas,* of a unity that encompasses difference, *off*-stage performances generate experiences of different ways of being that refuse to be so readily contained. Together, performances on and off stage in Kuranda allow people to attempt to resolve tensions between unity and diversity, between their experience of the universal as fellow human beings sharing a common place and their experience of the particular socio-political relations that confront them.

NOTES

1. Some sections of this chapter have been previously published in Henry (1998) and have been included courtesy of the editorial board of the *Australian Journal of Anthropology.*
2. Aboriginal people were first included in the Australian census in 1971 in conformity with the 1967 repeal of section 127 of the Constitution.
3. In 1971, the population of Kuranda was 345. By the census of 1976, however, the population had jumped to 481, an intercensal variation of 39.42 per cent. The rapid growth continued through the 1980s and is reflected in a population of 661 in 1981, an intercensal variation of 37.42 per cent. In comparison, the 1976–1981 intercensal variation for Mareeba urban area was only 9.23 per cent.
4. Ravenshoe is a small country town further west in the Mareeba Shire.
5. 'Murris' is a self-referential term used predominantly by Aboriginal people throughout large parts of Queensland and northern New South Wales. Non-Aboriginal people sometimes use it to claim familiarity with Aboriginal people.
6. Allotment 2, section 11 (R860) and portion 531 (R1467). The lease has since been extended.
7. Taussig (1993: 35) suggests that the womb can be seen as 'the mimetic organ par excellence, mysteriously underscoring in the submerged and constant body of the mother the dual meaning of reproduction as birthing and reproduction as replication'.
8. In 1984, when the electricity board threatened to cut down four advanced palms outside Frogs Restaurant in the main street of Kuranda, a band of eight women dug around the roots by hand and then arranged for a backhoe to move the trees so that they could replant them at the amphitheatre.
9. 'Noise pollution' generated by the amphitheatre is an ongoing issue of dispute in the town, as evidenced by numerous letters of complaint to the editor of the Kuranda paper and to the Mareeba Shire Council. This can be linked to broader town conflicts associated with the concepts of landscape, soundscape and environmental protection that I discuss in the next chapters.
10. See Kapferer (1986: 191), who states that in performance 'the Particular and the Universal are brought together and are transformed in the process. The particular is universalised beyond the existential immediacy of the individual's situation so that it is transcended, even while its groundedness and specificity

are maintained, to include others in what is essentially the same experiential situation. Concurrently, the Universal "is given a focus, an experiential content, in the immediacy of the individual's situation" (Natanson 1970: 126)'.

11. Such as the Kuranda Community Victorian & South Australian Bushfire Appeal on 27 February 1983 (with over A$8,678 raised), the 'North Queensland Bandaid for Africa' famine relief concert organised by members of the Ananda Marga sect, the 'Give Your Heart to Africa' appeal for African famine victims in 1986 and the Asian Tsunami victims in 2005, as well as innumerable fundraising events for local accident victims and for local community groups.

12. Such as Junction Theatre's 'Peter Pan' (21–22 December 1985), 'Sleeping Beauty' (13 December 1986), 'Alice in Wonderland' (11–13 December 1987) and 'Snow White and the Seven Dwarfs' (10 December 1988).

13. For example: Shed Theatre's 'Can't Pay? Won't Pay' by Dario Fo (1991), 'A Stretch of the Imagination' by Jack Hibberd (1991), 'Who?' by Jack Hibberd (1991), 'The Taming of the Shrew' by William Shakespeare (1992), 'The Glass Menagerie' by Tennessee Williams (1993) and 'The Proposal' by Anton Chekov (1993), as well as Junction Theatre's 'Weatherwise' by Noel Coward (1985), 'What If You Died Tomorrow' by David Williamson (1987) and 'The Three Marketeers' by Ric Ephraims (1992).

14. In 1996, the Spring Festival became an event organised and run by the Shire Council, with the Amphitheatre Society simply involved like any other volunteer community organisation.

15. See Judith Kapferer (1996) for an excellent description of this event, which she includes as a case study in her analysis of Australian cultural practice and the 'dream of community'.

16. 'Kuranda Reggae Festival', last accessed 26 January 2005, http//www.kurandar eggaefestival.com (site discontinued).

17. Such performers include Red Gum, the Bushwackers, Bullamakanka, Tansey's Fancy, Galapagos Duck, The Fureys, Slim Dusty, Charlie Pride, Kev Carmody (born in Kuranda), Lee Kernaghan, Eddie Quansah (leader of afro reggae group Osibisa), Goanna, Eurogliders, Midnight Oil, John Mayall, Eric Bogle, The Band, Kate Ceberano, The Black Sorrows, INXS, Jenny Morris, The Wailers, Paul Kelly, James Morrison, Hunters and Collectors, Tommy Emanuel, Joe Cocker, Margaret Urlich, George Thorogood, Tooth Faeries, UB40, Divinyls, Cruel Sea, Wendy Matthews and James Brown.

18. However, it should also be noted that the regional biennial Aboriginal dance festival at Laura has also been significant in this respect. Kuranda was first represented at this festival in 1986. Since then, a large group of dancers – who performed first as the 'Mona Mona Dancers' and later as 'Mayi Wunba' – has won numerous prizes at the festival.

19. This concept was introduced to Kuranda by Don Freeman and Judy Halperin. Don Freeman had trained in theatre in the USA and had founded a touring company there. He then collaborated with Judy Halperin to write, produce and direct plays, as well as head an experimental theatre project in India for four years, before coming to Kuranda and establishing the Tjapukai Dance Theatre.

20. Catherine Morris, Janice Starck, Rob Crapper, Carl Neil and Gawain Barker.
21. I have not been able to locate any records of attendance. A writer/performer in *Timewarp* estimates a total attendance at the three repeat performances of 'at least 1000'. These included 'just about everybody in Kuranda' as well as visitors from Cairns and as far afield as the Daintree. Because at least one third of the performers in *Timewarp* were Aboriginal, Aboriginal people were also well represented in the audience.
22. This is a reference to conflict associated with the Kuranda markets, which I discuss in the next chapter and which I have also analysed in Henry (1994).

Chapter 4

Commodifying Place

The Metamorphosis of the Markets

The marketplace and the main street are another two hot spots of social conflict in Kuranda. In this chapter, I trace the metamorphosis of what began as a periodic community market for locals into a permanent tourist attraction in the town. In the next chapter, I consider the social dramas associated with the transformation of the main street of the town in the face of the increasing impact of tourism during the 1980s and 1990s.

While the 1970s, settlers were sometimes credited with having fostered the creation of the tourist industry in Kuranda, it is important to note that the town has had a much longer history as a tourist destination. Of course it was not the shopping that brought tourists to Kuranda at the turn of the century, but rather the exotic natural beauty of the surrounding countryside, the mystery of the virgin rainforest, the drama of the Barron Falls in flood, and the rugged cliffs of the gorge. An early tourist brochure waxes lyrically:

> No township in the world has such splendour within its environs ... Come to Kuranda for a tonic, for a rest, to enjoy the best mountain air, the most golden sunshine, and the richest sight of tropical jungle in the Commonwealth (*The Glory of Kuranda* n.d.).

During the 1920s and 1930s, Kuranda was popular with honeymooners who would stay at one of the hotels and visit tourist attractions with romantic names like 'Fairyland Tea Gardens' or 'Paradise', which was originally called 'The Maze'. Both of these places were on the other side of the Barron River from Kuranda. Tourists would take boat rides there for morning and afternoon teas and join guided walks in the rainforest along carefully tended pathways that had been enhanced with strategically placed feature plants:

> Gold type or camera cannot convey or adequately express the beauty and wonders of "The Maze" – a jungle of exquisite tropical scrub, babbling

brooks and miniature waterfalls; wonderful ferns, palms and tree-ferns; beautiful orchids, aspleniums, elkhorns, staghorns, and other epiphatic growths – all glorious aids to the beauty and inviting coolness of the forest bowers (*"The Maze": Nature's Wonderland,* tourist brochure c. 1923).

Given its well-established identity as a tourist destination, it was perhaps inevitable that when the new settlers arrived in Kuranda during the 1970s, their practices of 'curling up', or burrowing into place, would eventually be affected by the economic forces already in operation. A case in point was the new settlers' practice of bartering and exchanging goods outside of the monetary economy through community markets.

From Community to Commodity

Between 1971 and 1978, a number of events, referred to as markets,[1] were held in different people's 'backyards'.[2] There was no particular designated marketplace. The markets were mainly based on a bartering system. One person would bake bread, another would provide organically grown fruit and vegetables, yet another handcrafted leather goods and so on. As one of the participants reminisced:

> They were markets where it was a bartering system. We used to go to these markets and we'd take what we had. It was an all day affair and everybody jumped into the river and threw their clothes off with gay abandon and smoked lots of dope. It was a very happy atmosphere; I mean, there wasn't the heavy drug scene. It was really just marijuana which was relatively harmless in a sort of way. And I think that's how the market thing started and went on for a couple of years (Joan Dods, pers. comm. 8 July 1994).

The hippie settlers introduced the markets in order to gain relative independence from shop-bought goods. During the mid-1970s, inspired by this backyard market phenomenon, John Bax decided to run a periodic market in the courtyard behind his shop. Bax owned a coffee shop called 'Mr Sunshine's' that was located in the Kuranda Honey House complex, which included a shop that sold honey to tourists and which was at that time located on the main highway at the entrance to the town. John advertised the market with a large banner that read 'Market here every Sunday'. This banner later assumed symbolic value in terms of the narrative history of the 'origin' of the market concept in Kuranda and in the debates about who should be given credit for the first market. When he sold the lease on his coffee shop, John sold this banner to the owners of the Honey House complex. The Honey House owners effectively treated the banner as a bill of sale for the market idea, and they used it on 6 August 1978 when they launched what is generally understood to be the first Kuranda tourist market. This particular Sunday market was held on the Honey House land and sponsored by the Kuranda Tourist Association, an unregistered association of local business people. It had about fifteen stalls and was so successful that those involved decided to run markets on a permanent basis in this location. The Kuranda Tourist Association continued to operate the markets for a number of years until community members, including the owner of the Honey House land, formed their own association. This association, the Kuranda Markets Association, operated the markets as a community venture until 1986, after which the Honey House owners assumed it as a private business.

The act of taking the markets, which had been separate individual events, and tying them to a particular place was the first step in the markets becoming a focus for social conflict in Kuranda. While they were unfixed in time and place, the markets were difficult to politicise. In becoming localised, however, they became subject to state apparatuses that began to reconstruct the marketplace as 'disciplinary space' (Foucault 1977). In other words, both stallholders and marketplace owners had to comply with the Mareeba Shire Council By-Laws and Regulations. Building standards were imposed on stall construction and the sale of food and beverages became subject to health regulations. The history of the development of the Kuranda markets provides a good case study of such transformative processes as Braudel (1986) has described in relation to village markets in medieval Europe, which were swallowed up by towns and forced to submit to the laws and controls of 'urban authorities'.

That the land was privately owned was also a significant factor in stallholders' experience of the marketplace as disciplinary space. As in the case of Rosebud Farm and other communal ventures in Kuranda, landownership provided the basis for social stratification, and by virtue of their land tenure, the marketplace owners were able to assume ownership of the markets as a private business. In the early stages of the Honey House markets, the owners provided the land to the Kuranda Tourist Association for free. Proceeds from the hire of stall space were used to employ management staff, to advertise the markets and to promote the town. Profits were donated to local charities and community organisations. The owners of the land at this stage did not see running the markets as a business venture in and of itself. The impetus for running the markets was the expected spin-off it might generate for the Honey House and other businesses. The business people of the town had begun to see the positive economic potential of the image that Kuranda had gained during the seventies as a haven for people they referred to as 'drug smoking hippies' and 'weirdos'. They had realised that this apparently negative image actually attracted many a spending visitor to the town.

The owners of the Honey House also saw the markets as a means of providing employment for 'the considerable number of unemployed people about the place, hippies and craft people' who had converged on the area. Of course, many of these people (potters, leatherworkers, glass blowers and artisans of all description as well as horticulturalists) did not think of themselves as unemployed. They saw themselves as living – if not always successfully – a subsistence lifestyle independent of state welfare and outside the definitional constraints that categorised people as either employed or unemployed. Nevertheless, few managed to maintain themselves completely independently of state welfare. Most people at one time or another had had to rely on some form of social security or, if they came from more privileged backgrounds, on trust funds or support from their families.

Market Traders

During the first few years of operation of the Honey House markets, traders (stallholders) were mainly residents of Kuranda and the surrounding district, and they stocked their stalls with their own locally made handicrafts and fresh produce. The stallholders from Kuranda were mainly 1970s settlers, but there were also members of old settler families who embraced the opportunity to sell their home grown produce and craftwork. A number of Aboriginal people ventured into business as market traders, but few were Kuranda locals. According to the original market owner-manager, Jim Mealing:

> I was always a bit disappointed in that. We had a long term Aboriginal family that ran a stall in there. But they were Aboriginals that came from Brewarrina in NSW up to Mareeba. They did a fantastic job. Dennis was there almost from the inception, but he's from Mareeba. We had a group that used to come in from Herberton and another Aboriginal lady who painted, who was married to an Australian or Englishman. She was from the Northern Territory; did magnificent dot painting. They were there for a long time, but then she became ill ... We've had Aboriginal groups come in on training programs and I always used to provide stalls and that for them. But they'd go through a training program and then it wouldn't continue. I couldn't understand why. They're always complaining there's no work for them. There's something there they could do, get in and make stuff. I actually created an Aboriginal products stall, but the people that

provided me with materials were from Mareeba and other places; none of the locals (Jim Mealing, pers. comm. 5 March 2005).

Nevertheless, I came across a market stall in 2005 that was, in fact, run by local Indigenous people. The salesman was from the Torres Strait, but he had grown up in Kuranda. He said that he was working the stall for his Aboriginal 'sisters', who had made the boomerangs and other objects on sale. The stall had not been operating for very long. More recently, a cooperative of Kuranda Aboriginal women have opened a shop (*Djurri Dadagal*) in the main street as an outlet for local Aboriginal handicrafts.

During the first few years, the markets were staged once a week on a Sunday. Local stallholders, who were mainly artists, craftspeople, small farmers and horticulturalists, had all week to produce their goods. However, the market proved to be so successful that by 1986 it had grown to approximately 150 stalls every Sunday and had begun to draw large numbers of both domestic and international tourists. Given this growth, the owner-managers of the market decided that the market should run on weekdays as well. As a result, local artisans and primary producers found it difficult both to produce their goods and to staff their stalls. Some began to employ salespeople to work their stalls, while others gave up the markets altogether and eventually established a cooperative arts outlet in the main street.

The popularity of the markets began to attract, as stallholders, regular traders from nearby Cairns, Mareeba and the Atherton tablelands, as well as itinerant traders from elsewhere in Australia and overseas during the tourist season. This change in the type of stallholder brought with it a change in the nature of the products sold. The markets were flooded with goods from Asia that itinerant traders, often English and American backpackers, bought cheaply for resale in Australia as a means of funding their travel.

Market Patrons

During the early years of operation, the markets mostly attracted a local clientele supplemented by a few domestic and international tourists. The marketplace was directly accessible from the highway at the entrance to the town, and there was ample parking for private cars. People came up the range from Cairns by private vehicle or by train, as the price of a ticket at the time was reasonably affordable. Today, however, the markets are perceived to be 'just for tourists'. A number of factors led to this change in market clientele. These include the dramatic rise in international tourism during the 1980s and the transport developments that led to spatial transformations that affected traffic flow in the town. The owner-manager of the Kuranda Markets analysed the situation thus:

> A few things affected the market. After the by-pass was built through Kuranda, Mareeba Shire re-planned the streets and car parking in Kuranda and a result of that was that most of the car parking around the Kuranda markets was wiped out. Once the car parking was wiped out, then we were almost completely relying on rail passengers. When Skyrail [the cable-car from Cairns] came on we were expecting things to escalate and things to get busier. Instead what happened was Queensland Rail really put a nail in the coffin. Prior to Skyrail operating Queensland Rail was running three trains on market days and charging eight dollars a fare from Cairns to Kuranda. When Skyrail commenced, Queensland Rail went into an agreement with Skyrail to even out the fares in the tourist areas so that Skyrail was charging approximately what it cost to go to Green Island and Queensland Rail upped their fares to comply with those two. We ended up with Queensland Rail charging twenty-eight dollars one way as against a previous eight dollars. The increase of fares virtually wiped out all of our Cairns customers, all the locals. Then we were reduced to where we had two trains running, with mainly international and interstate people coming, and Skyrail the same. From that time on our clientele just changed from locals to international people and that meant that an enormous number of the stallholders weren't viable. They just couldn't sell things [fresh produce] to people that were flying in and out of Cairns and travelling by bus or travelling by train. And from that point the markets started going downhill. That was the *main* reason and of course helping that then was the entrepreneurial migration into Kuranda of all the shopkeepers (Jim Mealing, pers. comm. 5 March 2005).

During its first decade, the marketplace was an important weekly gathering place for people who lived scattered around the Kuranda area. People treated the markets as a community meeting place and a place where they could socialise with other locals. One elderly woman, it is said, set up her stall every week for years with the same bottles of home-made jam, pickled chillies and chutneys. When people wanted to buy them, she would say they were sold because she wanted an excuse to come to the markets the next week. The markets were her social life, and she set up her stall each week just in order to be able to interact with everyone.

However, as a result of the influx of tourists, local residents increasingly started to avoid shopping at the markets, or else they would do a 'hit and run' and make sure they did their marketing before ten o'clock in the morning, when the first trainload of tourists arrived. Many of the stallholders I interviewed lamented the loss of community spirit:

> I don't know what will become of the markets. As a focal point for this community this one has probably ceased to have any particular impor- tance to the community, whereas it was a very important part of the com- munity. It was a meeting place. I mean, I saw a lady just now walk through who I hadn't seen for six months, but in the old days I would have seen her once a week here. You know, it was a *genuine* place where people would come as a social thing (Ron Edwards, 9 January 1994).

The Kuranda marketplace was central to the development of a sense of collective identity among the new waves of townspeople from the 1970s onwards. Yet it also was – and still is – the social space where locals most immediately confront global economic forces. As such, it has been the site of a number of social dramas through which townspeople attempt to situ- ate themselves locally in relation to one another yet at the same time to respond to the wider social and economic networks that they feel to be beyond their control. I focus below on two of these dramas, which Kuranda people call 'the Market War' and the 'War Memorial War'.[3] I leave discus- sion of a third drama connected with the markets, which I dub the 'Main Street War', for the next chapter.

The Market War

What Kuranda people call the 'Market War' occurred over a period of about eighteen months during 1986–87. The story I recount here was pieced to- gether from interviews with traders, marketplace owners, managers and others involved in the war, as well as from newspaper reports, minutes of trader's meetings, and the minutes of meetings of the Mareeba Shire Council.

By 1986, the Kuranda markets were thriving. Space was at a premium and there was great competition for stalls. In June of that year, in the middle of the tourist season, the Kuranda Markets Association told the traders that they were to be issued with occupancy agreements. The agreements would require them to pay a premium of A\$1,500 in order to secure the right to operate their stalls for a five-year term. This was in addition to their normal rental per market day, which at that time was seven Australian dollars. The proposal caused a huge outcry among traders and a meeting was quickly called. About 120 traders attended the meeting and unanimously rejected the proposal, which 'a gentleman from Perth' was said to have suggested to the owner-manager of the markets. This 'gentleman from Perth' became the focus of much resentment among the 1970s settlers, as he represented the outsider business entrepreneurs that had begun to threaten their way of life. Ironically, people who themselves had 'invaded' Kuranda during the 1970s and 1980s in search of an alternative lifestyle now confronted a new wave of settlers attracted by the economic potential of the tourist industry. In the marketplace, tensions took the form of a competitive price war among T-shirt sellers. Traders who had been in Kuranda since the 1970s push and who specialised in hand-painted and screen-printed T-shirts were resentful that market management was allowing the newcomers to sell cheap mass produced T-shirts. The owner-managers' proposal to introduce a lease agreement at a time when tensions were already running high due to the T-shirt price war led to a dramatic escalation of the conflict among traders, as well as between traders and management.

The introduction of the lease agreement was linked to changes in ownership of the Honey House that signalled the final stages of the metamorphosis of the markets from a series of events orchestrated by the community into a single privately owned profit-making business venture. This transformation was completed through the sale of the Honey House and market place. The owners of the Honey House sold their business, as well as the associated land on which the markets were held, and then formed a new company in order to buy the markets back. The repurchase took place in July 1986, whereupon the owners began to operate the markets as a private business. However, since the owners had also been the key members of the Kuranda Markets Association (KMA), the changed status of the markets was not as obvious as it might have been if new personalities had been involved. Many Kuranda people at the time had no idea that the markets had become a private venture rather than a community controlled affair.

The intense negative reaction of the traders to the A$1,500 lease agreement led to its being abandoned almost immediately, but this was not the end of the matter. The traders formed another association known as the Kuranda Rainforest Stallholders Association (KRSA). The constitution of the KRSA lists as one of its objectives 'to be non-profit making; non-political; non-sectarian and non-racial', and not only traders from among the 1970s alternative lifestyle settlers in Kuranda, but also small business entrepreneurs from the region and itinerant stallholders from elsewhere could be found under its umbrella. In general terms, most of the stallholders could be thought of as 'seekers of alternatives' in their self-conscious rejection of formal sector work and in their search for economic alternatives. Working in the markets was particularly attractive because it offered an autonomy of action that formal sector work did not provide.

In its formative days, the Kuranda Rainforest Stallholders Association mainly investigated legal issues on behalf of the stallholders. One of the association's very significant findings was that a part of the land on which the markets were held was not actually Honey House land, but rather an adjoining closed road reserve named 'Booroo Street' on the original town plan. The Kuranda Markets Association (KMA) had leased the area in question from the Queensland Lands Department.[4] It was discovered that under the original permit, the KMA had no legal right to collect money, allocate stalls, or remove stallholders from Booroo Street. Therefore, members of the KRSA who already had stalls on Booroo Street – as well as others who subsequently moved into that section of the market – refused to pay for their stalls. The KRSA then applied to the Lands Department for the permit to occupy the road reserve, arguing that it was a more representative body of the markets as a whole.

Booroo Street had been gazetted as a public road with the official birth of the town on 23 October 1888. Although planned and mapped, the street had never actually been constructed, and became a 'lived place' only a hundred years later when it became a place of resistance for market traders. The resistance represented by the occupation of Booroo Street was not merely a case of stallholders united against the market management. The traders were themselves split into two camps: those who supported the owner-managers (KMA) and those who supported the KRSA. Booroo Street became KRSA territory, separated from the rest of the marketplace by a barbed wire fence that was erected, according to KRSA members, by the KMA. Rumour and gossip spread like wildfire. Stallholders on the KRSA side assumed that many of those on the KMA side were there because of blackmail and fear that they would be 'dobbed in' to the Taxation Department for avoiding taxes on their market earnings or to the Commonwealth Employment Service for claiming unemployment benefits to which they were not entitled. The following extracts from my interviews with stallholders in both camps indicate the extent to which the conflict escalated:

> And we had situations where, because these people were told if they didn't pay they'd be kicked out, there were actual fistfights in there between different people. This is in the middle of the damn market, with people going past. One gentleman started bringing a shotgun with him in his car, because he felt so threatened, and there were people bringing steel pipes and all sorts of things along. There was all this kind of authoritarianism, you know; this fascism was around. And there were people who were actually being forced into making commitments, on very little information, about where their allegiances lay (Stallholder 1, 4 January 1994).

Oh they used to put barbed wire up in the market, Sunday morning early before the stallholders came. When the stallholders came they couldn't get in (Stallholder 2, 19 January 1994).

At one stage they tried everything they could to stop me going in there and to stop other people going in [to Booroo Street]. They'd actually come down during the night with a big ditch digger and dug this big trench about three foot deep and two foot wide right across the front so we couldn't drive in there. Someone went home and got a spade, so we started filling this ditch in and the policeman was there trying to stop us. It was really heavy, people punching us and carrying on and everything. We managed to fill it in a little bit and then someone in a four wheel drive started to drive over the ditch and one of these guys stood in front of his car and wouldn't move and almost got run over (Stallholder 3, 18 January 1994).

The KRSA members were determined to find a site for their own markets. While waiting on a decision from the Lands Department about the use of Booroo Street, they submitted several proposals to the Mareeba Shire Council for alternative sites. However, the owner of the Honey House Markets was also a Shire Councillor, so they did not have much confidence in this approach. One night, members of both factions drove to Mareeba for the Shire Council Meeting:

It was a real cauldron. When we drove back we actually feared for our lives on the road, because we came out of that meeting and [the KRSA] mob hadn't done terribly well and we represented, we were not part of [the KRSA] mob. We were still trying to keep the middle ground so therefore we were [on the owner's] side and as we came out of that meeting there was incredible abuse hurled at us and I was fearful. I thought, 'Where's our car? How do we get to the highway?' and all this sort of stuff, because there had been talk of guns, you know at that stage (Stallholder 1, 4 January 1994).

A trader from the KRSA faction admitted that he had filled the back of his four-wheel drive with sticks and iron bars in case there was a fight after the meeting. He added, 'I used to go out at night, guerrilla war, and all that sort of thing. I put on wigs and all sorts of things'.

Eventually it became untenable for the traders to remain on Booroo Street. One of the proposals that the KRSA put to the Council was that an area of land across the road should be rezoned as another marketplace. (At the time, there was a settler museum called the 'Heritage Homestead' on the proposed area of land.) The proposal was eventually approved and the KRSA stallholders moved from Booroo Street. They installed the required drainage, paved the pathways and built new stalls (Figure 4.1). Neverthe-

Figure 4.1. Market Stall, Kuranda, 1997.
Photographer: Rosita Henry.

less, conflict between the two factions continued. One Sunday, stallholders arrived to find that someone had slashed the canvas roofs of their new
stalls.

On the median strip between the two marketplaces, someone erected
a confusing sign with arrows pointing in opposite directions. Above the
entrance to the Honey House marketplace, a huge banner read 'Original
Kuranda Markets', the emphasis on 'original': a reminder to locals of the
Market War and the continuing contestation of place. This banner was later
replaced by a fixed sign with the words 'Original Kuranda Markets Here'!

Transcendence of Market Limits

When walking through the main street of Kuranda as a tourist, it is difficult to know where the marketplaces start and end. In spite of all the signs
– or perhaps because of the signs – Kuranda itself has become one large
marketplace, as far as tourists are concerned. Retail shops along the main
street have doors that open in such a way as to give the shops the appearance of market stalls, and many of the new shops built in the last few years
have been deliberately designed to evoke market stalls. (A significant dif-

ference, however, is that shopkeepers are locked into tenancy agreements with prohibitive rents when compared with a daily market stall fee.) Thus the market – a periodic event identified with and belonging to the community – was transformed into two privately owned businesses. Although the stallholders in the Market War of 1986–1987 won the battle against the lease agreements, it could be argued that they did not win the war. As one of the stallholders commented, despairingly, 'I had sort of a freedom kick; I thought we could do things right in Kuranda, but now it's all too late. Kuranda is gone, finished; Kuranda has lost. It's no freedom; you can't ever win against the baddies on top'.

The Heritage Markets have been bought and sold as a business venture several times, and Jim Mealing, the owner of the Honey House Markets, put the market itself 'on the market' after building an adjoining complex of permanent market stalls for which it was necessary to enter into tenancy agreements. The new owner has upgraded and renovated the market place and constructed new stalls for lease (see Figure 4.2). Numerous signs at the entrance celebrate its identity as the 'Original Kuranda Markets' (see Figure 4.3). In the thirty-three years it has been running, the market has apparently accrued heritage value, and tourists are encouraged to read about the history of the markets on an information board placed at the entrance.

Figure 4.2. Market Stall, Kuranda, 2011.
Photographer: Rosita Henry.

Figure 4.3. Market Signs, Original Kuranda Markets, 2011.
Photographer: Rosita Henry.

State Elections and Local Politics

The timing of the state government elections further complicated the market situation. The National Party, with Joe Bjelke Petersen as premier, was still in power in 1986, but the owner of the 'Original Kuranda Markets' was standing for election to state parliament as the Labor Party representative. The two factions in the Market War thus eventually became divided along party lines: stallholders who supported the owner in the Market War were thought to be strong Labour Party supporters, and the other faction, members of the KRSA, became associated with the National Party. These factional alignments had more to do with parochial strategies of power than with support of party policies or identification with an overarching political ideology. As a KRSA stallholder admitted:

> I joined the National Party because of the Markets. I went to [the National Party Representative] and said, 'Look what these people are doing to us'. He said, 'Oh yeah, you are a bunch of commos. You all belong to the Labor party. We can't help you'. I said, 'I'm not. I belong to your party'. And next minute he came and said, 'Look, we'll make you a member of the National Party and we'll do things for you'. Then things went ahead and we got that

second market. Things really went ahead (KRSA stallholder, pers. comm. 19 January 1994).

The Market War was referred to in State Parliament (10 September 1986) by a National Party member, Mr Menzel. Under the protection of parliamentary privilege, the member was free to malign the character of the Honey House owner. A KRSA stallholder read his speech after it was published in Hansard, photocopied it and pinned it up on the notice board outside the post office in Kuranda every day during the election period, replacing it each morning because by nightfall someone had removed it.

The dramatisation of state politics in the Kuranda marketplace demonstrates the way in which local places and local identities are made in articulation with wider, cross-cutting economic and political forces. The Market War must not be interpreted as merely a local expression of party politics generated from outside; rather, the state elections were harnessed to existing factional interests in the Market War. National and state politics are themselves local phenomena. They are a means of expressing and polarising locally significant issues and parochial identities. In other words, global forces are always articulated and experienced in local situations.

Kuranda people call the market conflict a 'war', and indeed many recognisable symbols of war were present: barbed wire, trenches, guns and other hand weapons. The question is how to understand and interpret this war. It could perhaps be interpreted as Geertz (1973) did the Balinese cockfight: that is, as an enacted 'text' of the social order, the sort of analysis Gell (1982) undertook in his paper 'The Market Wheel: Symbolic Aspects of an Indian Tribal Market'. However, I prefer to interpret the Kuranda market conflict as a social drama in which, through particular spatial practices, people sought to secure the dominance of their own constructs of community by attempting to 'arrest the flow of differences' (Laclau and Mouffe 1985: 112).

The traders culturally constructed their explanation of the Market War in terms of economic or material factors. For example, it was argued that because the market had grown so much, stall space had become a premium and 'a supply and demand situation' developed where the shortage forced prices to 'go through the roof' (Eve Stafford, pers. comm. 4 January 1994). It was also argued that the marketplace was extremely run down. All the paths were dirt (mud during the wet season), stalls were roughly constructed, and there were poor toilet facilities. In general, the traders felt that the owner-managers should be putting some of the fees they charged for stall space into upgrading the marketplace.

Yet such explanations of the conflict do not account for the intensity of the dispute or the interest that the wider Kuranda population took in it. The

Market War was not confined to those people who were actually involved in the business of the market as traders and owners. It attracted the participation of a keen audience of local residents. In order to understand how the market became a hot spot of conflict, one needs to consider the nature of the relationship between people and place: how people constitute themselves in the making of place by articulating the contradictions between identity and difference, between community and commodity.

The Market War was fostered by the metamorphosis of the markets into a private business and the tension between the concepts of community and commodity that this metamorphosis generated. The Kuranda people resisted those who would commodify their place for sale to tourists. The market tenancy agreement symbolised the invasion of 'big business' into Kuranda and a consequent loss of the locals' power to maintain the identity of Kuranda as their home place. This tourism-generated commodification of place is keenly felt by many Kuranda residents.

The Three Marketeers: A Performance of Place

The significance of the Market War to the wider Kuranda community was given expression in a theatre production staged in the Kuranda Amphitheatre by local amateur theatre group Junction Theatre. The play, called *The Three Marketeers,* was written by Ric Ephraims, a Kuranda resident. The play presents Kuranda as being at risk of contamination by economic greed infiltrating from outside the community. Outside business people corrupt local business entrepreneurs, who are then tempted to sell out their fellow Kurandans. In the play, the owner of the marketplace is represented as taking over the markets. In the first scene, he announces:

> There's those three silly guys running that juice stall. Take a look at them, long hair, way out clothes, bare feet ... and that music they play. They're freaks, I tell you freaks. They don't fit in with the way I want things to be. ... I will monopolise these markets – *the big takeover* – first this puntsy little scene ... next, this puntsy little town...

The market owner captures Goldie, the hippy heroine, and holds her for ransom by threatening to push her off a bungee jump located in the marketplace. (The play thus comments on the absurdity of the bungee jump that for some years provided tourists with the 'unique opportunity' of bungee jumping from a crane into an artificial rock pool in the centre of the Heritage marketplace.)

The stallholders, or marketeers, rescue Goldie after a sword fight on a cable car (a reference to the then yet to be constructed Kuranda Skyrail, which I discuss in Chapter 7) and win the battle for the markets. The marketplace owner sees the error of his ways and is 'born again'. The play ends, however, with two new characters arriving on the scene, in business suits and ties, discussing their 'big plans' for the markets.

The theatrical production provides a comedic commentary on the social drama of the Market War. It is a performative means of providing an insider situational analysis, one that does not just allow people to reflect on their own social situation, but that is itself a generative practice by which people make place. Like the Kuranda amphitheatre performances I discussed in the last chapter, *The Three Marketeers* explores the relationship between community and commodity and expresses resistance to a situation that renders the emplacement of the 1970s settlers uneasy. Although the Market War was a particular social drama that occurred over a period of eighteen months in 1986–1987, the markets continued to provide a focus for contested identity in Kuranda. This is evidenced by the eruption in 1993 of conflict over the relocation of the Returned Serviceman's League (RSL) War Memorial.

The War Memorial War

In January 1993, the Kuranda sub-branch of the RSL was given Council permission to erect their proposed new war memorial 'opposite the Honey House shops'. To the RSL, this meant directly in front of the entrance to the Heritage Markets. A relatively unobtrusive rock with a plaque attached was placed at the site. However, the grander RSL plan was to eventually relocate the honour boards that were located at the railway station to the new memorial site. This would involve constructing a substantial concrete block wall that would partially block the entrance to the Heritage Markets from view. The proposal led to protracted and bitter conflict among some Kuranda residents.

The dispute was seen by many to be an extension of the Market War, as the president of the RSL was also the owner of the Original Kuranda Markets. Whether it was truly an extension of the original conflict or not, some people interpreted the plan to erect the memorial directly in front of the Heritage Markets as a deliberate move by the owner of the Original Kuranda Markets to obstruct entry. In addition, it was suggested that the honour boards would cause embarrassment to the owner of the Heritage Markets (particularly given the Japanese and German tourists visiting the markets who would be unavoidably confronted with the cenotaph). The owner of the Heritage Markets and other residents of Kuranda also objected to the location of the cenotaph on the grounds that it would be 'sacrilegious' to site it in front of the markets. After letters of complaint from the owner of the Heritage Markets and others, the Mareeba Shire Council resolved to advise the Kuranda RSL that the memorial had to be relocated to a nearby park. The concrete block wall, however, had already been constructed around the memorial, and the rock could not be moved without damaging the wall. The conflict eventually made front page news in the *Cairns Post*, which reported:

> Factions warring over placement of the memorial verbally agreed to a truce to end the bitter debate which began 18 months ago when Kuranda RSL branch sought Mareeba Shire Council approval for a site. Since then there have been accusations of commercial blackmail, secret deals, vandalism and misrepresentation of RSL members, culminating in a dawn 'raid' by some RSL members yesterday to move the 9 tonne memorial back to their preferred site. It was the third time in less than a week that the memorial had been moved (*Cairns Post*, 10 November 1993).

It is clear that the cenotaph issue was seen by many Kuranda residents as being part of the continuing conflict between the two marketplace owners as businessmen. They interpreted it as a matter of one businessman trying to put a spoke in another's economic wheel. This interpretation not only reflects the dominance that is culturally granted to economic factors, but also the determining effect that is attributed to individual personalities. Yet I suggest that there was more at stake than the economic interests of the market owners. The RSL War memorial is a powerful symbol of Australian identity and occupies a central place in most Australian towns. For the RSL to put it in front of a marketplace frequented by foreign tourists is telling indeed. The dispute over the location of the cenotaph is, I suggest, essentially an example of spatial practice marking the right to define Kuranda as more than just a tourist town, but as a place with a local population who identify as Australians. That is, the cenotaph asserted Kuranda's identity as an Australian place, albeit one that was regularly invaded by international tourists. Placing the cenotaph at the entrance to the markets was a strong statement of Kuranda's Australian identity; so also, however, was the claim by residents – including dissenting members of the RSL – that it was sacrilegious to locate it in front of the marketplace, as was their demand that it be moved. Because the marketplace is seen as the community's contact with the outside and thus represents its borderland or frontier, it provides a fertile arena for social conflict that generates identity in and of place.

The Kuranda Market War was not simply a contest between traders and market owners. The Market War stirred the imaginings of the wider population of Kuranda, and the market became a focus for disputes about representations of Kuranda. It became a site of contest between people whose imagined home place was the small village – where they could stage their own events that remained relatively free of influence from national and trans-national economic and political forces – and people who could not imagine any place except in terms of such market forces and demands. Many of the people that settled in Kuranda during the seventies and eighties saw Kuranda as a place of escape from the outside world, a haven in the rainforest. They wanted freedom from what they considered to be oppressive legal and political constraints imposed by the State, and they wanted the relative autonomy to grow their own food, to express their creativity and to savour the products of their own labour. The Kuranda markets enabled them to participate in the economy relatively free from constraint. They did not have to sign leases or contracts. They could spend their days working at home and sell their products from market stalls once a week without having to pay any overhead. The introduction of tenancy agreements and of government by-laws posed a threat to these ideals.

While they draw on communitarian ideologies, these counter-culture values are not incompatible with liberal individualist ideology and the concept of a free market economy. This is why the speed at which the markets transformed from hippie bartering to a system based on capitalist commerce is not so remarkable, and this is why it is not incongruous that by the 1990s, a number of the original hippie settlers were upstanding members of the Kuranda Chamber of Commerce.

Thus in introducing the market concept to Kuranda, the hippies also inadvertently planted the seeds of dissolution of their 'imagined community'. The markets increased in number and overflowed into the townscape. They drew the global economic forces of circulation, production and consumption that many of the 1970s settlers had sought to escape into the very heart of the town. They brought Kuranda to the attention of capital, speculators and developers who colonised the main street with the shops that have begun to 'conquer and devour' not only the markets but the very town itself (Braudel 1986: 68).

Many of the social dramas that break out with regularity among local residents are expressions of the residents' attempts to harness these global market forces and to define a sense of local community in the face of them. Digging trenches, defining boundaries with barbed wire, breaking out of the disciplinary space of the marketplace by erecting stalls outside its boundaries, marching in protest in the main street, creating their own 'spatial trajectories' (de Certeau 1984: 115), erecting, damaging or removing signs, writing letters to the editor, graffiti, gossip, narratives and staged performances: these are all examples of the spatial tactics through which people attempt to construct and transform place – contesting the identity of places by displacing others and emplacing themselves – in a continuing struggle to acquire the power to define and control their own lifeworlds.

NOTES

1. Plattner (1989: 171) defines the term market to mean 'the social institution of exchanges where prices or exchange equivalencies exist', and the term 'market-place' to refer to the localisation of the market 'in a customary time and place'. In Kuranda, people use the word 'market' to refer to a specific community event, rather than to the market as a social institution, and they tend to use the plural 'markets' to mean more than one event, as well as more than one marketplace.
2. The word 'backyard' as used in Australia generally evokes the expanse of lawn behind a house situated on what used to be the standard rectangular suburban block (a quarter of an acre). In Kuranda, however, the new settlers, particularly those on tenancies-in-common, spurned this type of backyard and avoided definite fenced boundaries. Houses were hidden away in little pockets surrounded by encroaching forested areas. The idea was to clear as little growth from the land as possible.
3. Portions of this chapter have also been published in Henry (1994) and are reproduced courtesy of the *Australian Journal of Anthropology*.
4. Under Permit to Occupy No. 3533.

Chapter 5

Planning Place

Main Street Blues

You can't any longer call it a village in the rainforest. It's just a load of shops in the rainforest.

—1970s settler

The Kuranda markets were a key force in building the reputation of the town as a tourist destination. They served as a good training ground for a number of the shopkeepers in the main street today who originally began as stallholders in the marketplace. The markets provided the impetus for some of the 1970s settlers to establish businesses that catered for the tourists, and a new wave of settlers inundated the town during the 1980s and 1990s in the wake of the burgeoning tourist industry. At the same time, concern grew among Kuranda people about their apparent powerlessness in the face of development in the town and the resulting dramatic changes to both its natural environment and built fabric. Building construction in the town led to regular disputes about town planning and in particular about developments that affected traffic flow through the main street to the markets. The concept of strategic planning, which had developed within corporations and state bureaucratic agencies as a management tool, began to infiltrate the daily lives of Kuranda residents. Planning is generally accepted as a joint problem-solving project between government and the public, a 'rational, professional activity, aimed at producing a "public good" of one kind or another' (Yiftachel 1995: 216). There is little recognition that planning is also a project of creating dominant realities that operate to block out other realities (Lefebvre 2009). As Greed (1994: 53) comments, 'plans are useful tools in the process of legitimating one's world view'.

Planning Disputes

In 1992, the Shire Council and the Queensland government agreed to raise additional funds through a transport levy to deal with problems of 'wear and tear and overloading of infrastructure caused by visitors to Kuranda' (Mareeba Shire Council, 1995: 1). However, the council continued to be seen as 'the enemy' by many local residents:

> The community was unified within itself against the enemy, the council; because they were sort of the ruling body but they live in Mareeba and Mareeba's whole *modus operandi,* whole style, is different to the Kuranda style. Just what should have been happening in this different environment wasn't being addressed from that different environment in Mareeba. They were talking about development, just encouraging as intense development as they could (Kuranda resident, pers. comm. 9 November 1995).

As explained in Chapters 3 and 4, an entrenched distrust of the Shire Council had already taken deep root among Kuranda locals. According to one of the 1970s settlers:

> You had people like developers, land speculators, real estate agents [on the Shire Council] and if you look around you will find that quite a lot of very good land historically was bought up by councillors, because they knew what was going on. So there was all that kind of stuff going on but it was also that Mareeba was so different to Kuranda. That was the cringe factor, you know. Like, Mareeba was the bad taste capital of North Queensland, and everything that they did just looked awful, and of course there was the whole thing with, you know, the hippies. It was just that ideologically the two communities were just *so* different (1970s settler, pers. comm. 7 January 1997).

In response to this situation, a residents and ratepayers organisation, the Kuranda Consultative Committee – later renamed Association for Regional Kuranda, or ARK[1] – applied for and secured a grant from the Commonwealth Office of Local Government to carry out a 'visioning exercise'. The idea was to agree upon an identity for Kuranda that would guide all future development projects. Because of its grant success, ARK was able to negotiate co-funding from the Shire Council to employ a planning consultant to carry out a full study and develop a strategic management plan for the town.[2] Kuranda people saw community involvement in planning as a way of challenging the power of the Mareeba Shire Council, which they saw as supporting the interests of private land developers and tourist operators against the interests of the townspeople. A town plan, as a tool of state control and government regulation, might enable them to hold local government agents accountable and provide a means to rein in corporate and state interests.

Two 'vision workshops' were held during 1993 in order to gauge the main concerns of Kuranda people – or, in planning parlance, 'the major local stakeholders'[3] – about the town and their vision for its future. The first workshop was held at the local primary school and was attended by approximately 139 residents, including only two Aboriginal people. At the end of the day, eighty-six of these residents had committed to joining eight different 'working groups'[4] to help the consultants develop the strategic plan. This is a relatively high level of public commitment, given the population of the town. The second workshop was held specifically to cater for Aboriginal people. It was assumed that Aboriginal people had been too 'shy' to come to first workshop, as they felt overwhelmed by the non-Aboriginal participants. The second workshop was held at Ngoonbi Farm, owned by the Ngoonbi Aboriginal Corporation, because the organisers thought that Aboriginal people would feel more 'comfortable' in their 'own place'. Seventy-two people attended the meeting. Whatever their particular reason for not attending the first workshop, it must be noted that Aboriginal people are rarely to be found at any general community meetings for a number of reasons. Firstly, they are already overwhelmed by the requirement to attend meetings of the various Aboriginal corporations. Secondly, some feel that even if they do attend general community meetings, their voices are rarely heard and what they say has little effect.

The 'Kuranda Strategic Management Plan' study took seven months to complete and won an award for excellence in 1994 from the Queensland 1994 Royal Australian Institute of Planners. Its broad aim was to 'provide an integrated strategy for the development and management of Kuranda' (Mareeba Shire Council 1995: 2). Part of the planning consultant's brief was to prepare and document the principles upon which a new statutory development control plan (DCP) would be based.[5] The resulting Development Control Plan 2 – Kuranda Village was adopted by Council on 15 April 1997. The principal aim of the DCP was 'to manage the use and development of land within and adjacent to Village of Kuranda, such that its character and function as a Village in the Rainforest is preserved and enhanced' (Mareeba Shire Council 1995b: 5).[6] In the vision workshops, both Aboriginal and non-Aboriginal participants had emphasised the identity of Kuranda as a 'Village in the Rainforest'.

Planning continued in Kuranda under the auspices of the Kuranda Village Promotion Program sponsored by the State Department of Tourism, Small Business & Industry through its Queensland Main Street Program.[7] A community 'future vision' workshop was held under this program, and new committees and working groups were formed that specifically focused on Coondoo Street, the main street of Kuranda. Because of the many disputes that had arisen in relation to tourist development proposals, some Kuranda business people and other residents decided that a united approach to tourism policy was needed. Therefore, the Kuranda Village Promotions Program advertised for a consultant to formulate a plan to promote tourism.[8] In the resulting plan, Kuranda is treated as a product for tourists and its identity as a home place is muted. In fact, no distinction is made between product and place. Kuranda is represented as a product that must be 're-made' and 'made real' for marketing purposes. Kuranda is construed by the consultants as lacking authenticity, and therefore, for the purposes of marketing, Kuranda people are urged to strive to present the town to the outside world as an authentically *lived* place, not just a tourist product. Much of the tension and dispute over planning and development in Kuranda arises out of this contradiction between the idea of Kuranda as a home place and the notion of the town as a product for tourists. Some residents wrestle with the contradiction, while others line up determinedly on one side or the other.

Traffic Flow

During the 1980s, the shops along the main street of the town began to compete with the markets for the tourist dollar. This competition led to disputes among the townspeople that were framed in terms of a discourse about the planning and management of traffic flow within the town. The minutes of the meetings of the Kuranda Chamber of Commerce[9] reveal that the issue of traffic management dominated debate in Kuranda with regard to town planning throughout the 1980s and 1990s.[10]

The Kuranda Strategic Management Plan included the formulation of a Transport Management Plan to deal with the issue of bus circulation in the village.[11] The plan that was eventually adopted took a staged approach that limited the access of buses to the main street and provided a parking facility for them outside the village centre. This plan, which was based on the idea of enhancing Kuranda's village atmosphere by pedestrianising its main street, led to intense conflict both among villagers and between villagers and representatives of the transport industry. A number of people feared that their businesses would suffer if buses were prohibited from driving up and down the main street. In particular, those business people located at the top end of the town felt that the tourists arriving by train and cable car (Skyrail) at the bottom end of town would require bus transport to the top end where their businesses are located. The following extract from a letter to the editor of the *Cairns Post* expresses some of the terms of the dispute:

> I am amazed at the damaging misinformation being circulated by business operators and bus companies. The supposed steep hill from the sta-

tion precinct is in fact a moderate incline taking you past the interesting Bottom Pub with views of the Barron River, then along a lush and well treed walkway with a sighting of the quaint old wooden lock-up, and immediate arrival at the first of the Kuranda shops, with seats and refreshments. This is a leisurely four-minute stroll. Here is another fact – people in buses do not spend money, people walking do. One of the aims of the strategic management plan is to improve walking access, and shade and seat the visitors. We already have an unusually compact village with the majority of attractions no further than a 10 minute walk in any direction … I wonder how many of the pro-bus business operators will spend their next holidays in a noxious, fume-laden, bus-choked village similar to the one they would continue to foist on us – yes Kuranda (*Cairns Post* 20 June 1996: 20).

People with businesses located at the top end of the town wanted the traffic plan changed so as to allow for some bus movement directly from the railway and Skyrail stations to the top end. One of their concerns was that if people walked from the stations, they would spend all their money at the bottom end of town before they even reached the top end. Business people thus became polarised: top-enders, including the market owners, against the bottom-enders, shopkeepers and others in the main street:

When we started off [the market] we only had about twelve businesses [in the main street]. Suddenly we got an increase of people coming in building shops. We've got over 200 businesses in the main street, which is between the rail terminal and the markets. So we were just not getting anybody at the markets, and of course the war continued and all these shopkeepers saw all these people coming up the main street and they started telling people, well that's the markets. The main street's the markets. We retaliated by creating a courtesy bus service. That helped us out then. Both the Kuranda markets and the Heritage markets plus all the shops in that area all got together and created the courtesy bus service. Now that put new life into our end and helped build it up. Now the final nail in the coffin: these shopkeepers coming into the main street have been opposing the bus service and everything like that (Jim Mealing, pers. comm. 5 March 2005).

On the Buses

While some Kuranda residents would have preferred that tourists stay away altogether, others were ambivalent about the issue because they depended on the industry for their livelihood. They wanted to be able to cater for the tourists while maintaining the integrity of the village as their home place. Their vision of a village in the rainforest entailed a commitment to protect that rainforest environment. The concern over the negative impact of tourism, therefore, came to be centred not on the tourists themselves as visitors but on the environmental impact of the large buses or coaches that had in increasing numbers been bringing those visitors to the town (Figure 5.1). Members of the transport industry in general – and particularly the bus operators – were seen to be the villains. The bus issue became a focus for conflicts that flared among various interest groups within the town, sparked by the fact that in order to keep their buses cool, the drivers would keep their motors running while they were waiting for their passengers. In a letter to the *Cairns Post*, F. Taylor wrote:

> I'm 'outing' a bus for flouting the law, and I have witnesses. The full-sized bus arrived outside Kuranda Markets at 11:25 am on 11–7–96, disgorging its cargo of Japanese tourists. Leaving the engine running, the bus driver struck up a conversation with another eating an ice cream further along the pavement. It is illegal to keep the motor going while the driver is not in attendance. Copious diesel fumes pumped out for the next half-hour over

Figure 5.1. Tourist Buses, Kuranda, 1995.
Photographer: Rosita Henry.

hundreds of tourists walking in both directions. Apart from the noise, we were gasping for clean air and feeling sick to the stomach 50m away (*Cairns Post* 22 July 1996: 9).

Gonzo, one of the 1970s settlers and a creative jeweller who operated a small business in town, told me that if I interviewed everybody in Kuranda and recorded them, I would 'record for two, three days as people told you stories, where they pulled the keys out of the bus ignition or where they were insulted by a driver; *wars* were going on' (Gonzo, pers. comm. 17 February 1997; original emphasis). Gonzo was involved in several incidents in which he personally took direct action against the bus situation. The detail and narrative style of his accounts reflect the fact that he was called upon to represent himself in Court as a result of his actions:

So I'm walking down the street one day and there's this bus running out in front of the markets and as I walked up I saw the motor running, the driver sitting in the vehicle in the air conditioning reading his newspaper and having a cup of tea. So I knocked on the door. He opened the door and I asked if he would turn the motor off. And he refused and told me to fuck off and, you know. So then I walked away, and went up to the Post Office. Did what I had to do. I came back, it was like twenty minutes later, and he's *still* there; his motor's *still* running and he's *still* reading the paper. And I went, 'Well fuck this', you know, and I knocked on the door and said, '*Would you turn this damn thing off! You've been twenty minutes here. What, to cool your butt? You've got another hour and a half before these people are going to be back*'! You know. Anyway he just shut the door in my face. So I walked back up to town, where I got myself a good marker pen with a real thick nib, and I walked back again and on the back of the bus I wrote, 'This is an unreasonable bus driver. He will not listen to logic. He will keep this motor running to cool his butt, at the same time polluting the atmosphere of the rainforest'. So that was the arse end of the bus, and then I went and did the side of the bus and then I did the front of the bus … And so I went down to Court and I pleaded not guilty. It was 'Wilful Damage'. Ok, so I pleaded not guilty and defended myself. I'm real good on the floor. I'm not real good at the law. So I looked it all up and I figured I had this beat and my defence was provocation. I was provoked. I'd been provoked for years and this was like *it*, you know. So I started my defence that way and the prosecutor said, 'Provocation is not a defence under the law for Wilful Damage', and I went, 'You're kidding me!' So he [the magistrate] found me guilty and instead of the A$2,860 worth of damages, as I demonstrated that with eucalyptus oil we could take this stuff off and they didn't really have to repaint the whole bus, he said, 'Yeah, you're right

A$100 damages, three months to pay, no recording of a conviction'. But I was put at the same time on a one-year's good behaviour bond.

The second incident, I was walking along the sidewalk by the butterfly farm and there was a small coaster bus, like twenty-one, twenty-four passenger. Looked around for the bus driver; could not see him anywhere. There were old people there who were obviously the group. As I walked by the bus, by the back sliding door I just flicked the handle in and it wasn't locked and I went 'Aw beauty'! So I slid the door open. I walked in up to the front, reached over the seat, turned the key off. Walked out of the bus, closed the door, and because that same group of people were like there, like sort of walking the sidewalk, I just went around the bus then out on the street to continue to the market ... I got about halfway down the bus ... I turn around, and here comes the bus driver charging down, a big guy ... and so he came like this at me you know. I just went *boompf*, just pushed him against the side of the bus, you know, not hard, just enough for his force to move him against the side of the bus ... So then he opens the door, the driver's door, as if to like bang me with the door, you know, gets into the bus, turns the motor on *again!* And I put my hand on his arm and said, *'Eh! At least wait until they get into the bus!'* and he turned like this and went *boompf* and kicked me away ... I had a hold of his arm and as I pulled like that, he had a hold of the key and the key was in the ignition and so it ripped that little wire thing off the key. I ended up with the tag, he ended up with the wire, and the key was still in the bus running. I tossed the tag back in the bus and just walked away. So he went down and filed charges of 'Assault' and 'Tampering with a Vehicle', and so we went to Court and I lost [laughs] ... But I got the minimum fine too so that was all right, something like eighty bucks for tampering with the vehicle, three hundred for assault, and then one hundred and ten in court costs, so four hundred and ninety all up (Gonzo, pers. comm. 17 February 1997; original emphasis).

That Gonzo was not alone in his battle against the buses is evidenced by the fact that he was able to pay for his fine with donations from many sympathetic supporters.

Place or Product?

Just as the bus issue was beginning to settle, a development proposal for an 'edu-tainment' centre called the 'Kuranda Heritage Park' sparked renewed conflict in the village. It also became a testing ground for the effectiveness of the Strategic Management Plan and its offspring, the Development Control Plan. The dispute reached such intensity that the *Cairns Post* (28

June 1996: 5) reported it under the headline 'Town Plan under Siege'. The developers of the park argued that their initiative was a response to the increasing number of theme park attractions in the Cairns area that were competing with Kuranda for tourists. ARK and the Kuranda Chamber of Commerce both objected to the proposal because it involved a large area of the town being fenced off and given over to tourists as a theme park. The president of ARK addressed a Mareeba Shire Council meeting on 4 April 1996 as follows:

> Locals find this concept of a 'Kuranda' theme park (inside a fence inside their town) demeaning and insulting. It undermines the integrity of the village ... The scale is inappropriate and will 'swamp' the town, it does not complement the 'village in the rainforest' – being more like a 'Dreamworld' GOLD COAST type development ... The project also seeks to create an 'imitation' Kuranda inside a fence with admission price around $25.

Significantly, in his address the president quoted directly from the Strategic Management Plan and the Development Control Plan (DCP), detailing how the project conflicted with the plan. The theme park proposal provided a testing ground for the plan and the dispute was phrased in terms of the value of the real over the simulacrum, as well as of the natural environment over a culture of rank commercial greed – as the following extracts from various letters to the editor of the local papers illustrate:

> Putting a fence around a large portion of our town and charging $25 admission reeks of greed and shows a non-caring attitude in regard to Kuranda ... Greed has obviously replaced green (*Cairns Post* 16 April 1996: 9).

> Somewhere along the line tourists will realise that butterflies exist outside of sanctuaries, rainforest may be experienced without a cover charge and T-shirts may be bought anywhere in Australia (*Cairns Post* 16 April 1996: 9).

> The 'edu-tainment centre' is in reality a real estate deal. And that's the greatest failing of the tourism industry in Kuranda – increasingly it has nothing to do with tourism. It's all about real estate speculation and property development. As far as locals like me are concerned, Kuranda does not have an image problem. It has an integrity problem. And we're sick of being tainted by greedy 'conpeople' who treat tourists as wallets on legs (*Cairns Post* 22 April 1996: 9).

This dispute about the edu-tainment park reveals that objections to development in the village are not solely based on the technicalities of town planning and traffic control, but on a vision of the village as a home place, as *lived* rather than simply performed for tourists. That the development company subsequently withdrew its application to build the theme park was hailed by many townspeople as both a victory for the plan and a vindication of all the time and effort they had put into the planning process.

Nevertheless, the traffic plan section of the Kuranda Strategic Management Plan continued to be a hot topic of dispute in the village. Some people argued that the situation had changed in Kuranda in the two years since the community strategic planning exercise and that a plan had to be flexible enough to allow for such change. The Mareeba Shire Council commissioned a consulting firm[12] to do an updated traffic study in October 1996. The consultant's report concluded that 'bus and coach use of the upgraded Coondoo Street would not be desirable' (Mareeba Shire Council 1997: 31). However, the Far North Queensland Tour Operators Association and local business people at the top end of town continued to lobby for changes to the plan so that buses could collect tourists from the railway and Skyrail stations at the bottom end and bring them to the top end. The president of the Kuranda Tourist Association argued that the restrictive ban on buses through the main street was a 'fundamental and fatal flaw' in the Kuranda Strategic Management Plan (*Cairns Post* 29 June 1996: 3; *Tablelands Advertiser* 3 July 1996: 9), and tourist operators addressing a Mareeba Shire Council meeting warned that the Plan was 'suicidal' (*Cairns Post* 6 July 1996: 5). As the disputes about the main street reveal, while some residents supported tourist developments in the town, many villagers reacted against the town being made over solely as a product for tourists. Involvement in the town planning process was one way that residents attempted to reclaim the village as their home place.

Reclaim the Village!

In addition to the transport issue, there was conflict in Kuranda over the particular design and materials used in buildings and also over the location of public buildings. Cases in point are the library and the building that locals call 'The Ark'. Kuranda residents had been lobbying the Mareeba Shire Council for a library for many years, and various committees worked on different plans regarding where the library building should be located. In April 1994, in anticipation of a funding success, a new library working group was formed at a public meeting called by the ratepayers and residents association. This group, with the voluntary assistance of a local architect, produced a concept plan based on a site next to the Kuranda Amphitheatre. The idea was to encompass the library within a larger complex that would include a community centre with a stage, meeting rooms and the Kuranda branch office of the Shire Council. The architectural design was released for public perusal and consultation. People appeared to be satisfied with the building design itself. What generated intense public debate, however, was the site of the complex. Some residents considered that the library should be located in the village centre rather than near the amphitheatre. They called a public meeting on 28 January 1995 to discuss the issue. I was present at this meeting at which yet another working group was formed to consider possible alternative sites for the library. As they left the meeting, a group of people chanted in unison: 'Reclaim the village! Reclaim the village!' As a means of presenting the two sides of the dispute, I quote from a letter written by Kuranda artist Henri Hunsinger in response to observations delivered at the meeting by a member of the Library Working Party:

> The work done by your group is very impressive and I would be in full support for it except for your assertion that: 'Although the aim to reclaim the village may be desirable it is not very practical. The town has sold out to commercialism and bears almost no resemblance to the Kuranda village we all loved'. Even though the village has been over commercialised, we have just invested an incredible amount of time to find a vision for it! The village still functions with its Post Office, Bank, News Agency, Chemist, etc. and remains the main focus of the community at large. If we want the future library to be used by everyone, and to become an integral part of community life, it should be built as close as possible to the other services which are grouped in the village, and which make the village a village, even though one which is over commercialised.[13]

It is clear that the dispute regarding the library was another expression of the resentment that had been building up among Kuranda residents against what they saw as the invasion and transformation of their town. 'Reclaim the village' became a catch-cry among Kuranda people who sought recognition that their town was the living place of a local community and not just a product for tourists.

The Village Concept

The village concept has, in fact, given rise to some debate in Kuranda, a debate that is reflected in its built fabric. The main street, for example, boasts an odd mixture of what people refer to as 'heritage style' buildings – those with wooden facades and verandas painted in what are called 'heritage' colours – and arty new buildings painted in bright 'modern' colours.

Clearly for some people the idea of a village evokes the past, and these people equate the enhancement of the village atmosphere of Kuranda with the preservation and reconstruction of the heritage style buildings. There is much resentment against developers who have demolished old buildings to give way to new shopping complexes, replacing timber and corrugated iron with concrete. Yet for other people, the description of Kuranda as a village does not evoke this heritage aspect, nor is their image necessarily one of an intimate little country town. Rather, the kind of village they envisage comes closer in style to an inner city village such as Greenwich in New York with its art galleries, coffee shops, and the like. Their image is one of a compact place, intimate in structure and scale and distinctive in terms of the artistic creativity of its built fabric, its local identity marked by the rainforest that surrounds it. The Kuranda Strategic Management Plan emphasises the importance of maintaining and enhancing the 'green belt' around the village and the 'green tunnel' of overarching trees through which one must travel in order to arrive at the village heart. Historically, however, Kuranda and the countryside surrounding it had been extensively cleared. Much of the growth in the area today is secondary growth.

The Ark

The village concept as it finds its expression in Kuranda is revealed in the response of residents to a proposal to construct a tourist shopping complex in the shape of a ship on the main street (Figure 5.2). There was much opposition to the proposal, dubbed 'the Ark'. However, the Shire Council gave approval for the building, and a local resident – who came to Kuranda as a self-identified 'hippie' during the 1970s and who plays a key role in village politics – backed the decision.[14] The reason she gave for her support is telling. In a letter to the Mareeba Shire Council (7 November 1996), she wrote:

> I am convinced that the project should be supported. It deserves to have its spirit of innovation recognised. Our desire was that Council recognise that Kuranda is not a 'Heritage village' as such where conformity is the norm … Our recommendation was that Council recognise Kuranda as a village not of the past but rather of the future. We wish not to be fusty but rather vibrant and creative. I believe this project is that hard-to-define thing – a real 'Kuranda' development, it is quirky but makes sense in its own way.[15]

After the Ark was approved, however, an application to house an indoor pistol and rifle range within the new shopping complex was put to Council.

Figure 5.2. 'The Ark' in the main street of Kuranda, 2011.
Photographer: Rosita Henry.

In spite of the public outcry against it, the Shire Council approved the application. The protestors appealed to the Planning and Environment Court[16], and a petition against the rifle range attracted over 500 signatures. Again the Village Development Control Plan was tested. A circular distributed to residents requesting support for the legal battle states:

> The truth is we simply cannot afford to lose. This appalling decision ... if allowed to proceed will open the floodgates once and for all. We must defend our town Development Control Plan as it is our only defence in what will undoubtedly be a long fight to retain our rights as residents. If we win this fight it will send a strong and lasting message to Council and unscrupulous speculators that we haven't given up our rights and won't!

However, the Development Control Plan and other plans – including the Mareeba Shire Strategic Plan – in fact worked against the interests of the objectors to the development. Mr Justice Daly said in his judgement that 'it is, of course, the maps, plans, and words of the planning documents themselves upon which this court and, indeed, the local government and public must concentrate' (Jean Anderson and Ors v. Mareeba Shire Council and Maytrend Pty Ltd 1998: 5). The judge found that there was 'no conflict with the planning documents as framed'. I cite this case not to point out the inadequacies of the plans themselves, but to demonstrate how the planning process operates as a disciplinary measure that directs the expression of resistance into a form that can be bureaucratically and legally controlled.

Bureaucratic strategies of power such as community planning processes *contain* resistance. The planning process as it operates in Kuranda is an example of the phenomenon in Australia and elsewhere of increasing governmental decentralisation and devolution of administrative and decision-making processes. Within the bureaucratic order there has been 'an apparent decline of hierarchical and corporatist forms of organisation and the emergence of new groupings and coalitions that deligitimise centralised political control and authority' (Long 1996: 39). In the case of urban and regional planning, the idea is to involve members of the community in the planning process. This apparent devolution of power was embraced by Kuranda people because it is entirely compatible with a distinctively Australian egalitarian ideology that operates to mask state effects.

Aboriginal People and the Main Street

Like other locals, Aboriginal people tend to avoid the main street during the peak tourist period of the day (10 A.M. to 3 P.M.) apart from the building owned by Ngoonbi Aboriginal Housing Corporation, from which the corporation runs its business activities. During the 1980s and 1990s, this building used to house the Jilli Binna Museum, which featured artefacts of rainforest Aboriginal people.

The spatial trajectories of Aboriginal people have changed with the changing face of the main street. During the late 1980s and throughout the 1990s, the Tjapukai Aboriginal Dance Theatre, located opposite the Jilli Binna Museum, was a lively meeting place until it was moved to Cairns. A coffee shop at the 'Strangled Mango' was popular for a time because the Community Development and Employment Program (CDEP) operated from the same building. However, the mango tree was diagnosed as diseased and removed, and the coffee shop closed. Young people congregate in pockets along the main street at night, and some shopkeepers are concerned about potential break-ins and robberies. Yet few such events occur, and when they do the perpetrators are as often as not non-Aboriginal youths. One shopkeeper, a 1970s settler, commented that the new shopkeepers were paranoid and that in his experience there were relatively few burglaries in Kuranda compared with other such towns. One evening he had accidentally left his shop window wide open, and when he came back the next morning, nothing had been disturbed or stolen.

Aboriginal people in Kuranda tend not to become involved in the planning issues that concern the business people and other non-Aboriginal residents of the town. Nevertheless, they are also worried about the impact of tourism. In particular, they are concerned about the increasing proliferation of arts and crafts that are falsely marketed to tourists as 'authentic' Aboriginal products. A march down the main street in demonstration against this was organised to coincide with the Kuranda Spring Fair in September 2004. People had heard that shipments of didjeridus and boomerangs were being sent to Indonesia to be painted there more cheaply before being returned for sale in Kuranda. Marchers chanted, 'Kuranda town don't let us down. Employ our people here today'.

During the past thirty years, Kuranda Aboriginal people's spatial experiences of the town have been increasingly defined in terms of tourist movement through the town, the town planning practices of the settlers and the approvals by the Shire Council for changes to the built fabric of the town. Many Aboriginal people are concerned about the impact that these developments will have on their lives:

> We wonder what's going to happen to the Aboriginal people with all this development going up. Will there be jobs for our people? Will they be able to accept us into their community? Will we be able to cope with what is happening in Kuranda or is it going to put us in a place where there are too many things happening? We don't like it. These are the questions. We still asking questions. What's going to happen to us when more people come into Kuranda? Sometime when we go into town we sit down and we watch people coming up in the tourist train, line of them from the station coming up into Kuranda. We watch them with amazement and I guess at the same time they look at us in amazement. Some of them have never seen Aboriginal people before and we've never seen a line of white people like that before. We sit down, we look, we take notice, but we're not in a position of speaking out what's in our mind (Lyn Hobbler, pers. comm. 26 June 1995).

Aboriginal people are as concerned about changes to the built fabric of the town and the loss of the old buildings as many of the non-Aboriginal residents, even though these are 'white man's' houses:

> We said, 'Why they had to pull Fitzpatrick's down and build brick hotel?' It was upstairs and downstairs. I used to work there … It was nice. They didn't have to pull it down. They could have just renovated it if they thought it was old. Them verandas right around looked real nice, but they pulled it all down and the old homes in Coondoo Street [the main street].

> They lovely old homes that the white people had … I think development,
> well that's the government and that's the white man for you. I don't like
> it. Because we used to have all these trees in the street and it was really
> a village amongst the trees, but they pulled it all down and built all these
> modern brick homes and I think they are just destroying Kuranda. But,
> you know, that's just government. But we can't say anything. We got to live
> with it (Marita Hobbler, pers. comm. 26 June 1995).

It is clear that older Aboriginal people in particular began increasingly to
feel the pressure of the tourist boom and the influx of new settlers into the
area. Yet unlike many of the non-Aboriginal residents, they felt powerless
to say anything about the changes or to take direct action in resistance
(such as the action Gonzo took against the buses described above). At first,
there was hope that the new shops would bring employment opportunities,
but these have not materialised: 'All these development coming to Kuranda,
where is it leaving our black children? They can't get job. No matter how
fair-skinned you could be, you still can't get a job. As long as you're black,
you're black'.

In contrast with the 1970s settlers, who are thought of as 'friendly', more
recent settler-entrepreneurs drawn to Kuranda for the tourist industry are
considered 'racist':

> White people in those days were all friendly. Everybody knew us when we
> moved in from Mona Mona. And this is all *new* development and they're
> *new* people. They come from south, or Cairns. They're not going to offer
> our people any jobs … They're going to push black people out and out like
> in early days. Because in the early days our people were camped right in
> the main street but they were pushed out … here and there, and then sent
> out on government mission (Marita Hobbler, pers. comm. 26 June 1995).

Kuranda Aboriginal people assess the quality of their relationships across
socially constituted racial boundaries according to whether they 'know' the
white people in question and whether they are in turn 'known' by them.
What does to 'know' someone mean in this context?

Knowing the 'Other'

The settlers who lived in the old houses along the main street were known
in the sense that they belonged to families who had lived in the area for
generations. Aboriginal people knew them by face and by name and knew
which people would treat them with respect and which might treat them

badly. These settlers may have been racialist in attitude and practice, and not all of them were 'friendly', but Aboriginal people had grown accustomed to them. Their practices of social interaction were predictable. In turn, on the other side of the racial divide, long-term settlers felt comfortable because they recognised these particular Aboriginal people as belonging to Kuranda, as Mona Mona people, and they 'knew' them as individuals and as members of families.

One of the strategies Aboriginal people use to ensure that settlers 'know' them and recognise their connection to place is though the names they give their children: 'We name our children after our old people because then the old settlers remember us'. Time of residence in Kuranda is a factor in whether a person is recognised as a 'friendly' local, not just because the person becomes 'known' as an individual, but because the person has also had time to constitute a set of kin relations. Many of the 1970s settlers who came to Kuranda as young single people subsequently formed partnerships and had children. Their children have in turn reproduced. In some cases, elderly parents have joined them in Kuranda, so that up to four generations of a family may now call Kuranda home. Some of the children of the 1970s settlers have married or formed partnerships with Kuranda Aboriginal people, and some have had children who are embraced by their Aboriginal relations. As Marita Hobbler commented about the younger generation:

> They're all at one with the Aboriginal. The kids, you'll see white and black together, camping, and all friends. They come to our homes. They go right into black person's home up in Mantaka, Kowrowa. I can go to my son's place and there you see a lot of teenagers, white and black all together … When we have dance, everybody come, white and black people, all the young ones (Marita Hobbler, pers. comm. 26 June 1995).

Being part of larger multi-generational families helps to localise or emplace settlers and contributes to their acceptance by Aboriginal people. They are recognised not merely as settlers but as settler families. The significance of 'family' among Aboriginal people in urban areas and rural towns (see Babidge 2004, 2010) is expressed in Kuranda in terms of how Aboriginal people interact with settlers. To be part of a settler family – the larger the better, and the more generations the better – provides a non-Aboriginal person with acceptance by Aboriginal people and recognition as a local. When I first started fieldwork in Kuranda, I found immediate acceptance among Aboriginal people because they knew my family. During our very first meeting, Aboriginal elder Lyn Hobbler asked me to help him write his life story. Surprised at this show of trust, I responded, 'But don't you want to get to know me first?' He replied, 'I know you; I know your family'.

Spatial Politics

In her study of the town of Katherine in the Northern Territory, Merlan (1999: 111) discusses transformations in Aboriginal spatial practices. She notes: 'Aboriginal people extensively redefined their daily lives and practices in relation to the place-dominating character of settler presence and projects, though without necessarily representing this to themselves as the grounds of their actions'. In contrast, many Aboriginal people in Kuranda *do* recognise and represent settler projects as constraints on their actions (where they walk, sit, congregate) and on their relations among themselves. They trace histories of changes in the main street and in the places of significance to them there:

> They've all been moved [Aboriginal places in the main street] so we move on and find another place that we can get attached to ... As soon as Aboriginal people make a place for themselves where they feel comfortable, they come in to change it. Whether it's intentional? Going back to the Mango tree, they removed the seats so we couldn't sit there anymore ... The post office area changed. They put all that new development there. Ok, we moved from there ... I see a lot of people just come in and do what they have to do and head straight back out again because it's not as it used to be, when we could hang out. And that's where I think one of our problems is, because that's where information was passed on. That's how ideas were developed. You could get to hear what people felt about something. Because we haven't got that meeting place in town anymore, there's all these misunderstandings and tensions and pressures and bad relationships developing that are really splitting us all up so much so that everybody's gone off and set up their new organisations [Aboriginal corporations]. Now we have to have a formal meeting. Just getting information out now is not happening how it used to and not as effectively as it used to and, like I said, misunderstandings are developing. Regardless of the technology that we have with our fax machines and phones and what not, there's nothing as good as coming together face to face, because you can really see for yourself how that person feels about something and you can show that you understood what that person said (Rhonda Duffin, pers. comm. 10 November 1995).

In other words, change in the built fabric of the town is linked to increasing conflict among Aboriginal people and to the rise of Aboriginal bureaucratic organisations. One of the elders also complained to me about the loss of the seat under the mango tree where she used to sit waiting for transport to Cairns:

> The bench under the Mango tree ... That's where we used to sit; warm ourselves and get a tan but you find no more seats there anywhere. That's why we doesn't like too much buildings going up knocking the trees down. That's what I mean. It's not the same. Kuranda's not the same to us now like it used to be. I think it's still our place where we should have something to say about it, but don't have nothing to say (Esther Snider, pers. comm. 18 June 1995).

Merlan (1999: 192) has observed that in the town of Katherine in the Northern Territory, 'many Aborigines feel comfortable sitting on the ground, do so regularly in camp life ... do not find it inherently demeaning [or] threatening, and station themselves in these locations in the middle of town to sit and watch what is going on, taking special notice of the movement of familiar Aboriginal people'. This is true also for Kuranda, although I have never observed Aboriginal people in Kuranda sitting on the pavement. In the past there used to be patches of lawn outside the grocery store, near the hotel and at the post office where not only Aboriginal people but also hippies, tourists and other travellers used to sit. However, these areas have now been paved. Today, people find alternative seating on the stairs and the rock walls of the refurbished town.

Aboriginal people respond not only to changes in the built fabric but also to changes in the ownership of businesses in the town. When one of the hotels changed hands and there was talk that the new owner was 'racist', most Aboriginal people took their business to the other hotel. This is also the case with non-Aboriginal residents. A particular coffee shop in the main street is popular because of its reputation for welcoming locals who tend not to spend much money but who might sit and talk for hours over just one cup of coffee. Other businesses have reputations for wanting people to move on fast so as to clear tables for the tourists:

> I feel like we've lost the main street. It's really lost its image there. I love the coffee shop. The pub as a meeting place doesn't really work in Kuranda anymore for my friends because of that whole police culture. The coffee shop's taken it over, you know. I still go across the road [to the pub]. Maybe you can have a drink in the pub between say three and five, but if you stay longer, you're going to get into trouble. But the coffee shop's taken over from that and you get some really interesting discussions up there. Mainly everyone's gone by the time the tourist train arrives at ten thirty, you know (Ronnie Bruce, pers. comm. 8 January 1997).

Occasionally, Aboriginal people will join their friends at the coffee shop, or they'll stop to chat as they pass by but the coffee shop tends to be frequented mainly by tourists and non-Aboriginal residents. Aboriginal-only groups are rarely to be found sitting at the café tables. Although there are no rules and regulations about which coffee shops people may use, people tend to segregate along these lines anyway in response to subtle social pressures partly conveyed through bodily demeanour. On both sides of the socially constructed racial divide, people sense that some people on the other side feel discomforted by their close presence.

Planning as a State Effect

Relationships between people and place are constituted through such social practices as community planning and through people's political engagement with one another in the disputes that the process of planning 'gathers'. The state seeks to draw people into a project of decentralised planning, but as Lefebvre (2009: 179) points out, 'How can the centralised state take responsibility for decentralization? This is a façade, a caricature'. Community planning is, I suggest, a 'state effect' that acts to control and steer place memory in particular directions. Trouillot (2001: 126) argues that state processes and practices appear in multiple sites and 'are recognizable through their effects'. Influenced by Jessop (1990), who coined the term 'state effects' and who argued that their source lies in 'state projects', Trouillot defines state effects as including:

> (1) *an isolation effect*, that is the production of atomized individualized subjects molded and modeled for governance as part of an undifferentiated but specific 'public'; (2) *an identification effect*, that is, a realignment of the atomized subjectivities along collective lines within which individuals recognize themselves as the same; (3) *a legibility effect*, that is, the production of both a language and a knowledge for governance and of theoretical and empirical tools that classify and regulate collectivities, and (4) *a spatialization effect*, that is, the production of boundaries and jurisdiction (Trouillot 2001: 126, italics in original).

Power is not only imposed from above by a 'big brother' state. State effects find their expression in, and are distributed through, multiple agencies, including non-government organisations, private industries, corporations and various other entities.

In their everyday interactions with each other and in relation to place, people continually propagate state effects. The planning process as it operates in Kuranda reveals the collusion of people in state projects and in the bureaucratic order. Yet community planning activities, planning disputes and conflicts about changes to the built fabric of the town are also practices that work to build alliances against state effects and against corporate strategies of power that threaten to displace people. Through their political engagement in planning processes, people make place in both collusion and collision with state effects.

Casey (1987: 197) posed the question: 'How are we to account for the power of place-as-remembered?' His answer is that places are empowered both by the inherent features of place itself in its landscape character – its variegation, its sustaining character, and its expressiveness – and by the *lived* bodies that occupy and animate specific places. Yet he does not adequately discuss the particular occupying and animating practices that define bodies as *lived.* My aim in this chapter, as in the book overall, is to understand the nature of those practices. The intimate relationship between people and place is not given, but is made by the activities of social actors. It is made through planning disputes as well as through everyday spatial practices, through meeting, sitting, watching, eating, drinking and socialising as well as busking, parading and protest marching. It is made through the spatial and temporal trajectories that people take as they rhythmically weave the fabric of their relationships with one another through the paths they take through the town.

NOTES

1. The name Association for Regional Kuranda was in fact deliberately chosen for its acronym ARK, as in Noah's Ark. The association has since been renamed Kuranda Ratepayers and Residents Association to more accurately reflect the interests it represents.
2. The company hired was C&B Consultants Pty Ltd. In the course of producing the 'Kuranda Strategic Management Plan', its successor the 'Kuranda Village Masterplan' and the 'Kuranda Village Development Control Plan', C&B Consultants Pty Ltd sub-contracted a number of other architectural firms and planning consultants. These included Clouston Pawsey Prouse, Guy Architecture and Interior Design, Burchill Bate Parker & Partners Pty Ltd and the Centre for Applied Economic Research and Analysis at James Cook University.
3. The 'major local stakeholders' were categorized as follows: i) local residents; ii) Aboriginal people; iii) larger businesses; iv) smaller businesses; v) market operators; vi) market stallholders; vii) tour operators; viii) the Mareeba Shire Council; ix) Queensland Rail; x) Skyrail.
4. These working groups were called: Development Control (Environs), Development Control (Village), Waste Control, Landcare (Forest), Transportation, Landscape and Streetscape (Village), Community Facilities, and Arts/Culture/Heritage.
5. The existing DCP, entitled 'Development Control Plan 1 – Kuranda and Environs', was gazetted on 27 July 1985. The new DCP was to apply only to the village itself as shown in DCP 2 – Kuranda Village Map. DCP 1 was to continue to have effect over those areas outside the boundaries of DCP 2.

6. To complement the new Development Control Plan, a group of residents also began to meet voluntarily in December 1994 to formulate another DCP for the Kuranda environs. Some of the members of this group had already been involved in the Kuranda vision workshops in early 1993. The group – which at each meeting averaged some twenty members, including developers, conservationists, land holders and other interested residents – met every fortnight for over a year. All their hard work was recognized when the four people who produced the final proposal document for a DCP for the Kuranda Environs won an award for excellence in the category of community planning from the Queensland division of the Royal Australian Planning Institute in 1995.

7. This program was a government initiative to enhance business performance within town centres by bringing together local government, business people and community representatives to formulate management plans that would compare to the kinds of integrated management strategies under which large shopping centres operate. The Kuranda Village Promotion Program was funded by the department to the tune of A$20,000 per year for three years, supplemented by the Mareeba Shire Council and the Benefited Area Rate contributed by Kuranda businesses.

8. The consultancy was awarded to Le Page and Company and resulted in the Kuranda Village Promotion Plan.

9. The inaugural meeting of the Kuranda Chamber of Commerce was held at the bottom pub on 23 November 1983.

10. Motions passed at the meetings of the Kuranda Chamber of Commerce include several against keeping the motors of buses running while empty (see Minutes of Meetings, 1 October 1990; 7 January 1991) as well as motions against buses in the main street (4 November 1991).

11. A Department of Transport survey was conducted on Wednesday 11 August 1993 over a twelve-hour period during the height of the tourist season. The surveyors counted 120 bus movements entering the village via Rob Veivers Drive, the main entrance to the village from the highway. These movements comprised sixty-two large coaches (forty-nine seats) and fifty-eight small coaches (twenty-two seats).

12. Connell Wagner.

13. Letter dated 29 January 1995, from Mr Henri Hunsinger to Ms Lynne Provan. The letter was copied and distributed among residents interested in the library issue.

14. This woman has been referred to by a more recent settler as one of 'the three battle tanks of Kuranda', community-minded women who are seen to be very active in village politics and who are given credit for being powerfully influential.

15. See Chapter 2 for a discussion of the significance of ships and boats to the new settlers.

16. See *Jean Anderson and Ors v. Mareeba Shire Council and Maytrend Pty Ltd* (Kuranda Shooting Gallery Appeal), Appeal No. 48 of 1997, held before His Honour Judge Daly, 13 February 1998.

Dancing Place

Cultural Renaissance and Tjapukai Theatre

*You could see that excitement was brewing up amongst the
Elders too because they'd been waiting to see something like this
themselves. Because it was all the stuff that was taken away
from their generation that now was reawakening and was coming through again. Like the culture was there! It was all there!*
—Willie Brim

While the hippies and other new townspeople were busily burrowing into
Kuranda – establishing the markets, creating the amphitheatre, battling
against the Shire Council and blueing over the main street – Aboriginal
people had begun to reassert their own identity in place through a cultural
renaissance. The rapid transformation of Kuranda in the wake of the emplacement practices of the new wave of settlers and the subsequent rise in
tourism had a dramatic impact on practices of sociality among Aboriginal
people. During the 1980s, just twenty years after the Mona Mona mission
had closed, a younger generation of Aboriginal people began to seek to re-
engage with their Aboriginal heritage. 'Cultural revival' became the catch-
cry of the day. In this chapter I discuss this phenomenon, focusing on social
dramas associated with the establishment of an Aboriginal dance theatre
in the main street of Kuranda and, some years later, its transformation into
a cultural park in Cairns.[1] The Tjapukai Dance Theatre – in tandem with
the Tjapukai Aboriginal Cultural Park – has been hailed as 'an instructive
best-practice example' of private sector employment and enterprise development for Aboriginal people (Finlayson 1995: 4). The dance theatre has
been a key factor in the emergence of a specific locally based Djabugay
tribal identity. Following Kapferer (1995a), I argue that the Tjapukai Dance
Theatre provides a performance space for playing with the categorical identities generated by the dominating and encompassing practices of bureaucratic colonialism and a native title claims process that denies Aboriginal
people recognition of their lived experiences. Aboriginal people are called

upon to demonstrate their authenticity by being able to trace cultural *continuity*. Yet a common refrain among Aboriginal people in Kuranda during my fieldwork in the 1990s was 'We don't live that way anymore'. One of the ways people have responded to this situation is through public cultural performances.

The Djabugay Renaissance

Today the name Djabugay[2] is used to refer to the 'traditional owners' of the Kuranda area. According to Dixon (1977: 6), strictly speaking, Djabugay is the language name, while Djabuganydji refers to the 'speech community'. However, people commonly use Djabugay to refer both to the people and the language. Djabugay, along with other tribal and language names, had virtually disappeared from *public* use during the mission days when people began to call themselves Mona Mona people. As one woman told me, 'We only heard this Djabugay in the last recent years now, really since the theatre you know ... I myself think, because I can remember on the mission nobody spoke of Djabugay. Nobody spoke of Djabugay when I was in Oak Forest. We were just Mona Mona people'. In response to my question about how the Dance Theatre was named, a member of the first group of dancers responded as follows:

> Well one of the elders decided on that. See, I hadn't heard of the Djabugay, the name Djabugay, until I was in my twenties. Now my grandfather didn't even tell me that. My Dad speaks about it a lot now, but even he was mouth-shut about the whole situation. That explains a lot of my radicalness, you know, when I was younger ... We were being forced to believe absolute crap, that Cook discovered Australia; and at the same time your tongue is slowly being snipped away out, while your elders are passing away behind your back. There's this language that's dying and going out the back door while you don't even know about it (Willie Brim, pers. comm. 13 August 1997).

A Djabugay elder stressed to me that it did not matter whether or not they knew their tribal names; what was important was that they knew their kin connections:

> When Tindale [1930s] and them come, we was in the dorm and we used to go up and take our photos and we didn't know they was questioning our old people. So it comes from Tindale when they interviewed our old people. I was only small. They had to lift me up for the photo. We didn't

know our family tree and we didn't know until we read it what tribe we were. *We knew who our relations were* (Esther Snider, pers. comm. 18 June 1995; original verbal emphasis).

Many Aboriginal people experience themselves as having a lack of 'traditional knowledge'. They say that their culture was taken from them by the missionaries and see themselves as having to work hard now to fill this void. Their identity is founded upon an absence. Being Djabugay is itself the very practice of filling this void, a counter-hegemonic challenge to the bureaucratic practices that deny them access their own means of becoming-in-the-world. Being Djabugay is an articulation of the politics of identity that is, according to Morris (1989: 225), 'an expression of resistance to attempts to make Aborigines experience themselves in the terms defined by the dominant society'.

Djabugay in the Historical Record

Early anthropological and linguistic research indicates that the Aboriginal people living in the Kuranda area prior to European contact spoke the one language but belonged to several different small politico-family groups (Tindale 1938–39; McConnel 1939–40). A number of researchers (Sharp 1938–39; McConnel 1939–40; Seaton 1957; Tindale 1974; Dixon 1977 and Patz 1991) have documented the general territory within which this language was spoken. Lauriston Sharp (1938–39: 256–57) produced a map that roughly located 'Tjabokai' as a tribal group based on data primarily gathered in the course of 'field surveys' conducted during 1933, 1934, and 1935. Ursula McConnel (1939–40: 59), in order to record tribal names[3] and territories as accurately as possible, travelled through the country with her informants and did detailed fieldwork rather than relying on interviews carried out at mission stations and reserves. She writes, 'I have accepted the distinctions recognised by the natives themselves, choosing as my informants in each case members of the tribe under consideration, not members of neighbouring tribes, travelling as often as possible in their company to the grounds they claimed as their own, and locating them simultaneously on a surveyor's four-mile map' (McConnel 1939–40: 60). Nevertheless, McConnel (1939–40: 59–60) recognised the problematic nature of her project, noting: 'One is not dealing with a static situation, but with the shifting sands of culture change ... Local groups, bound together by a homogeneous culture, and only slightly differentiated from each other in dialect, are in the process of splitting off into distinct tribal entities'.

Tindale, during his surveys of the Mona Mona mission in 1927 and 1938–39, recorded residents who identified as 'Tja:pukai'.[4] He recorded 'Njakali' or 'Nyakali' as an alternative name for the Djabugay, as well as 'Buluwai' and 'Irukandji' as different tribes, later providing a detailed account of the location of their boundaries (Tindale 1976: 21).[5] It is beyond my scope here to fully discuss the problematic issue of language and tribal boundaries in Australia.[6] As Dixon (1976: 231) notes in his account of such boundaries before European contact on the eastern coast of north Queensland, in this area a 'tribe' was not defined solely according to linguistic criteria, but was rather a political unit composed of various local groups. According to Dixon (1977: 5–6), there may have been a number of 'groups speaking the Dya:bugay language: Dya:bugay, Guluy, Yirgay, Bulway and Nyagali'.[7] He is uncertain as to the political identity of these groups, although he notes that 'nowadays the name Dya:bugay (which is said to have been originally the name of the dialect spoken on the coast, towards Port Douglas) appears to be used by speakers to refer to the whole language, and Djabuganydji to refer to the whole speech community' (Dixon 1977: 6). Today, most descendants of Djabugay speaking local groups – in other words, people of the area around Cairns through to the other side of Kuranda and along the coast to Port Douglas,[8] except for Yirrganydji and some Bulwanydji – tend to identify as 'Djabugay people'. This includes those people who have read early anthropological sources such as Tindale's genealogical charts of 1938 and who are aware that at that time, their predecessors identified themselves more specifically in terms of local group affiliation.

According to some Djabugay people, Djabugay is a tribal group that encompasses all the people who trace their descent from Djabugay speaking ancestors. In particular, Nyagalindji (Nyagali), Gulunydji (Guluy), and Bulwanydji (Bulway) are considered to come under the umbrella of the Djabugay Aboriginal Tribal Corporation. However, the Yirrganydji, as coastal people, categorically distinguish themselves from the Djabugay people in the Kuranda area and have their own separate tribal corporation. Encompassment by Djabugay is contested, and processes of identification and differentiation remain fluid. For example, during a visit to Kuranda in 2004, I was told by a man who in 1996 had identified himself as Djabugay that he had recently discovered that he is actually Bulway. He said that he no longer identifies as Djabugay.

Language Revival

In 1961, the linguist Hale (1976) did a study on the Djabugay language. He thought that there were at that time approximately fifty fluent speakers. However, Cassells (1977: 1) was only able to identify three 'fully fluent' speakers: Gilbert Banning, his mother Buttercup Banning and Gilbert Martin. In 1978, Patz (1991: 248–9) was able to reliably identify two other competent speakers, Keatie Street and Roy Banning. The Banning family, because they were camped under the protection of a local farmer at Red-lynch, near Cairns, were able to evade the 'round-ups' and therefore escape missionisation and the disciplinary power that had suppressed the use of the vernacular among other Djabugay speakers.

During the 1980s, Roy Banning began to work with Sue Robertson, a Kuranda resident with some training in social anthropology, on the compilation of a Djabugay dictionary. From 1987 on he continued this language work with Michael Quinn, who had studied anthropology at Sydney University and who had settled in Kuranda as part of the alternative lifestyle wave. Together they developed material on Djabugay that was suitable for instructional purposes (see for example, Banning and Quinn 1989; Quinn and Banning 1991, 1992). Quinn was able to secure government funding[9] for himself and Banning and 'other Djabuganydji descendants' in their efforts 'to preserve the Djabugay language for further generations' (Quinn 1992). Djabugay language classes began in 1987 at the local primary and high school, and the language was taught principally through song. Most of the lyrics were composed by Quinn and Banning. Over the years, other Djabugay people have contributed songs, and today there is a repertoire of such music that Djabugay people consider belong to them and that they use to mark their vibrant presence and continuity as a people. Some of these songs are now also danced at the Tjapukai Aboriginal Cultural Centre and elsewhere[10], and they have been presented to national and international audiences.

These efforts to revive the Djabugay language have had a significant impact on contemporary Aboriginal identity politics in Kuranda. The 'official' documentation by anthropologists, linguists, and other researchers of Djabugay as the encompassing name for the language of the area assures not just its recognition today by state authorities, but also its contemporary political significance as an identity category. Yet, whatever it meant to be Djabugay (or Djabuganydji) before European settlement, and what it might have meant to people in the Djabugay camp on the Mona Mona mission, it means entirely something else today.

State Projects and White Brokers

The tribal category called Djabugay, as it operates today, is a construction that arose in response to the confluence of a number of other forces: the global tourist industry, state bureaucratic policies of multiculturalism and Aboriginal self-determination, native title, and opportunities for government sponsorship of community cultural projects. Contemporary tribalism in Australia is a response not just to the demand for 'tribal' culture in the booming tourist industry, but also to the rationalising and categorising techniques the state uses to control Indigenous peoples. Such techniques are evident, ironically, in state programs that are designed to foster the 'reconstruction' and 'revival' of Aboriginal culture. With the rise of multiculturalism and the move away from the policies of Aboriginal assimilation, from the 1970s onwards Australian governments increasingly began to provide funding for projects that celebrated the cultural diversity of the nation. This support, however, was founded on a problematic concept of culture that tended to shift attention from the violence of structural inequality in Australian society to cultural diversity. The differences between Aboriginal and non-Aboriginal are considered to be strictly and almost mystically 'cultural', and thus the social, political and historical conditions of inequality go unrecognised. Yet as Bottomley (1987) argues, a mastery of expressive cultural forms is recognised everywhere as a form of symbolic capital. It is through the negotiation of such symbolic capital that people who lack power in the nation are able to make claims they otherwise would not be able to make. 'Traditional' practices such as dance and song, carving, painting and weaving are modes of performance that are only apparently neutral. Such performances are in fact dynamic, embodied strategies of political and economic engagement, not static representations of culture.

An important force in the Djabugay cultural revival movement was the involvement of particular non-Aboriginal members of the Kuranda community. Some of the counter-cultural settlers, many of them visual and performance artists, played an important role in fostering the cultural renaissance in Kuranda by helping Aboriginal people access government funding for cultural projects. As seasoned applicants for grants, they were able to secure money that could be used to finance various Aboriginal heritage workshops. As discussed above, especially influential in the Djabugay renaissance was the work of local anthropologist Michael Quinn, who began to collate all the Djabugay language data that had been recorded and who produced an extensive range of teaching materials with the assistance of the few remaining fluent speakers and of grants from various government schemes. Another example was a dance – or *corroboree* – reconstruction project brokered by a former member of the Australian Dance Theatre, Ibena Cundell, who had settled in Kuranda during the late 1970s. She was able to secure government funding to conduct a series of workshops that enabled Djabugay elders Maggie Donoghue and Enid Boyle to teach younger women some of the dances they had remembered.

Although the cultural renaissance was essentially funded by the state and through the private enterprise dealings and support of local non-Aboriginal residents – of the type that Collman (1988: 14) in his study of Aboriginal response to bureaucracy in Central Australia has referred to as 'white brokers' – it is important to note that Aboriginal people in Kuranda see the renaissance as having been generated from within their own community. White interlocutors who secure grants and organise cultural workshops tend not to be recognised as having any *generative* role. They are simply considered to be facilitators of a process of knowledge transmission that had already existed within the Aboriginal community. A comment about the anthropologist Michael Quinn exemplifies this view:

> Well Michael came here as an anthropologist and as a linguist and all he wanted to do at first was study the language. And, you go back six years ago, we was renting a place down here in Oak Forest and I used to just go and check on him because I knew he was working with Uncle Lalfie and a few of the Elders around here ... He was actually writing the language down, recording and actually putting it down so it won't be gone. And it had to take a little guy from Wales to come over here to do that, you know. To me, I honestly felt that, he's been *possessed* by my Uncle, by Uncle Lalfie who died, you know like, and because Michael is a strong believer in a lot of spiritual things that he's been taught (Willie Brim, pers. comm. 13 August 1997).

Such skills as bush food recognition and preparation, weaving, dancing, and knowledge of the Djabugay language are thought of as having been exclusively embodied by the elders until someone or something enabled their release or revelation. For Aboriginal people, the fact that the release or 'cultural revival' was and continues to be facilitated by state funding and by white brokers does not undermine the authenticity of the cultural practices and beliefs that have been revealed. Aboriginal people treat non-Aboriginal interlocutors as mere conduits for the release and transmission of the knowledge already held in trust by the elders in their role as mediators with the 'Old People', the ancestors (Langton 2002).

An Aboriginal Museum

As part of the Djabugay renaissance, in 1982, in response to government policies, two members of the Kuranda Aboriginal community took the opportunity to train as museum technicians. They then worked to establish a museum, which they named Jilli Binna ('eyes' and 'ears'), in a building in the main street of Kuranda owned by the Ngoonbi Aboriginal Housing Cooperative. The existence of the museum inspired a group of young people to take a museum studies course at the Cairns College of Technical and Further Education (TAFE) in 1990. Through the course, they were able to identify the potential for transforming the museum from a static display 'into a cultural resource centre focussing on the revitalisation of Djabugay cultural heritage' (Duffin et al 1992: 1). As part of their course, students were given the opportunity to visit the Australian Museum in Sydney, the South Australian Museum, the Queensland Museum and the John Oxley Library in Brisbane in order to access and collect family history records, photographs and items of material culture. An important result of this project was the students' gaining access to many of the genealogies originally collected by the anthropologist Norman Tindale during his field trip to the Mona Mona mission in 1938, which were held in the South Australian Museum. Copies of these, along with reproductions of Tindale's photographs of Mona Mona people, were then stored at the Jilli Binna Museum and were widely accessed by people of the community who were eager to trace their family histories. The museum eventually closed during the 1990s, mostly due to the fact that it could not be sustained financially, and some of the artefacts were relocated to the Tjapukai Cultural Park in Cairns. The demise of the Jilli Binna museum can be attributed to the impact of state policy and to a project-based approach to Indigenous development that funded short courses and training workshops for Aboriginal people, but without providing continuing support to ensure long-term sustainability and future job prospects for trainees.

Djabugay Rangers

Another influential part of the cultural revival in Kuranda was the introduction of a TAFE Aboriginal Ranger training program and the 1991 establishment of the Djabugay Community Ranger Program. Rangers were paid under the CDEP (Community Development Employment Project, popularly known as 'work for the dole') and supplemented, while working on designated projects, by wages from the Department of Environment and Heritage. Djabugay Rangers became a significant force in the assertion of a Djabugay identity. They saw themselves – and were generally accepted in the Aboriginal community – as being directed by the elders and therefore as having the authority to be the official keepers and representatives of the traditional knowledge that marked Djabugay identity. They became the Djabugay front to the outside world, as exemplified in the native title mediation process and in the negotiations with state government regarding cultural heritage management, cultural tourism and the archaeological site surveys associated with developments.

Dance Festivals

The cultural renaissance was also fostered by the 1983 establishment of a dance festival for the Aboriginal communities of Cape York Peninsula.[11]

This festival – now known as the Laura Aboriginal Dance and Cultural Festival and from its beginnings sponsored by the state government – brought dance groups from different Aboriginal communities in Cape York into competition. At the first festival, state support for Aboriginal dance was publicly declared by the then Premier of Queensland, the Honourable J. Bjelke-Petersen, who announced the dance competition winners. The director of the Department of Aboriginal and Islanders Advancement, Mr Pat Killoran, donated the main trophy shield.[12] Although the festival is still funded by the state, the state's presence is today less obvious, and the organisation of the Laura event rests in Aboriginal hands (specifically, the Ang-Gnarra Aboriginal Corporation) with Aboriginal people as hosts and presenters. At the 1997 Laura Festival, the dance ground and the land surrounding it was handed back to the traditional owners, the Western Kuku Yalanji, under the Aboriginal Land Act of 1992 (Qld). Some of these traditional owners were past residents of the Mona Mona mission and are today residents of Kuranda. The festival represents itself as a continuation of the traditional practice of gathering for ceremonial purposes. Yet at the same time, it is a self-conscious performance of Aboriginal culture for tourists and an opportunity for various government agencies to represent themselves in a sideshow of stalls around the main dance arena (Henry 2000, 2008).

Kuranda people first sent a team to the festival in 1986, calling themselves the Mona Mona dance team in reference to their historical connection with the Mona Mona mission. Lance Riley, an elder who grew up in the dormitory at Mona Mona and who self-identified as being of Kuku Yalanji heritage and not Djabugay, trained the dancers. As an Aboriginal elder, Lance Riley (pers. comm. 17 February 1997) reflected: 'My little boy was two, two-year-old, that was the youngest [in 1986]; he's about thirteen now. I talked all about the importance of keeping our culture alive to them as they were growing up'. After its success at the Laura Festival, Lance Riley established his dance troupe on a more permanent basis, making regular tours to the Woodford Folk Festival in southern Queensland. He also took the troupe overseas. The group would swell when the Laura Dance Festival was being held to include any Aboriginal child from Kuranda who wanted to dance. In fact, in 1997 there was a complaint from supporters of other community dance groups about the dominance, in terms of sheer size, of the Kuranda contingent.

Since the troupe represented the Kuranda Aboriginal community at the festival and because of the widespread association of Djabugay with Kuranda as 'the tribe for Kuranda', the Mona Mona Dancers came to be increasingly referred to by many participants and visitors at the festival, both Aboriginal and non-Aboriginal, as Djabugay dancers. However, not all of the dancers identified themselves or were identified by the elders as Djabugay. Some simply used the more encompassing identities of 'Mona Mona people' or 'Kuranda people'. Others began to stress different tribal affiliations, such as Kuku Yalanji or Muluridji. Increasingly, tensions arose among Kuranda Aboriginal people over who could legitimately identify as Djabugay, tensions that were linked to disputes about the ownership and management of the old Mona Mona mission site and its native title status. These tensions affected the composition of the dance team in performances at the Laura Festival: in response to these questions about native title rights and about who had claim to Djabugay identity, Lance Riley renamed his dance group Mayi Wunba (which he said was the Kuku Yalanji name for 'sugarbag', or bush honey). Lance Riley sadly passed away in 2002, and his wife, Joyce Riley, has taken over management of the group while his eldest surviving son leads the dancers. The dance team dedicated its performance at the 2003 Laura Festival to the memory of their father and grandfather.

Revival, Revelation and Continuity

The phrase 'cultural revival' as used by Kuranda Aboriginal people does not necessarily signify that what is being 'revived' no longer exists in the here and now, nor that there has been a discontinuity with the past. 'Revival' here is perhaps more accurately translated as 'revelation'. People trace the continuity of their dances from the 'Old People' who lived in the camps attached to the mission and who continued to perform rituals, particularly funerary rites, while their children were confined in the mission dormitories. Some elders told me that they remembered certain songs and dances taught to them by their parents and grandparents before they were removed to the dormitory. They claimed authenticity of their knowledge on the basis of direct transmission through physical presence and through first hand observation – through 'being there'. Others, although they spent all their childhood in the mission dormitory separated from their parents and grandparents, still strongly identified with the soundscape, having often heard the rhythms and the sound of the clapsticks coming from the direction of the camps all night long, particularly after someone had died. Today, people who grew up at Mona Mona and their descendants sometimes hear the sound of the clapsticks of the 'Old People' at night when they are camping at Mona Mona. Together with Roy Banning, Frank McLeod and Michael Quinn, Ashley Coleman wrote a children's book based on memories of a corroboree that his father had witnessed at Mona Mona and passed on to him. He introduces the book as follows:

Knowledge of this *warrma* (corroboree) was passed on to me by my *nyumbu* (father), Dan Coleman who saw it when he was eight or nine years old at Mona Mona S. D. A. Mission. He remembered that George Carroll was singing and some of those performing were Toby Brim, Tommy Hobbler, and Paddy Newbury. Dad and a mate had sneaked out of the dormitory one night to watch the old Djabuganydji people do this *warrma* in the *dulgu* (scrub). Boys in the dormitory were flogged with lawyer cane for speaking their own *ngirrma* (language) and were not allowed to attend corroborees . . . My *nyumbu* remembered some of the lines and worked with Michael Quinn and Roy Banning to compose the remainder (Coleman, McLeod and Quinn 1993: 1).

Djabugay elder Enid Boyle confirmed:

We used to have our corroborees when we were small growing up in the camps [the Djabugay camp on the periphery of the mission] ... Yeah at night, evening times when the old people like to get together you know, have their dancing and singing. Well, in the day they'll go out and get a heap of wood, you know, out in the bush. Make two big fires, and the dancing and singing would be done in the middle of the fires ... Well I was brought up that way with knowing my traditions, my lifestyle. But as I say, when they put me in the dormitories that all changed. They picked us up, put us away in the dormitories. We stayed there until we had to get married or until superintendent shipped us out to different white people who wanted worker. Domestic labour they wanted, and that's how I went ... As a child, the Kuranda tribe, people from Kuranda and Redlynch, we weren't really in the compound. We were just out of the compound, because my tribe were, you know, still in their wild state.[13]

While people on the mission who were living in the camps were able to continue some practices, the missionaries forbade non-Christian ritual activity among those people who had been 'assimilated' into the mission fold:

When I was growing up we had it on the mission [in the Djabugay camp] most of our corroborees .... but the missionaries when they heard the clapstick, you know, they didn't like to hear that, you know. They sort of cut it out and it gradually died out then until now this generation is trying to revive it (Florence Williams, pers. comm. 6 July 1994).

However, during the 1950s, after having banned it for at least thirty years, the mission did allow some dancing to be performed. According to Lance Riley:

The old people teach us [to dance]. It used to be something like the Laura
Festival out at Mona Mona. Dancers came from Malanda, Tolga, Kairi
... This is going back to the early 50s ... Mareeba used to come in there.
Mossman used to come up. Molloy people, they used to come across there
too; one big weekend (Lance Riley, pers. comm. 17 Feb 1997).

The mission opened its gates during this period to busloads of tourists who
would arrive on organised trips each Sunday and Wednesday afternoon.
They would do tours of the mission and be provided with displays of boomerang and spear throwing and opportunities to purchase artefacts made
on the mission (Queensland Parliament, 1952: 37). During the late 1940s,
the missionaries had begun to encourage the teaching of what they called
'native crafts' to children removed from their parents and placed in the dormitories. As Superintendent Pastor G. Peacock reported to the director of
native affairs (Queensland Parliament, 1951: 38): 'We are keeping before
them many of their native crafts for, not only are they useful to them, but they
are also of great interest to people who visit these areas'. Therefore, although
practices of discipline and punishment on the mission in general worked
towards erasing memory, there were other forces that worked against this
erasure. The economic situation of the mission and the attractiveness of the
tourist dollar meant that particular skills were 'kept before them'.

Memory, Continuity, and Performance

The policy of multiculturalism as it has been practiced in Australia has
tended to treat people and peoples as if they possess cultures, and therefore cultural identities, as though such things were tangible objects. Thus
the concretisation of cultural identities as an objective property of persons
and groups is partly an effect of bureaucratic state policy and practice.
Although cultural identities may be recognised as being contemporary
constructions, the constructions are thought to be traceable to fixed attributes that come from a given past and that continue into the present
through transmission and acquisition. In the case of Indigenous Australians, identity categories acquire respect, legitimacy and recognition within
the state jural and bureaucratic order according to how well they can trace
their cultural continuity from 'time immemorial'. Thus identity politics
for Indigenous Australians has become about establishing the categorical
legitimacy or authenticity of native title tribal identities in terms of their
cultural continuity. In turn, cultural continuity is seen as being dependent
upon the transmission of particular practices through time. But what does
transmission through time mean? In considering this question, I refer to
the analytical distinction a number of scholars have made between history

and memory. Roach (1995: 46), for example, contrasts history with collective memory, which he defines as the transmission of cultural practices through performance. Similarly, Connerton (1989: 13) distinguishes what he calls 'social memory' from 'historical reconstruction' in which knowledge of all human activities in the past is considered possible only through the knowledge of their traces. These traces are given the status of *evidence*, proof of the phenomenon's authenticity, while memories, including body memories, are not granted such status.

In the context of the native title process and the operations of state bureaucracy in general, historical reconstruction is privileged. The High Court in the Mabo case held that native title is extinguished when 'the tide of history has washed away any real acknowledgement of traditional law and any real observance of traditional customs'. In order to establish categorical legitimacy as native title holders, claimants have been asked to demonstrate the continuity of their attachment to country in terms of documented historical evidence of continuity of transmission and acquisition of culture.[14] Yet Aboriginal people challenge the requirement for such evidence with performances of memory based on an idea of culture as something embodied. In other words, they lay claim to the possibility of body memory or embodied acquisition of culture. For example, as Willie Brim (pers. comm. 13 August 1997) stressed to me: 'No, none of us guys [had danced before], but we knew, we knew. It was there, but it was a matter of just bringing it out of ourselves'.

Such responses have been criticised as essentialist and have given rise to impassioned debate among anthropologists (see for example Hollingsworth 1992; Lattas 1993). I am in concert with Lattas (1992: 162), who argues that essentialism needs to be historicised, contextualised and understood as 'a language for embodying cultural continuity and for internalising notions of struggle, solidarity and resilience'. Yet, the statement that 'it was there, but it was just a matter of bringing it out of ourselves' should not be categorised as a mere expression of strategic essentialism; there is more to it than that. Brim's emphasis was on the performative dimension of identity: the *action* of 'bringing out', as opposed to the thing that is brought out. The statement hints at a particular understanding about the nature of the world and an ontology that accepts that some truths remain 'inside' until the conditions are right for their revelation. Such an interpretation is in keeping with Aboriginal cosmology elsewhere in Australia (see for example Myers 1986; Merlan 1999; Sansom 2001; Greer 2009, 2010). Sansom (2001: 33) writes that in his experience, Aboriginal people 'distinguish between inner truths and outside appearances in all aspects of being'.

A Djabugay weaver one told me that unlike weaving and language, dance came naturally to their children and that although they had dance practices for festivals in order to coordinate their movements with others in the group, individuals really did not need to be taught how to dance. For the performances on stage, the Tjapukai dancers might have to be taught particular routines, but they argue that they already carry within them the rhythmic potentiality to dance. On numerous occasions, I have observed Aboriginal children adopting various dance poses and movements while at play. Perhaps they bring to their festival performances the body memories, demeanour, manner and style with which they carry themselves through life. Cultural continuity is not something given, but is made partly through 'dressage', or how one is 'bent' to the ways of one's society and how one learns through rhythmic repetition to hold oneself (Lefebvre 2004: 39). In other words, cultural continuity also expresses itself in 'bodily hexis' (Bourdieu 1977: 93). Lefebvre (2004: 39) distinguishes between education, learning and dressage, noting that 'knowing how to live, knowing how to do something and just plain knowing do not coincide'. According to Tjapukai dancer Willie Brim:

> Myself, I used to muck around, when all the boys used to go down the river and party on and stuff and we used to get into dancing and stuff like that. But to be actually taught, that didn't come until 1987, when Uncle Lalfie Thompson, Granny Danny Coleman, they were the two main elders who sat down and decided to show us leg movements ... They got interested because we asked them ... you could see that excitement was brewing up amongst the elders too because they'd been waiting to see something like this themselves. Because it was all the stuff that was taken away from their generation that now was reawakening and was coming through again. Like the culture was there! It was all there! (Willie Brim, pers. comm. 13 August 1997).

Cultural transmission does not only occur cognitively, through structured learning events, but also through bodily movement and posture in the ordinary practice and playfulness of everyday life.

The Tjapukai Dance Theatre

The Tjapukai Dance Theatre was spawned by a new settler theatre production called *The Odyssey You'll Ever See*, directed by Don Freeman and staged at the Kuranda Amphitheatre in 1986 (as mentioned in Chapter 3). Following the success of *The Odyssey*, Don and Judy Freeman, in cooperation with the now well-known Kuranda Aboriginal musician David Hudson, decided to form an Aboriginal dance company that would perform regularly for tourists in Kuranda. The Freemans approached Aboriginal elders in Kuranda who responded positively to the idea. The concept of setting up a dance group was something that they had already discussed among themselves: 'We were thinking of setting up next to Jilli Binna, but the know-how of how to go about setting it up was an obstacle plus the managing side of it all. The set up was out of our reach, you know, to set up a business' (Willie Brim, pers. comm. 13 August 1997).

In 1987, the Tjapukai Dance Company started to perform in a rented space under a small shopping complex in the main street of Kuranda, before moving to its own theatre, also in the main street. By 1995, aside from the CDEP (Community Development Employment Project, the Tjapukai Dance Theatre had become 'the single largest employer of Aboriginal people in Kuranda' and had 'grown from a business with a capital base of $45,000 to a theatre complex employing 37 Aboriginal people and turning over $1 million (gross) annually' (Finlayson 1995: 5).

Don and Judy Freeman and David Hudson, under the guidance of a number of Djabugay elders, jointly wrote the show that was performed in the theatre. It told the Dreamtime story of Woonun, a young hero who challenges an evil spirit being. The show introduced the performers as Djabugay, rainforest people, and the Djabugay tribal territory and its boundaries were announced. During the performance, the seven male actors/dancers explained the uses of various items of material culture: how to throw a boomerang, play the didjeridu and hurl a spear using a throwing stick (*woomera*). They also explained the totemic meanings of each of their body paintings. Various dances, such as the cassowary dance, the brolga dance and kangaroo dance, were then showcased. The show concluded with a dramatic demonstration of fire making followed by more dancing and the finale song, 'Proud to be Aborigine', excerpts from which were distributed on a flyer given to the audience on their entering the theatre:

> Proud to be Aborigine
> We'll never die, Tjapukai
> Always be our identity
> Proud to be Aborigine.

Finally, an invitation was issued to the tourists to come from the audience onto the stage to take posed photographs.

The show was so successful that the troupe was invited to Brisbane to perform at the World Exposition in 1988, and Tjapukai won the first of many cultural tourism awards in 1989, the Pacific Asia Travel Association's Gold Award for 'cultural development'.[15] This led to a whirlwind world tour with the Australian Tourist Commission, Qantas and Ansett Airlines to promote the Australian tourist industry. The show was performed fifty-eight times in sixty days across four continents, and many more overseas tours have been made since.[16]

What's in a Name?

Djabugay elders suggested the name for the dance theatre. It was to have unforeseen repercussions for the company, as it linked the theatre very firmly to Djabugay as a particular people or tribal group. Don Freeman (pers. comm. 8 April 1996) admitted, 'Knowing what I know now, I probably would not have chosen that name, because there were tremendous political implications'. Although ownership of the business was originally mostly non-Aboriginal, the Djabugay came to see the business as rightfully theirs. Resentment built up, and some Djabugay people argued that they were being exploited, as the theatre was 'making money from our culture'. Moreover, they argued, the use of their name meant that they were answerable to other Aboriginal groups for what was presented to the public. As Finlayson (1995: 15–16) notes, there was some hostility 'from Aboriginal quarters complaining that the dances "borrow" too heavily from other Queensland Aboriginal groups'. The representation of the songs and dances as being Djabugay left the Theatre Company, and therefore the Djabugay people, open to criticism concerning the authenticity of their performances. In particular, there were complaints about the use of the didjeridu, which Aboriginal people of the Kuranda area had not traditionally played.[17]

The popularity during the 1990s of Tjapukai Dance Theatre T-shirts and bomber jackets among young Aboriginal people in Kuranda attests to their close identification with the theatre. Given this situation, it was politic for the theatre management to allow local Aboriginal people to watch the performances for free whenever they wished. During many of the shows, therefore, there would be a group of children watching their fathers or uncles or brothers dance. Not all the Tjapukai dancers were Djabugay by descent, although some had historical connections through the Mona Mona mission and/or were related through marriage. Yet some of the children thought that because their fathers were Tjapukai dancers, they were therefore Djabugay by descent. There came a point in time when almost all Aboriginal children in Kuranda thought of themselves as Djabugay, and this caused some concern and dissent among their elders. As one woman argued, although she was not Djabugay, she had grown up at Mona Mona and her kids had grown up in Kuranda thinking they were Djabugay. She had not thought there was a problem with that, but due to social pressure she now felt obliged to tell them they were not Djabugay. Nevertheless, she felt that as her children were born in Kuranda they should be given a chance to work at the Tjapukai Dance Theatre (pers. comm. 25 January 1996). By

1996, native title claim policies and bureaucratic practices had begun to dominate everyday life, resulting in an increasingly problematic and concrete binary opposition between Djabugay and non-Djabugay in Kuranda.

Beyond the Tjapukai Theatre Stage

Tjapukai dancers with whom I talked during my fieldwork in the 1990s saw themselves as ambassadors for their people. They did not see their dancing for the Tjapukai Theatre as being just a job like any other. Rather, they saw themselves as being representatives of Djabugay people in the wider political context of their dealings with agencies of the state. Thus when the National Native Title Tribunal mediations were held in Kuranda, the government representatives and officers of the tribunal were taken to see performances by the Tjapukai dancers. In a different context – and against the wishes of the Theatre management – the Tjapukai dancers, in full costume, joined their people in protest demonstrations against the Skyrail development (Chapter 7).

Performance spilled out of the frame of the theatre and into the world at large as dance became a public practice of continuity for the Aboriginal people. Today, small groups of young people of various ages can sometimes be found roaming around Kuranda in body paint and dance costume on their way to busk in the main street (Figure 6.1). The performances are for

Figure 6.1. Young Aboriginal Buskers, Kuranda, 1999.
Photographer: Rosita Henry.

tourists, but they inscribe Aboriginal people in a very public way upon the streetscape and soundscape of the village, and they are a means of clearly marking Kuranda as an Aboriginal place. During the 1990s, being a dancer – whether with the Tjapukai Dance Theatre or as a busker in the street – seemed like the modern equivalent of the traditional young warrior fronting up for his people. To become a dancer was sought after by many young men not only because it brought economic opportunity in a context where there was otherwise almost total unemployment, but also because it became recognised among Aboriginal people as not merely a job but a status category. Kuranda Aboriginal people could often be heard to talk with possessive pride about 'our dancers', or 'our boys'.

Tjapukai Performers

The first Tjapukai dancers were members of the reggae band 'Mantaka'. They were suggested as appropriate by one of the elders because they were used to performing in public and would therefore not be too shy. This first Tjapukai dance team went through an intensive dance course taught by Aboriginal elders[18] and arranged through the Cairns College of Technical and Further Education (TAFE). This has not been the case for more recent recruits to Tjapukai. Increasingly, Aboriginal children in Kuranda began to be exposed to public dance performances and to have opportunities to learn by observing their fathers, brothers and other relations dancing. They can be observed incorporating movements into their play activities. Many have participated over the years in the Mona Mona/Mayi Wunba Dance Troupe performances at the Laura Festival. Others have had lessons at school as part of the Djabugay language program.

The first Tjapukai dancers chose particular totemic names for themselves for the show based, where possible, on anthropological records of a grandparent's totemic affiliation. Willie Brim explained that he had adopted his grandfather's totemic name, which he had discovered in Tindale's anthropological records. Similarly, the dancers had adopted the designs painted on their bodies from old photos:

> We looked back into the old Mona Mona photos, back into the archives, and actually there's records of like my grandfather, his totem, his clan and his tribe, his father and the same with all the other families who were rounded up. They were taken in and their totems were recorded. And not only that, there were early photographs of the guys; how they were painted up. So then we could pick out which family was which and say that's your design and don't stray away from it and stay as close as you can to that design because *that's you* (Willie Brim, pers. comm. 13 August 1997).

It is the fact that the names and designs come from particular named ancestors that provides the claim for authenticity of the contemporary performance. Both the actual medium of transmission and the fact that the totems and designs were rediscovered through historical traces and anthropological records collected by non-Aboriginal people is of little note to Willie; he does not see this as challenging the authenticity of the performances. The historical and anthropological records are treated merely as a means of accessing something that is already embodied and is embedded in place, enabling its revelation through the intercession of the Old People.

Today, many Djabugay people give their children Djabugay names at birth, so there is a younger generation of dancers growing up who will already have Djabugay names and who do not need to go to the historical records. These names are sometimes (but not necessarily) chosen according to what might be understood as an inherited totemic affiliation. Sometimes a name is simply given to a child because the name has a nice ring to it. A child who was not given a Djabugay name at birth may be given a name later because of a peculiar personality characteristic, or older people might choose their own names. Thus performers employed at Tjapukai today already have totemic identities. Similarly, the management does not assume a role in designing the body paint of the performers. Performers paint themselves using design elements corresponding to their own totemic names. While some performers look to the old photographs for design elements, others develop their own body decoration based on what they have observed others doing. As the then managing director of Tjapukai Don Freeman (pers. comm. 20 April 2005) put it: 'They paint themselves. They come with a name and they design their own body paint and it tends to evolve, and it depends who is in the audience how much care they take on the day. We don't monitor what they choose as their body decoration'. The dancers generally help one another to 'paint up'. While particular elements of the designs are iconic of totemic identities and may be fixed, dancers express their own creativity in how they put these elements together on their bodies.

The Tjapukai Aboriginal Cultural Park

The Tjapukai Dance Theatre closed its doors in mid 1996 and reopened as the Tjapukai Aboriginal Cultural Park in Cairns. By the time of its closing, the Theatre, located as it was in the main street of the town, had become a focal meeting place for Aboriginal people. The show was performed every day by several teams of dancers who worked in shifts for a total of seventeen performances a week. Other Aboriginal employees staffed the theatre's reception area and local Aboriginal men did backstage work such as sound and lighting. The workers would come outside and sit on the steps during their morning tea or coffee breaks, and one or two dancers would advertise the next show by sitting or standing at the door in full costume. The front of the theatre thus became a gathering place for relations and friends of the dancers and other employees (and a good place for an anthropologist to do fieldwork!). There was a sense of ownership of place that did not correspond to any actual ownership of the business or title to the theatre property. There was pride among the people as well as a sense of belonging, a greater feeling of a legitimate right to be in that part of town, so that even during their days off many of the workers would come by and 'hang out' outside the theatre. Given this situation, it is understandable that the closure of the theatre in Kuranda caused a deep sense of loss among Aboriginal people, and that its move down the range to the Cultural Park was traumatic. Andy Duffin (pers. comm. September 1996) said, as we chatted one day in the main street, 'I feel the heart has been torn out of Kuranda'.

The Tjapukai Aboriginal Cultural Park was born during a period of political unrest in Kuranda over the construction of the Kuranda Skyrail, a cableway that runs above the rainforest canopy from the foothills of the mountain range through the Barron Gorge National Park and terminates at Kuranda. There was much protest from environmentalists and from both Aboriginal and non-Aboriginal residents of the Cairns and Kuranda area against the construction of the Skyrail, a social situation that I discuss in the next chapter. Identifying themselves as rainforest people, Djabugay joined forces with environmentalists over the issue of potential damage to the rainforest and over the government grant of a private enterprise lease in the national park. They lodged a native title application over the park and engaged in direct action against Skyrail, participating in protest marches and joining a blockade. Ironically, behind the scenes negotiations were taking place between the owners of the Tjapukai Dance Theatre and Skyrail to go into partnership. The plan was to build an Aboriginal Cultural Theme Park near the Skyrail terminal at the foot of the range, a project that would mean the closure of the Tjapukai Theatre in Kuranda. This development drew the Djabugay Tribal Aboriginal Corporation into protracted negotiations with Tjapukai and Skyrail in order to achieve some equity in the venture. They argued that the Tjapukai Dance Theatre had been operating as a commercial business for eight years with their name, their land and their culture as the product. They wished for equity in the business in recognition of the value of their name and the international reputation that their performances had built up over the eight years that the theatre had been in operation in Kuranda. Although they opposed the Skyrail, Djabugay people recognised that even with environmentalist support, they were powerless to prevent its construction. Since their priorities also included jobs and a secure economic future for themselves and their children, they made an agreement under which the Djabugay would be gifted some shares in the Cultural Park and would be given the opportunity to purchase further shares at a later date. In addition, the long-term Aboriginal staff of the Tjapukai Dance Theatre negotiated a small separate shareholding.[19]

The move of the Tjapukai Dance Theatre from Kuranda and the creation of the Tjapukai Cultural Theme Park at the bottom of the range embroiled Djabugay people in a whole new set of contestations. The Yirrganydji Tribal Aboriginal Corporation had lodged a native title claim for a swathe of country along the coast from Cairns to Port Douglas that encompassed the site on which the new cultural park was to be built. Since they had an interest in the land on which the park was to be located, the Yirrganydji asserted their entitlement to be part of the project. Tension-filled, protracted negotiations between the Djabugay Tribal Aboriginal Corporation and the Yirrganydji Tribal Aboriginal Corporation eventually led to a working agreement. Although some Djabugay preferred that the Yirrganydji, as historically Djabugay speakers, should come under the general Djabugay umbrella, they were forced to recognise the Yirrganydji wish to remain autonomous. Because of the particular interest that the Yirrganydji claimed to have in the land, the Djabugay Corporation agreed to the Yirrganydji taking up 40 per cent of the opportunity to purchase shares that the Djabugay had negotiated with the original owners of the dance theatre. The Djabugay stressed, however, that the land on which the cultural park was to be built was actually common ground, and that, significantly, it had been a meeting place where people from Kuranda had come together with people from the coast for ceremonial purposes.

The Djabugay and Yirrganydji formed separate corporations to hold their respective partnership shares in the Tjapukai Cultural Theme Park: the Djabugay chose the name Buda:dji for their organisation, and the Yirrganydji chose Irukandji. It was agreed that Buda:dji would at all times own a greater partnership share than Irukandji: Buda:dji was to own 15.82 per cent and Irukandji 10.3 per cent. In addition, it was agreed that Djabugay elders would be paid an annual fee (A$20,000) 'to ensure the cultural authenticity of operations' (*Tjapukai Aboriginal Partners' Newsletter*, June 1997). The Aboriginal and Torres Strait Islander Development Corporation (CDC), which was established by the federal government to encourage Indigenous people's participation in the mainstream economy, also invested in the company (19.93 per cent) with the idea that its shares would eventually be acquired by Buda:dji and Irukandji. In addition, the CDC provided the Djabugay and Yirrganydji corporations with a loan to enable them to buy, as equal partners, the freehold title to the land for lease back to the

Tjapukai Cultural Theme Park for a fifty year term, with an option to renew for another fifty years. In 2001, the CDC was taken over by Indigenous Business Australia (IBA), an entity that was established as an independent statutory authority by the Aboriginal and Torres Strait Islander Commission Amendment Act of 2001.

From 2003–4, Tjapukai employed between eighty-five and one hundred staff members, depending on the season. Of these, 85 per cent were Aboriginal people, although not all of them identified as Djabugay. The business offered career opportunities beyond the cultural performance area. As Don Freeman commented:

> Forget the dancing; there is also food and beverage, and retail, customer service, technical [employment opportunities]. The dancers form only a third of our Aboriginal workforce. Of seventy-five, I think only twenty-four you would class as performers. We call them cultural demonstrators because it's not just dancing. I mean you are expected to talk bush food and medicine, boomerang and spear throwing lectures. I think one of the advantages of this place over the old show in Kuranda is that there are ten different things that people are expected to do (Don Freeman, pers. comm. 20 April 2005).

Tjapukai lays claim to being the largest private employer of Aboriginal people in Australia. Although some of the original performers left the company when Tjapukai moved from Kuranda, a number of the employees have worked for the company for over twenty years and now some of their children are also employees. According to Don Freeman:

> There is a new workforce, which is virtually a new generation. A fair few of the children of those original people now work here. So it is the second generation. And obviously those are kids that grew up with Tjapukai. Everybody that comes is pretty much buddied, taken through the whole thing, taught the scripts, and taught the dancing. But the big difference, of course, is that all the men that come now have grown up with this and there are very few kids in Kuranda that couldn't do the Tjapukai shows from beginning to end. The actual performance skills [as opposed to the dance movements] have to be taught. It gets taught here. We try to do rehearsal and training for an hour every day (Don Freeman, pers. comm. 20 April 2005).

In 2009, Don and Judy Freeman sold their interest in Tjapukai to Indigenous Business Australia. That same year Indigenous Business Australia

(IBA) held almost 100 per cent of the company, as it had also purchased the shares held by the Buda:dji and Irukandji Corporations and was in the process of acquiring the remaining 3.57 per cent of shares held by Ngandjin, representing the long-term Aboriginal staff of the original Tjapukai Dance Theatre. IBA has employed David Hudson as creative director and plans to renovate and refresh the cultural park – which had not been making a good profit in the past few years – with the understanding that Djabugay and Yirrkanydji corporations would be able to re-invest in the company in the future. It will be interesting to follow the fortunes of Tjapukai now that the company is owned by a government statutory authority and now that Don and Judy Freeman – who, as part of the 1970s–1980s wave of counterculture settlers in Kuranda, had developed long-term relationships with local Aboriginal people – are no longer personally involved.

Tjapukai Park Shows

The following is a description of the Tjapukai Cultural Theme Park when it was first set up in 1996. Since the transfer in ownership to IBA in 2009, there have been some minor changes and further developments are being planned.

In the foyer of the park is a museum display of material culture used traditionally by the rainforest Aboriginal peoples of North Queensland. Visitors are directed first into this space, which also features especially commissioned paintings of Dreaming stories by Kuranda Aboriginal artists Lynette Snider and Coralie Wason and a huge mural by Zane Saunders entitled 'Heart of my People'. On either side of this space, which is called 'The Magic Space', are two theatres, the Creation Theatre and the History Theatre. Depending on the timing of the shows, visitors are directed to enter one or other of these theatres after taking in the museum displays and art works (Figure 6.2).

The History Theatre

The History Theatre screens a film that documents the history of the Djabugay people within a wider context of the imperialism of the West over the world's tribal populations. The film includes old photographs and film clips from the Mona Mona mission days and scenes re-enacted by Kuranda Aboriginal people that show first contact, resistance and violent confrontation with the white settlers. For the Kuranda Aboriginal people watching the film, it is like opening a family album. Almost all men, women and children

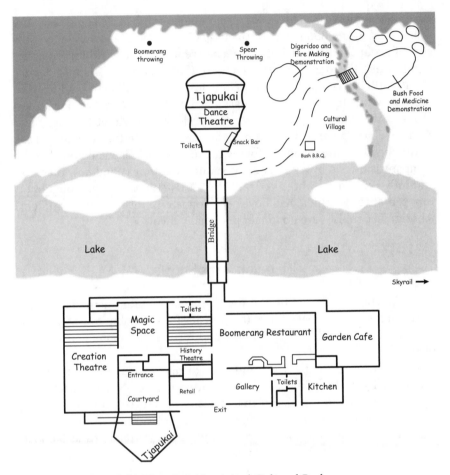

Figure 6.2. Plan of the Tjapukai Aboriginal Cultural Park.
Courtesy of Tjapukai; Redrawn by Rurik Henry.

who identified as Djabugay in 1996, as well as some who did not, took part in the filming, particularly for the last scene, a snapshot of the community gathered together as if at a family reunion.

The film is a history of invasion and colonisation that ends on a positive note of Djabugay survival and hope for the future. Many visitors come out of the theatre disturbed by the violence of the European settlers as portrayed in the film, the re-enactment of a massacre of Aboriginal people near Kuranda as passed on through oral history, and the violence of their removal and institutionalisation at the Mona Mona mission. On numerous occasions during my fieldwork, I observed members of the tourist audiences exiting the theatre in tears after watching the film. The theatre represents a defining feature of contemporary Aboriginality, a shared history of colonial violence and oppression.

The Creation Theatre

In the Creation Theatre, a number of performers enact a creation story supported by a laser display of the totemic world born out of a cassowary egg and holographic images of the totemic ancestors. The performance celebrates the continuity of the Djabugay connection to country. The show begins with the following statement in Djabugay, which is then translated into eight languages via personal headsets:

> You have come from far away to see us, to listen to the Djabugay language ... to listen to the Storywaters. Be joyful! My name is messenger ... the one with the word. Listen!

Michael Quinn scripted the creation story for the show at the request of the Djabugay shareholders in the Cultural Park. The story is presented as but one example of a universal human propensity to imagine the origins of the cosmos. First, the Djabugay creation story is placed on equal footing with other creation accounts, particularly the Upanishads, the Koran and the Bible. Then the narrative is particularised, brought back to and anchored in place in the concluding words of the messenger:

> Very near to here is Bida the pool on the Barron River where Damarri lost his leg. Yirrganydji elders were invited to ceremonies here and travelled up the river by canoe. Djabuganydji young men were given their initiation cuts and learned their responsibilities as men. Here they left their boyhood behind them and learned to follow the law and listen to the Storywaters.

Michael Quinn collated the creation story from several different sources during his over twenty years of work on the Djabugay language. These sources included oral accounts by Djabugay people as well as various written records. Among his sources, for example, was 'The Legend of Durren Dae (Dream Time)' by Douglas Seaton (1952). According to Seaton, this 'legend' was told to him by a Djabugay woman. Quinn translated Seaton's account into Djabugay with Roy Banning's help and then read it to Djabugay elder Lalfie Thomson. According to Quinn (pers. comm. December 1997), Lalfie Thompson already knew the myth and was astounded that Michael had learned it from an independent source. For Lalfie it was knowledge he had learned from his grandfather and had heard as a child around the campfire. He remembered it as a very important creation story.

After the introduction by the messenger, actors – speaking their parts in Djabugay and interacting with enormous holograms of totemic beings that represent their respective moieties, *gurabana* and *guraminya* – perform the creation story. Djabugay people consider the use of language to be an important marker of their identity. Language, dance and other performative activities are closely linked. Through the performance of language, the formalised movement of dance, demonstrations of cultural knowledge of bush food preparation and the use of traditional items of material culture, Djabugay people reach back to their roots and seek public recognition of their connection to place within a state bureaucratic discourse and native title framework that demands evidence of 'cultural continuity'.

The Dance Theatre

Behind the building housing the History and Creation Theatres and on the other side of an artificial lake lies the open air Dance Theatre. A timetable issued with the tickets directs visitors to the Cultural Park to proceed from one theatre to the next and then outside across the bridge to the Dance Theatre for a twenty-minute live dance performance. Then they are encouraged to move on to the boomerang and spear throwing demonstration spaces and the smaller stages where educational bush tucker and medicine talks and a short workshop on how to play the didgeridu are held. These various live performance spaces are interspersed with static displays of traditional camp life, fireplaces and traditional dwellings. Along the bridge is painted *buda:dji*, the rainbow serpent (a carpet snake), to guide the visitors across the water.

While the History Theatre and the museum present Djabugay identity in terms of historical evidence of past cultural practices and of colonial oppression, the Creation Theatre and the Dance Theatre celebrate Djabugay continuity as the collective memory of embodied relationship to ancestors and to country. At the Dance Theatre, one of the dancers announces to the audience that both dances 'passed on from our ancestors and dances created in their memory' are performed in that space (Figure 6.3). The performances are not just for tourists but are potentially commemorative ceremonies. I say potentially because their commemorative aspect lies dormant during the ordinary day to day performances for tourists. It is when Djabugay people are in the audience that the commemorative aspect of these performances springs to life. This was particularly evident on the first day of the Cultural Park's operation, when it was opened for the Aboriginal community. For Djabugay people this became not only a day of celebration among themselves of their identity as Djabugay, but a day of remembrance, of commemoration, in which the past was brought forth into the present to be borne forward into the future (see Casey 1987: 256).

Figure 6.3. Dancers Making Fire on Stage, Tjapukai Aboriginal Cultural Park, c. 1996.

Photographer: Rosita Henry.

Tjapukai by Night

In 2002, a night show was added to the Cultural Park program. Billed as 'Tjapukai by Night', the show includes a dinner banquet. Visitors enter via the Magic Space and are welcomed with a dramatic light show and the appearance of Djabugay ancestral spirits, including a live performer in the guise of 'Bulurru, grandfather, the rainbow serpent, the creator of all things'. Visitors are then ushered outside to join the Aboriginal performers at the 'ceremonial ground' on the banks of the artificial lake. Each person is provided with a set of clap-sticks, and then the performers teach the visitors to chant *biri* (fire) and *biri biri wayi* (rub the fire sticks together). Everyone is encouraged to sing and stamp their feet to the rhythm of the clap-sticks, moving around in a circle while the Tjapukai performers make fire by rubbing the fire-sticks together. After the fire is made, one of the performers lights the end of a spear and with the aid of a spear-thrower hurls it across to the other side of the lake where two other performers wait to launch their canoe. They paddle across in the moonlight and then lead the visitors down a fire-lit path to the restaurant. During dinner, there is a stage show that includes dances accompanied by didjeridu and clap-sticks and a short comedic skit. At one point, the lead performer draws the attention of the audience to the fact that these performances are not 'traditional', but that they are intended to celebrate the dynamic and changing nature of Aboriginal culture. The night performance is presented as pure entertainment, in contrast to the more educational message of the day shows. According to Don Freeman (pers. comm. 20 April 2005), 'This was developed mainly for the Japanese market as Japanese did not appear to be interested in the deep [educational] cultural experience of the day shows'.

There is a fascinating dialectical interplay between tradition and change that the performers clearly embrace and present in a playful way both in the night show and in the Dance Theatre during the day. The night show does not pretend to be anything other than pure entertainment, but it presents a very positive experience of interactive 'intercultural' exchange for both the audience and the performers. Members of the audience are invited to join the Tjapukai performers on stage to help make fire and to try dancing 'shake-a-leg', and after the show guests are invited to spend free time with the performers around a campfire. Here they are able to informally ask questions and perhaps learn something about the everyday lives of the performers, lives very different to what is represented on stage.[20]

Embodied Conflict: The Double-Headed Snake

Many Djabugay people have ambivalent feelings towards the Cultural Park. On the one hand they are proud of the Park. It is a vehicle for being Djabugay. It is not simply a representation of Djabugay but itself *generates* Djabugay as a very positive category of public identity. As one man told me, 'I used to think I was nothing, just a piece of dirt, but now I have pride. I'm Djabugay' (pers. comm. 16 January 1996). On the other hand, Djabugay people that I talked to in 1996 knew that they had been swept into a commercial venture in which they were shareholders but over which they had little control. For many, the experience was one of powerlessness. Over the years of its operation, there has been tension between Djabugay staff and the Cultural Park management, and on occasion employees have gone on strike over their working conditions. One dispute was taken to the Queensland Industrial Relations Commission. The Commission ruled that the thirty to thirty-five shows for which each performer was rostered weekly was "excessive", and that they should be paid 'about $30 extra a show for more than half of those' (*Cairns Post* 2 June 1998: 1). There was also concern that an agreement to give priority to the employment of Djabugay people in the park was not being honoured. Djabugay people feared that other Aboriginal people, more ready and able to perform in the style of speech and bodily demeanour that the management considered to be more attractive to tourists, would slowly and insidiously replace Djabugay employees.

Although there was a system in place that required cultural performances and presentations at the Cultural Park first to be approved by the Djabugay Aboriginal Tribal Corporation and by the elders, during the early phase of the Park's establishment there was much tension over this issue. Djabugay people sought to secure control over what was presented to the public and how it was presented. For example, it was initially planned that the Park would include a team of 'woman dancers' (Figure 6.4). However, at prac-

Figure 6.4. Women Dancers, Tjapukai Aboriginal Cultural Park, 1996.
Photographer: Rosita Henry.

tice sessions women complained that the director was trying to make them change the 'traditional dances' their elders had taught to them (during the corroboree workshops mentioned above) in order to make those dances more theatrically pleasing to a Western audience. One of the strategies that Aboriginal people use in relation to their dealings with dominating powers is to assert and insist on their right to authenticate their own cultural performances. The women's issue with the director was an example of this strategy. This use of the concept of 'tradition' as a discursive weapon of resistance, however, draws the resisters into complicity with dominating strategies of power by reinforcing the notion of a given, unchanging and factually discoverable past, one that may serve, in effect, to undermine contemporary Aboriginal claims.

The women's dance performances were eventually cancelled. According to the managing director, Don Freeman, this was mainly for economic reasons:

> The nature of the women's dance was that it happened separate to the men's dance, at least the stuff we were given, and required maintaining two separate and complete dance companies, and the business could not support it. It just didn't generate the cash flow necessary. Beyond that, it tended to drag domestic issues into the business in a much greater way, with kids and domestic disputes and family disputes. But all of that we could have dealt with. Primarily it was the economics of having to support additional performers, who in the end didn't generate any additional revenue (Don Freeman, pers. comm. 20 April 2005).

Tjapukai nevertheless employs Aboriginal women in other areas, and there are some Djabugay women who perform regularly in the Creation Theatre and who have for many years demonstrated the use of bush foods and medicines.

Story Place

The fact that the theatre was moved from Kuranda, where Djabugay people feel secure in terms of their rights to place, created a situation of fear and uncertainty. Stories began to circulate that the land on which the Cultural Park is built was a burial ground rather than a corroboree ground. Further signs of disquiet were expressed in stories about encounters a number of different people had with black snakes at the Park. When one of the woman dancers became ill, it was said that her dancing at the Park caused her sickness. She explained her experiences to me and I later recorded them in my field notes (16 July 1998) as follows:

From the first time she began to work in the Creation Theatre she was extremely frightened. It was dark in the theatre and she could always feel a presence standing behind her when she was in there. She thought it was probably a spirit being or one of the ancestor beings. She would always try to swap her shift with another woman when her turn came to work in the Creation Theatre. One day she noticed a group of Aboriginal people sitting under a tree on the edge of the rainforest. She said that she thought they were the 'Old People'. She explained that they were Aboriginal people who had evaded the round up and removal to missions and reserves and continued to live 'in their wild state' in the rainforest. She thought they had been attracted by the music and dancing and had come to watch. She said she was not the only one of the dancers who had seen these people. She had also seen black snakes on numerous occasions during the middle of the day. This she, and the others, thought was a warning sign about the dangers of the place. Eventually she became sick. She knew it was not the kind of sickness a medical doctor could cure so she consulted an Aboriginal healer. She regularly consults such healers. Her usual healer was not available so she was driven all the way to Cooktown to see another healer, who cured her. He took 'a stone' from her chest. It was 'the head of a double headed snake with terrible eyes'. The healer told her that working at the Tjapukai Park caused her sickness. He told her it was a 'story place' and that the dancing was causing the ancestors to reveal themselves. He told her that this was also why the dancers were fighting among themselves and that she should warn the others. She stopped working at the cultural park and warned the other dancers to do the same.

It is a widespread belief among Djabugay people and other Aboriginal rainforest groups that there are Aboriginal people who hide in the rainforest and continue to live there according to 'the old ways', and there are many stories of sightings of these people. Some people claim that they are living descendants of Aboriginal people who managed to escape the round-ups that led to missionisation and who cunningly continue to evade the white man. Others say that these 'Old People' are ancestors who occasionally make themselves visibly present to the current generation. In other words, they represent what Sansom (2001) has referred to as 'irruptions of the Dreaming'. One woman told me that she had decided to attend Djabugay language classes because she wanted to be able to communicate with these 'wild' Aboriginal people if she ever came across any of them. Sightings of the Old People who still live free in the rainforest mark the Aboriginal identity of places in a social situation where such an identity continues to be disputed. There were many such sightings at the Tjapukai Cultural Park during its establishment phase. As revealed in the experiences of the woman dancer recounted above, in her illness and through her healing, she became as one with place. Her experiences are an expression of the corporeal basis of her connection to place. Through her lived body, she animated and empowered the place with memories of the ancestors and of a lifeworld that continues to be lived by the Old People. As Marcia Langton (2002: 260) writes in her account of *Bama* philosophy: 'The dead reside in, and are coterminous with, particular places. It is the perceived existence of the spirits of the deceased ancestors in places that enlivens these places as powerfully effective'.

The spatial layout of the Park with its double-headed theatre complex resonates with the particular healing experience of the woman involving the removal of a double-headed snake from her body (see Figure 6.2). However, I shall not attempt to draw such symbolic connections here. My purpose is simply to emphasise the negative impact on Kuranda Aboriginal people of the move of the Tjapukai Dance Theatre from the main street of Kuranda. Experiences – such as the woman's described above – and the stories that circulate about such experiences express in culturally specific terms what it means to be in place and the serious discomfort that Aboriginal people feel upon being forced to move out of place. The woman's illness is also an example of the way in which social conflict becomes embodied. In the context of the Tjapukai Aboriginal Cultural Park, conflict had erupted between Djabugay people and the park management, for example, regarding wages paid to the performers and control over authentication of the performances. The Tjapukai Aboriginal Cultural Park became a site for conflict among the performers themselves and – at another level – a focus of tensions between Djabugay and Yirrganydji and of both these groups against the state.

Animating the Present with the Past

Opportunities for public performances such as the ones found at Tjapukai provide a means for Aboriginal people, whose everyday lives are oppressively over-determined by bureaucratic processes and the categorical relations arising out of such processes – to explore different possibilities of being. As Kapferer (1995a: 78) has argued in his analysis of the Tjapukai Dance Theatre phenomenon, 'It is in the play space of tourist practices that Aborigines are able to engage with dominating ideologies and to work new definitions of their situation'. Tjapukai is a site that allows Aboriginal people to play a part in redefining themselves through performance by making themselves visible on the national and international scenes.[21] When introducing the finale song at the cultural park, 'Proud to be Aborigine', one of the dancers announces to the audience:

This is an opportunity to showcase our culture and show we are not a curiosity but a relevant and integral part of twenty-first century Australia. We represent a new spirit of freedom. Freedom from dependence on government handouts. Freedom from a century of oppression and the cycle of poverty.

Yet this opportunity to achieve 'freedom' by 'showcasing' culture arises out of – and is structured and limited by – the political and economic constraints of the bureaucratic state and of private enterprise, as well as the demands of audiences who seek the experience of cultural 'otherness' and exotic primitive worlds.

Djabugay performances of dance, music and language respond to a bureaucratic order and a global demand for cultural alterity that constitutes identities in terms of the authenticity of their historical continuity. Yet Djabugay people themselves seek to demonstrate their authenticity by being able to trace *continuity* via a process of direct transmission of knowledge from their elders. Such a concept of transmission, however, raises the spectre of discontinuity due to colonisation and missionisation. Aboriginal people are thus forced to face a cultural lacuna that they have to fill in order to achieve recognition. They do this in apparent complicity with the dominant discourse by adopting concepts of culture and heritage and notions of a fixed tradition passed down either via material evidence collected and recorded by researchers or via narrative knowledge acquired directly from their elders. However, public performances also challenge this dominant notion of cultural transmission by positing the possibility of a mode of transmission through body memory, 'an unmediated access to the remembered past' where 'no mediation by mind and its machinations is called for' (Casey 1987: 178).

Music and dance performances are expressions of historical consciousness, a 'means by which Aboriginal people store and organise their pasts and their futures' (Beckett 1994: 99). Public performance provides an avenue for Indigenous peoples to deal creatively with histories of dispossession and to make sense of their futures. Such performance should not be scorned as a 'sell out' to the demands of tourist audiences eager to consume images of alterity. Nor should they be dismissed as the mere expression of cultural identity or of the traditionalist revival of a past long dead. In the context of public dance and other performances, Aboriginal people retrieve 'tradition' so as to put it to work to make sense of 'history' and to negotiate their way through state projects and structures of power within Australia and in relation to global political and economic networks. At the same time, they 'rediscover' tradition in contemporary innovation. Participation in the Tjapukai Aboriginal Cultural Park is an opportunity to evidence cultural vitality by publicly performing embodied knowledge. The performances are not only about continuing the links with ancestors and the past, but they are also a means of creating connections in the present. Performance in this context allows Aboriginal people not only to be the custodians of the past but also to be agents of change. As Mary Douglas (1995: 23) wrote: 'Time past is remembered, privately or publicly, when it can be used in time present to control the future'. Dance performances in particular are a tantalising opportunity to challenge a paradigm that assumes that remembering is merely a matter of cognitive recollection. Through the celebration of body memory and the embodied possession of cultural knowledge, Aboriginal people animate place. By moving into performance, they enable the past to reveal itself in the present so as to reach out to the future.

Notes

1. Portions of this chapter have been previously published in Henry (2000) and have been reworked here courtesy of *The Australian Journal of Anthropology*.
2. Aboriginal people in Kuranda have deliberately adopted the spelling 'Djabugay', partly to distinguish themselves as a people from the commercial venture of the Tjapukai Dance Theatre. The voicing of consonants is not significant in most Australian languages (i.e. there is no distinction between /d/ and /t/, /b/ and /p/, /g/ and /k/, and /dj/ and /tj/. Thus, the name Djabugay appears variously in the literature as Tjapukai, Tya:pukay, Tjabogai, Tchupaki, and so on. An early record of the name Djabugay appears in Meston's report (Queensland, Parliament 1896: 10) as 'Chabbuki'. Meston lists the 'Chabbuki' at Port Douglas on his list of 'Tribes Interviewed', and he notes:

   > The old Port Douglas tribe and a few of the Mowbray River blacks are camped a short distance along the beach from Port Douglas. Some of the men and women come daily into town and work for people who treat them fairly and feed them well. Their old hunting and fishing sources of food are also available, being very little affected by the small and scattered suburban settlement. On my return from the Daintree overland I met two of the Port Douglas tribe ('Chabbuki'), took two of the men to town, and gave them a bag of flour to take back to the camp.

   This camp remained in existence until the late 1930s, when the police removed the community to the Mona Mona mission. According to oral accounts recorded by Wood (1990), the population comprised predominantly Djabugay speaking peoples (Yirrganydji and Djabuganydji) and was located on the dunes of Four Mile Beach in a place that is 'probably now covered by the golf course of the Sheraton Mirage resort' (Wood 1990: 8).
3. McConnel (1939-40:67) refers to 'Tya.bogai-tyandyi' as a tribal name and 'Nyakali' as the name of a 'branch' or sub-group of the tribe. 'Bulwandyi' and 'Yirkandyi' are recorded as different tribes, 'on the south side' and 'low down' on the Barron River respectively.

4. Which he also variously spelt 'Tjapukai', 'Tjapukandji', 'Tja:pukanja', 'Tjabogai-tjandji', and 'Tjabogaijanji' (Tindale 1938–39, 1974, 1976).
5. Tindale, focusing on the ecological factors that affected tribal boundaries, writes:

> The northeastern boundary of the Tjapukai is clearly evident from the coast as lying at the top of the steep coast-facing scarp of the Macalister Range … The narrow coastal strip from Mowbray River south is Irukandji territory … At Red Cliff the Irukandji territory was reduced to a lowland of little more than a kilometre in width, although to the north and to the south it was much wider. Southward it extended to the estuary of the Barron River at Cairns, but only in the coastal strip.
>
> Inland the Barron River with its once dense rainforests was the coastal limit of the Buluwai, whose territory extended up on to the rough parts of the range in a south westerly direction, to Tinaroo on the Atherton Plateau. West of the area of Kuranda it was the change from rainforest to wet sclerophyll with some open patches of savanna and rainforest, sometimes much altered by burning, which marked the changeover to Tjapukai territory … The western boundary of the Tjapukai lay along the Barron river on the Atherton Plateau, the territory narrowing southward as the more rugged rainforested mountainous parts expanded towards Tolga. The Buluwai southern boundary lay at upland plateau from there south to beyond Malanda (Tindale 1976: 21).

6. The debate by ethnographers of Aboriginal Australia on this topic is detailed and complex. A review of the substantial literature the debate has generated is beyond the scope of this book. However, see Sutton (1995).
7. Hale (1976: 236) also notes Njakali /nyakali/ as an alternative name for Djabugay. Dixon's use of the colon in 'Dja:bugay' accords with the principles of the International Phonetic Association and indicates that the sound represented by the preceding letter is long. However, according to Patz (1991: 246), the 'a' in the first syllable is in fact short when compared with other vowels in the language that have a phonologically contrastive length.
8. For maps locating tribal and linguistic boundaries see Duffin and Brim n.d.; McConnel 1939–40; and Tindale 1974; Dixon 1977; Patz 1978 and Bottoms 1999.
9. The funding was sought through various government programs such as the Commonwealth government's National Aboriginal Language Program and the Wet Tropics Management Authority Community Support Program.
10. For example, at the Laura Aboriginal Dance and Cultural Festival.
11. Prior to this, the first regional festival to be held in Cape York was sponsored by the Aboriginal Theatre Foundation in 1972 and hosted by Aboriginal people from Lockhart River, Cape York. The festival was conceived and organised as a means of fostering 'cultural revival' among Cape York peoples. The success of the 1972–73 Lockhart Festival led to a repeat performance in 1974. The festivals enabled new relations to be forged among Indigenous peoples of Cape York. The Lockhart River Festival spawned the idea for an annual Cape York Festival to be hosted by a different community each year and to be supported

by state government funding through what was then called the Department of Community Services.

12. It is significant that the first festival was held just prior to the 1983 state elections and that Mr Killoran stood for election.

13. Enid Boyle's remarks were delivered at a Cultural Awareness Workshop organised by environmentalists during the anti-Skyrail protests on 3 July 1994; see Chapter 7.

14. See, for example, Justice Olney's decision in *The Members of the Yorta Yorta Aboriginal community v. the State of Victoria* (1998).

15. Other awards include: Queensland Small Business Award (1990), Queensland Tourism Awards (1990, 1992, 1993, 1994, 1997, 1998, 1999, 2000, 2002), Australian Tourism Awards (1992, 1993, 1994, 1995, 1998, 1999, 2000), Documentary film award for creative excellence at the 24th Annual US Film and Video Show (1991), Outstanding Contribution Award from Inbound Tourism Operators Association (1992) and the ATEC Awards (2001, 2004). They were also voted the best attraction in Australia by members of the inbound tourism industry.

16. Tours were made in 1991 to the USA, 1992 to Korea, Japan, and Singapore, 1993 to the USA, Austria, Canada, and the World Expo in Korea, 1994 to perform at the Commonwealth Games in Canada, 1995 to Japan, 1996 to Canada and the USA, 1997 to New Zealand, 1998 to Singapore and Guam, 1999 to Japan and the USA, 2003 to Taiwan and 2004 to Singapore.

17. According to Lance Riley (pers. comm. 17 February 1997), a young 'whitefella' first accompanied his boys on the didjeridu in 1986 while they were practicing for the Laura Festival, and he taught one of Lance's boys how to play.

18. These elders included Lyn Hobbler, Selwyn Hunter, Lalfie Thompson, and Dan Coleman.

19. Full details of the negotiations and agreement are discussed in Holden and Duffin (1998).

20. Of the five performers in a show I attended, only one was not from Kuranda. As we chatted around the campfire, he discovered that I was an anthropologist, told me his father was Djirbal and asked whether I knew of the work of the linguist Bob Dixon. He wanted to get hold of Dixon's work because working at Tjapukai had made him interested in learning more about the Djirbal people and language.

21. For example, the Djabugay name was again in the national and international media in 2002. On 2 March, during a visit by the Queen and Prince Philip, the prince, after being informed of the names of the two tribes in the Tjapukai Park, said 'Djabugay, Yirrganydji, what's all that about? Do you still throw spears at each other?' The remark caused a furore among Aboriginal leaders (see *The Telegraph* 2 March 2002 http://www.telegraph.co.uk/news/worldnews/australiaandthepacific/australia/1386542/Do-you-still-throw-spears-at-each-other-asks-Prince.html, accessed 17 June 2012).

Chapter 7

Protesting Place

Environmentalists, Aboriginal People and the Skyrail

> Trees, trees! Yes, yes! That is actually the binding of all of us,
> interest in keeping nature.
>
> —Uli Seidel, 22 April 1994

Between 1993 and 1995, a tourist development project – a passenger cable car through the mountain range from Cairns to Kuranda – became a hot political issue. As with the markets, the main street, the amphitheatre and Tjapukai, the development generated intense social dramas in the town. The responses of the local community to the construction of this cable car that passed through the Barron Gorge National Park and the newly listed Wet Tropics World Heritage Area were varied, but quickly became polarised. The cable car development, which was officially opened on 1 September 1995 under the name of 'Skyrail', became a heated topic of debate in both the private and public domains (see Figure 7.1). It began in the homes of local residents and in cafes, bars and other public meeting places, and it eventually spilled out into the streets and into the rainforest itself.

A good deal of anthropological and other writing has been produced on the relationship between Indigenous peoples, environmentalists and developers. For example, in Australia Maddock (1987a, 1987b), Brunton (1991), Merlan (1991) and Jacobs (1993) have all analysed the relationship between Indigenous and non-Indigenous interests specifically in relation to the mining of Coronation Hill in the Northern Territory, while Trigger (1996, 1997, 1999) has written more generally on the competing ideologies espoused by environmentalists, Indigenous peoples and the mining industry. On another front, Langton (2003) has discussed the complex issues that relate to environmentalist attitudes about the sustainable use of biodiversity in Indigenous homelands, Anderson (1989) has examined the relationship between the Kuku Yalanji people and the conservation movement in relation to the Daintree-Bloomfield road in North Queensland, and Weiner (1995a, 1995b), Brunton (1996), Fergie (1996) and Bell (1998), among numerous others, have discussed and debated the traumatic complexities of the

Figure 7.1. Skyrail from a Kuranda Street, c. 1996.
Photographer: Rosita Henry.

dispute that arose in response to the construction of the Hindmarsh Island bridge in South Australia.

This chapter is a contribution to this body of literature in the sense that I explore Indigenous and non-Indigenous responses to yet another development project: the Skyrail.[1] I argue that such disputes must not be read as simple binary contestations of values, worldviews, ideologies or primordial loyalties. Nor should they be interpreted as merely a struggle between two opposed social groups: the powerful against the powerless, Indigenous against non-Indigenous, greenie against developer, and so on. I attempt to escape the categorical imperatives that otherwise constrain interpretation by focusing my discussion on the discursive *fields*, practices and performances that *produce* such categories in the first place. I develop my argument by highlighting a particular moment of protest within the Skyrail dispute. Such moments, I suggest, are crucial to the understanding of how identity categories are made. Identities are not an expression of inherent properties of individuals or of groups, but are the result of social and cultural practices, and they are produced and articulated through performance.

Identities are not merely the result of selecting at will from a given collection of traits. Rather, they are structurally and historically produced; they are constituted, negotiated, tested and contested through social practice, through performative action and through various modes of representation.[2] The Kuranda Skyrail protest situation I describe below is such a productive moment of strategic action and resistance. The protest actions of the participants must be understood as *situated* practices rather than simply as cultural representations that are remote from the political and economic regimes that spawned them. As Peters points out:

> The improvisation of identity is wonderful if you have the cultural and finance capital to cushion you against the traumas of post-modernity, but most of the human species still lives out its days in localized spaces, dependent in various ways on the people they have known for years. The means of making one's identity a poetic work are inequitably distributed . . . We should neither drain the concept of culture of its ties to place and matter nor freeze it into absolute identity (Peters 1997: 91).

The conflict situation that arose in relation to the Skyrail development provides a revealing case study on how the various global discourses that concern environmentalism become entangled in practices of place and come to assume particular local signatures (see Figure 7.2).

Figure 7.2. Skyrail Protest, 1994.
Photographer: Rosita Henry.

Protesting Skyrail

The Queensland government gave approval in principle for the construction of the cableway in June 1988. Local residents immediately began to gather forces against the development, but their protest activities were put on hold in December 1988 when the area through which the proposed cableway was to be constructed was successfully listed as World Heritage. The Queensland National Party Government took out a High Court action against the listing, but in December 1989 the newly elected Labor Party Government withdrew the action and deferred decision on the cableway until a Wet Tropics World Heritage management regime could be established.[3]

In 1993, in anticipation of state government approval for the construction of Skyrail, a group of concerned people from Cairns and Kuranda met and formed an anti-Skyrail action group, which they named PAKS (People against Kuranda Skyrail). This group included not just environmentalists but also other local residents who were worried about the effects of the Skyrail on their place-world. It included representatives from the Djabugay Tribal Aboriginal Corporation, the Wilderness Society, and the Cairns and Far North Environment Centre (CAFNEC). The group began to distribute newsletters to keep people informed about the progress of its campaign. In response, some locals put out their own newsletter to undermine the PAKS cause. They called themselves PAPAKS (People against People against Kuranda Skyrail). Their first newsletter began in the following vein:

> Our mandate is to oppose the Greenie, Leftie, Pinko, Dole-bludger, Hippie, Feral, Artie Fartie, Mabo Do-gooder minority factions that will stop anything just for the sake of stopping it ... PAPAKS are real world people who don't scoot around the rainforest lustfully hugging trees, but in fact hate and detest trees – just look at what the rotten, stinking trees did to Sydney recently – trees are killers!

The People against Kuranda Skyrail (PAKS) meetings throughout 1994 were regularly attended by a significant number of Aboriginal people. I say significant because it is rare to find Aboriginal people in Kuranda in attendance at meetings that are driven by members of the wider community. Of a total of seventy-six people listed individually by name on the mailing and work group list of PAKS, eleven are Aboriginal, and newsletters were sent out on request to the Aboriginal settlements at Mantaka, Kowrowa and Mona Mona.

The formation of PAKS meant that Aboriginal people who were against the Skyrail could access allies in the settler community. However, PAKS organisers were as keen to harness the support of Djabugay people against the Skyrail as Djabugay people were to use PAKS. As Rhonda Duffin (pers. comm. 10 November 1995) commented, 'They [PAKS] needed our support as well, so I think it worked both ways; they came in asking for our support you know really, and we helped them. So we helped each other'.

A cultural awareness workshop was arranged in Kuranda to promote goodwill and understanding between Indigenous and non-Indigenous protesters. A trained facilitator from one of the environmentalist groups organised the workshop at which a Djabugay elder talked about her family's removal from the Kuranda area to the Mona Mona mission in 1916. She described her life growing up on the mission and the significance of the rainforest to her people. The workshop facilitator also arranged a visit by women protesters to the old Mona Mona mission site and a partnership system was established there between Aboriginal and non-Aboriginal women so that they could support each other in their combined campaign against Skyrail.

Direct Action: Spatial Practices of Protest

PAKS members were not united on the form their protest against Skyrail should take. Many thought that PAKS should confine itself to attempts at raising public awareness through media coverage, public displays, peaceful marches and letters, petitions, and submissions to the state and federal governments. Others thought that this was not enough and that direct action – such as blockades at the various Skyrail tower construction sites – would be required. To this end, some members undertook 'non-violent direct action' training, and a separate group, the Barron Gorge Wildlife Action Group, was formed. Members of this group remained part of PAKS, but also engaged in independent activities to physically obstruct the construction of the cableway. Direct action included erecting a bamboo platform at one of the tower sites to stop the construction company's helicopter from moving equipment from the site, dressing up as endangered rainforest species, and building a set and performing a skit inside the offices of the Department of Environment and Heritage in Cairns. Protesters also blockaded various Skyrail tower construction sites to prevent loggers from felling the trees. Some individuals and groups glued their hands together around trees, while others did 'tree-sits' that involved volunteers climbing and sitting for days on end high up particular trees that had been marked for logging. A ground crew supported the tree sitters by providing them with food and other requirements and disposing of their waste matter in buckets lowered by rope. One protester lasted 208 days in a tree before police posed as a television crew and tricked him into allowing them to climb up to his platform. The police used a block and pulley system to remove him and the tree was immediately felled (*Cairns Post* 11 January 1995: 1).

Aboriginal people of the Kuranda area also engaged in direct action against the Skyrail. Dancers from the Tjapukai Dance Theatre joined the protest demonstrations in full dance regalia, armed with didjeridus and clap-sticks. Others painted placards and joined the street marches that PAKS organised. One of the environmentalists in PAKS had this to say about the Aboriginal involvement:

> I remember that first big Cairns protest that we had where we were hoping we'd just get twenty people and, I think, we ended up with about 150. It just happened that way. What was absolutely beautiful was the Djabugay. They wanted to march in front, and that was brilliant. And they brought some signs that, you know, ours were white with red printing and writing, whereas the Djabugay had these ones that were just, artistically it was beautiful. They had Aboriginal paintings on them, and Aboriginal colours. For some strange reason, even their slogans were spot on. They were absolutely perfect (John Netz, pers. comm. 14 April 1995).

Aboriginal people also demonstrated at the tower sites and supported the tree-sitters by bringing them food. Some youths even took a turn tree sitting. Nevertheless, their views on the Skyrail were as divided as the views of the general population. Some Aboriginal people in Kuranda saw the development as an avenue for employment. In fact, as early as May 1992 the Chairperson of the Mona Mona Aboriginal Corporation had written to the developer asking for a meeting to discuss how a proposed new agency, the Djabugay Ranger Land Management, Conservation and Protection Agency, could assist Skyrail Pty Ltd (White 1995: 22–3).

Differences in response to the Skyrail corresponded to the already entrenched patterns of conflict among various factions in the Kuranda community regarding environmental values and the impact of economic development. However, the responses to the Skyrail cannot be adequately explained in terms of simple oppositions of values or categorical identities. Political manoeuvring regarding the Skyrail provided a forum for people's attempts to either undermine or to reinforce the hegemony of given identity categories. To illustrate this more clearly, I will describe a three-minute scene that one of the protesters captured on video during an anti-Skyrail protest at one of the Skyrail tower sites. There were no media personnel at the site, only the protesters, the police and the Skyrail logging contractors. In the video clip, one of the Aboriginal women points out that this is not a performance for the media and that they are not just putting on a show:

'We don't need no media. There's no media here. Our protest is from our heart and our heart is here'.

A Moment in the Performance of Protest

The protesters are mainly women and children, both Aboriginal and non-Aboriginal. They have seated themselves within the boundaries of a site to be cleared in the rainforest for one of the Skyrail towers. Non-Aboriginal women and children circle a number of trees, hands joined with super-glue. The police lead the Aboriginal protesters off the site, which is cordoned off with yellow tape. The Aboriginal protesters then stand outside the tape barrier protesting verbally as the police physically remove – in some cases even carry and drag – the non-Aboriginal protesters from the site. Some of the young girls are crying. It is apparent that at least one of them is in pain as they nurse hands that they had glued together and that police had torn apart. The protesters then stand together outside the barrier while the police protect the site so as to enable the loggers to fell the trees. The sound of chainsaws almost drowns out their voices as the protesters shout out to the police and the loggers.

In this short scene, this performative moment, place is made and community defined. We see and hear Aboriginal protesters asserting difference from non-Aboriginal Australians by calling on the police and the loggers to recognise the historical specificity of their experiences:

> The Government wants us to shut up. We're like a herd of cattle. They herd us here and there on missions ... Learn your history. We're the ones that suffered, not you. You don't even know our history.

However, we also hear them asserting their identity with other Australians: 'We're Australians. We're all Australians here'. We see and hear them defining community in the face of the state hegemonic power that the police and the loggers represent. An Aboriginal woman calls out to a distressed young protester by name and puts her arm around her to comfort her. Then she addresses her audience of police, loggers and other protesters:

> That's how much we know our locals in Kuranda. We're on first name basis. We mix. This is what you call caring. I'm loving up a white girl. We care for one another. We're here for one another. We're not here for ourselves.

This protest scene is indeed an articulatory moment, a moment in which place and identity are co-constituted. This performative engagement challenges and resists, while at the same time reproduces, the entrenched binary oppositions of dominant 'games of truth' (Foucault 1988b: 16).

A 'Game of Truth'

The initial task that PAKS set itself was a 'fact-finding' one. In February 1994, volunteers were called on to survey the Skyrail tower sites and count trees within thirty metres from each tower site. This is an indication of the form of discourse taken by the debate, much of which was waged in terms of disputed 'facts'. How much rainforest would actually be destroyed? Was it a fact that the total area to be cleared during the construction of the Skyrail would only be about half a hectare, as was claimed by members of the pro-Skyrail lobby group, or would the construction in fact necessarily entail swathe clearing? What, in fact, were the rainforest plant and animal species that the Skyrail would adversely affect? Was it a fact that the Skyrail would lead to fewer buses travelling up and down the range, thus relieving Kuranda of some of the pollution and congestion caused by their parking in the village? Was it a fact that the Skyrail would actually result in greater protection of the rainforest by replacing the more damaging walking tracks, or would it in fact simply supplement the already existing tracks and spawn the creation of new ones? Were there in fact Aboriginal sites of significance in the path of the Skyrail? In sum, the debate was waged in positivist terms: people debated about what was true or false according to what were perceived as objectively provable facts, and they called for environmental and social impact studies to be done to establish the truth or falsity of the factual claims being made. The terms of the dispute illustrate a major theme that Castells (1997: 123) identifies as being present in the global environmental movement: 'an ambiguous, deep connection with science and technology'.

Again and again the pro-Skyrail lobby attempted to make the anti-Skyrail protesters look foolish by demonstrating that they had their facts wrong. An article in the *Cairns Post* by freelance journalist Michael Sourial (1994: 8) entitled 'Protesters, credible or farcical?' expresses this discourse of the literal-minded well. Sourial argues that the actions of the protesters are farcical, and he uses a particular action by an individual protester to support his case. This action involved one of the protesters super-gluing her hands together around a tree at one of the tower sites. Sourial writes:

> The 'super-glue' incident was one of the true low points for this protest which has been marked by embarrassment. The protesters now, incidentally, deny that the young lady in question glued herself to the wrong tree, so let me clear up the doubt once and for all. I was there that day at Tower

Site 5 and that protester definitely glued her arms around a tree which was neither slated to be cut, nor in the way of any of the work being done. She may as well have glued herself around a tree in Botswana for all the trouble she caused (Sourial 1994: 8).

Yet the authenticity of human action is not simply a matter factual accuracy. What Keith and Pile wrote about the declaration of 'nuclear-free zones' applies, I argue, equally to the anti-Skyrail case:

> Assessed in the spirit of literalism, such designations were always manifestly absurd – given the failure of the contemporary nuclear device to respect borders ... So how should a nuclear-free zone be judged? As true or false? As real or metaphorical? As authentic or unauthentic? As true as a burning breast or as false as a bleeding heart? (Keith and Pile 1993: 10)

The environmentalist in question admitted to me that she did indeed intend to prevent that particular tree from being destroyed. As Castells (1997: 123) notes, 'Environmentalism is a science-based movement'. In the case of the Skyrail, both the pro-Skyrailers and the anti-Skyrailers were enmeshed in this 'game of truth', which required them to legitimise their positions by resorting to what Lyotard (1984: 28), following Wittgenstein, called 'the language game of science'.

The Djabugay protesters too were swept into this game in order to legitimate their native title claim. They had responded independently of PAKS by lodging a claim with the National Native Title Tribunal for Barron Gorge National Park. The Djabugay Tribal Aboriginal Council[4] (DTAC) had written already in October 1991 to the state minister for environment and heritage and the regional director of the Department of Environment and Heritage, among others, asserting that the Djabugay are traditional owners of the area and that the 'Barron Gorge is part of Djabugay spiritual heritage which should not be desecrated and spoiled' (White 1995: 15). However, the Department considered the developers to have discharged their responsibilities and obligations under the relevant cultural heritage legislation, the Cultural Record (Landscapes Queensland and Queensland Estate) Act of 1987, and the Skyrail was permitted to go ahead.

A cultural heritage survey prepared for Skyrail under the legislation concluded that there were no sites of cultural significance along the Skyrail route. Many Djabugay people were outraged by this report. They considered that it effectively 'denied them recognition of the continuity of their relationship with the country which the Skyrail traversed, and therefore their contemporary identity as traditional owners of this area' (Greer and Henry 1996: 20). However, DTAC's response to this denial expresses the hegemony of the scientific paradigm: the chairperson of DTAC sent a letter to various government ministers and department directors questioning the 'professionalism and qualifications' of the consultant and noting that he was not a qualified archaeologist (White 1995: 53).

In particular, the dispute focused on a number of scarred trees and stone arrangements. Although younger Djabugay people had been previously unaware of their existence, they did not doubt that these were Djabugay sites and said that if they had to produce tangible evidence of their heritage – particularly for the purpose of establishing native title – then here it was. As Rhonda Duffin put it:

> Then came the time to go and visit the sites ... I had only studied these things. The actual experience now to see it first hand ... that was what gave me the drive. We had to protect that. Just the feeling; and I still get that feeling that has more or less kept me going all this time ... It was just another thing to reinforce it, that it is really true. I could actually say it was *true*, it was *real* (Rhonda Duffin, pers. comm 10 November 1995).

Nevertheless Djabugay people, in the hope that the archaeologists would provide the scientific proof to establish the significance of the sites (and therefore the overall significance of the Barron Gorge National Park), requested four separate archaeological opinions.

Again the debate was a positivist one waged in terms of scientifically provable fact. Were the scarred trees in fact Aboriginal shield or burial trees? Were the rings of stones in fact Aboriginal sites, or were they made by more recent visits to the area by bushwalkers or timber cutters, or were they just old 'hippy' camps, as the pro-Skyrail lobby group suggested? Since the Aboriginal identity of the sites could not be established archaeologically, Djabugay people decided to enlist the help of the Federal Government by turning to the Aboriginal and Torres Strait Islander Heritage Protection Act of 1984. A reporter, Mr George Menham, was appointed in accordance with section 10(4) of the act to prepare a report to the minister for Aboriginal and Torres Strait Islander affairs for his consideration. Djabugay attempted to resist site-based definitions of heritage by articulating their claims to the reporter in terms of a concept of 'cultural landscape'. The following explanation by a Djabugay Ranger about what he told the reporter is an example of the kind of knowledge of a wider living landscape Djabugay people used to try to escape demands of the discourse of science and to evidence the significance to them of the national park and of places along the Skyrail route:

> I told him also of how Damarri is now sleeping. I told him if he goes back in to the Cairns area, from Machans Beach turn off, Holloways, all

of them, Yorkeys Knob, and you're looking backwards and forwards and you look at the skyline, just of the mountains, you can see Damarri lying down. I told of ... how the water fairy came about, and how they used to climb up one side of the mountain of Red Peak and go down the other side where now they are building Skyrail – where the Yirrigandyi could be, and the Djabugandji all camped below, once, when the Barron used to run that way. I told him of the camp there. Also the one in Woompera farm (Warrama) there, the camp there. Go back from Warrama, around the lookout; come into Mount Saddleback; from there along McAlaister Range (my area); walk back into Mona Mona; all that run. My grandma, being associated with that Red Peak and that place – travel along that ridge back into Mona Mona, and then back to Oak Forest. That's Guraminya side, you know. There's two sides. One Guruminya and one Gurubana.[5]

By phrasing their claims in terms of narrative knowledge and in terms of a landscape-based cosmology as opposed to a site-based one, Djabugay were claiming that the 'particular significance'[6] to them of places along the Skyrail route was based on a continuing process of being in relationship with those places. The 'particular significance' of a place for them is not so much that it acts as a fixed marker of given events in the past, but that it is a container for memories in the present.

I suggest that by their use of the concept of cultural landscape, the Djabugay meant landscape *as* memory, landscape as a lived memory-producing experience and as a product of the process of remembering 'which is forever being transformed' (Küchler 1993: 104). Barbara Bender (1993: 1) notes that landscapes are not given but 'are created by people through their experience and engagement with the world around them'. According to Morphy (1995: 204), in Arnhem Land people learn about their landscapes through the 'experiences and associations of their lives', by travelling through the land and by events such as birth, marriage and death. It is the lived experience of these events that creates the particular moments in which the landscape of the Yolngu is made visible. Djabugay landscapes can also be understood in such terms. Places are hidden unless events allow them to be revealed. In the contemporary context, such events include political moments like the Skyrail dispute. The authenticity of Djabugay claims to country was questioned within a language game of science that required the archaeological identity of particular sites to be established. However, cultural authenticity cannot be proved scientifically. Authenticity, I argue, can only be established outside of this game of truth by the contemporary practices of remembering that make the Aboriginal continuity of the landscape present to Aboriginal people themselves. As Rhonda Duffin noted with wonderment:

> And actually, when we went further into the rainforest we came across
> other things. Elders started *releasing* what they knew about it. It started a
> whole awakening (Rhonda Duffin, pers. comm. 10 November 1995).

It is upon their own sensory experiences and their engagement with the
country, as well as the experiences of their forebears, that Djabugay people
base their claims. Landscape is a living memory domain for Djabugay people who constitute themselves in terms of a continuity of *becoming* in place.
Djabugay people express their connection with land in terms of their feelings for and experience of a generalised domain that is alive with spiritual
forces and beings and that has an agency of its own (see also Langton 2002).
For example, when the Cairns/Kuranda train narrowly escaped a rockslide
on the track, Djabugay elders I met the next day in the main street told me
that the rockslide was actually the Dreaming ancestor Damarri's[7] response
to the construction of Skyrail (Esther Snider and Florence Williams, pers.
comm. 18 June 1995).

Many of the non-Aboriginal protesters similarly think of the environment as having an autonomous agency. They either anthropomorphise
nature itself, generally as female, or they think of it as being alive with spiritual powers. One protester told me that she firmly believed that the forest
was populated with Aboriginal ancestral spirits. On one occasion, she was
in the rainforest in the very early hours of the morning and saw a tall Aboriginal warrior there. She had heard stories from Aboriginal people of the
existence of spirit beings they call 'small men', so she had wondered why
he was so tall, but 'one of the Murris' told her later that there were also
'tall men'. This protester also related how she saw a giant cassowary appear
behind her and on another occasion a cassowary head and then the face of
an Aboriginal man emerging from a tree trunk. She said Djabugay people
later told her that their ancestors sometimes manifest themselves as cas-
sowaries. She said that the forest comforted her by telling her that it would
look after itself against the Skyrail. Nature would have 'her' own revenge.
As proof, she and another protester recounted the number of times since
beginning operations that the Skyrail has been 'out of action' due to storms
and lightning strikes.

Environmentalists and Aboriginal People

In general, environmentalists think of themselves as being part of a political
and moral crusade for a better world. Environmentalism has been characterised by Rubin (1994: 10) as being part of an ongoing saga of evangelical
reform: 'Indeed it is not far off the mark to say that environmentalism is

the temperance movement of our time. We know that it wants to save the earth. But we forget just how much it wants to save us from ourselves'. Environmentalism is based on a universalistic view of the world. Although environmentalists might 'act locally',[8] they assume a common humanity and common, human destiny. So called 'traditional' Indigenous ways of re-lating to the environment are celebrated as a contemporary expression of the way all humans must have once lived. Environmentalists have turned to Indigenous beliefs around the world for inspiration and guidance on how to formulate an alternative human environmental relationship. The follow-ing comments by environmentalist protesters against the Skyrail exemplify this search:

> This is the oldest rainforest in the world. It's the only rainforest that closely resembles what the planet looked like back then ... and when the Djabugay, when I realised, all of a sudden, that the rainforest people had no reason whatsoever to cut down a tree (they may take a section out of it for a canoe, which didn't kill it, or they may have taken out a section for food storage, or they may have taken a buttress out of one of the trees for a shield ... that didn't kill the tree). And here we are cutting down trees like there's no tomorrow ... That just, sort of, blew me away. It was a real inspiring sort of thing, that we could really learn something from these people (John Netz, pers. comm. 14 April 1995).

> I don't know, I guess I never trusted society. I knew there was something. You couldn't live in it. It wasn't natural. And so I always looked to primi-tive societies. Mainly I guess religion led me. Well I kind of looked at all religions and then I noticed there was one that ran through every one, one that was universal, and that was the old religion, and its been from the beginning of time, and that's how all primitive people live. It's with the earth. It's the earth religion and it's the way (Bronwyn Rohweder, pers. comm. 24 January 1996).

Thus Indigenous people are seen as a source of guidance for alternative ways of being in nature, and they have been romanticised as the 'first true conservationists' (Sackett 1991). In other words, as Trigger (1996: 55) puts it, in developing their holistic ecological vision, some environmentalists have 'co-opted alleged indigenous ethics regarding land use to their own cause'.

According to Marcus (1997), the celebration of the traditional ways of life of Aboriginal peoples by environmentalists and new age mystics actu-ally operates to further dispossess those same Aboriginal people. She ar-gues that new age mysticism regarding Uluru (Ayer's Rock) is driven by universalising sentiments that deny the unique identity of Aboriginal beliefs. As Marcus (1997: 46) puts it: 'Attempts to tap into the power of the Rock are seen by local Aboriginal people as simply more of what has gone before – now settlers are mining Aboriginal culture rather than the land itself'. Marcus and others view this as a form of 'cultural appropriation' (Marcus 1997; see also Jacobs 1994 and Lattas 1997). Environmentalists are seen as having appropriated Aboriginal culture and environmental values to further their own political causes. The celebration of Indigenous environmental ethics is thus treated as part of a primitivist discourse that operates to the disadvantage of Aboriginal people.

Yet this discourse can also be turned around to serve Indigenous interests. The concept of traditional culture and notions of Indigenous environmental values and knowledge have become tools by which Indigenous peoples all over the world can assert their rights in the contemporary context of national, state and international politics. For example, when Turner first started field work among the Kayapo in 1962, they were living in a village under the 'protection' of the Brazilian government's equivalent of Queensland's Department of Aboriginal and Torres Strait Islander Affairs, and they were dependent on this department and on the missionaries. During the 1960s, the Kayapo were not self-consciously aware of their cultural practices as being different from other peoples in Brazil; to them their ceremonies and social institutions simply represented the way they had always done things. As Turner (1991: 294) writes: 'They had, in short, no notion that their assemblage of received customs, ritual practices, social values, and institutions constituted a "culture" in the anthropological sense, nor any idea of the reflexive role of that culture in the reproduction of their society and personal identities'. Yet twenty-five years later, when he returned to do further research and ethnographic filming in the area, Turner (1991: 301) found 'a new level of cultural awareness and self-consciousness' among the Kayapo. Many Kayapo had begun to use the Portuguese word *cultura* – along with the language term that comes closest in meaning, *kukradja* – to mean 'a particular body of customary practices and lore' that requires self-conscious effort and concerted political action to preserve and reproduce.

The Skyrail dispute provides an example of the process of development of such a 'new level of cultural awareness and self-consciousness' in the Australian context. It was a case of some Aboriginal people actively and strategically allying themselves with environmentalists in order to resist the powers of oppression.[9] Celebrating the idea of culture is a means for Indigenous people to negotiate benefits for themselves within the context of contemporary political and economic relations that would otherwise leave them marginalised. The Skyrail protest was not simply a matter of environmentalists appropriating Aboriginal culture. Far from being helpless victims, Aboriginal people were active political agents in this process. In the

Skyrail dispute, Djabugay people forged an alliance with other protesters as a useful political strategy. Environmentalist discourse, which places value on traditional Aboriginal culture and which elevates Indigenous people to the status of 'original conservationists', provided an avenue for the Djabugay people to assert native title and heritage rights in the contemporary context of state politics. The Skyrail dispute also provided the Djabugay with a means of asserting a unique identity as rainforest people in a context of homogenising stereotypes of Aboriginality that contribute to their oppression. Andy Duffin, the chairperson of the Djabugay Tribal Aboriginal Corporation at the time, was quoted in the *Courier Mail* (28 May 1995: 1) as saying that 'it is the rainforest which keeps the Djabugay people going' and that their existence would 'fall apart without those forests'. Rhonda Duffin explained to me her involvement in the anti-Skyrail protest in similar terms:

> This rainforest, that's where our foods are. That's where our people lived. They protected the area; they took care of it; and we have the same responsibility. But it sort of goes deeper than that again that feeling that we got that we had to protect what rainforest is left, because you go into the future, you know. We tell our children that we are the rainforest people. If there is no rainforest, you know, how are they going to believe that we are the rainforest people? They'll be asking what is a rainforest? We are the rainforest people. I mean that was our survival, that rainforest, you know. That will continue to be our survival (Rhonda Duffin, pers. comm. 10 November 1995).

The fact that they had their own political agenda does not mean that Djabugay were not genuine in their dealings with the other protesters. The suggestion that people are using culture as a political tool is sometimes made with the cynical assumption that if something is political, it must therefore be inauthentic. On the contrary, political practice needs to be interpreted as part of the fullness of being human. It is not inauthentic practice, and neither is the way Indigenous people have come to use the concept of culture. Similarly, I do not wish to appear cynical about the intentions of the non-Aboriginal protesters. An environmentalist discourse that sought to establish the moral legitimacy of the protesters by romanticising Indigenous cultural practices and relations with the environment was indeed evident in the Skyrail case. However, many of the environmentalists were also very sympathetically aware of the historical oppression and contemporary social and economic plight of Djabugay people. They hoped for the success of the Djabugay native title claim not just because they believed that this would put a halt to the construction of the Skyrail, but also out of a genuine sense of fair play. As John Netz said:

So I got involved with the Skyrail campaign, but really what was far more fascinating for me was the cultural aspects. I mean, for me it's still people. The vast majority of Australians want reconciliation. I think the vast majority of Australians think of reconciliation as being something that's happened and it's okay now, but it's not. Native title is not working (John Netz, pers. comm. 14 April 1995).

When Djabugay people eventually came to an agreement with Skyrail Pty Ltd, there was disappointment among environmentalists but few recriminations. The Skyrail was being built in spite of their protests, and they respected Djabugay people's realisation that they could not fight this 'big monster' and therefore should focus on securing the best economic deal they could 'for the future' of their children.[10] This is not to say that there were no tensions between Aboriginal and non-Aboriginal protesters. For example, after the Cultural Awareness Workshop, an agreement was made that the non-Indigenous protesters would refuse to speak to the media unless the journalists first interviewed Indigenous spokespersons, to ensure that Indigenous voices were heard. Although it was made with good intentions, the agreement did not last long because Aboriginal spokespersons were not always available when the media arrived, and environmentalists became frustrated at missing good opportunities for press coverage.

While one of the Aboriginal elders told me that he was suspicious about the true motives of the environmentalists and wondered whether they were genuinely in support of native title (Lance Riley, pers. comm. 17 February 1997), most Aboriginal people in Kuranda saw the protesters as primarily working for their benefit. Esther Snider referred to the protester who sat up a tree for 208 days as 'a hero for Aboriginal people' (pers. comm. 3 January 1997). Yet the universalist tendencies of environmentalism were well articulated in a speech delivered by one of the key participants in the anti-Skyrail campaign during a rally, which he repeated for me during an interview:

> As a member of the local community, this is *our* forest, as a citizen of Australia, this is *our* National Park, and as a member of the international community, this is *our* World Heritage, *not* the exclusive property of Skyrail Limited (Steve Price, pers. comm. 12 April 1995; original emphasis).

These sentiments are also expressed in the slogans carried by the protesters: 'Economy poisons Ecology', 'Parks and People First Molly, Not Developer's Fees', 'No Development in World Heritage'. They voice not only the perceived incompatibility between environmental values and economic development but also the conflict between individualism and communal-

ism, between private ownership and the commons. The protesters' placards, I suggest, can be interpreted as statements of communal title. They
voice the protesters' reaction against what was seen as private appropriation of the commons. In contrast, the Djabugay were claiming the national
park through the native title claim and their direct protest action not as
common land, but as *their* land. The placards of the Djabugay protesters
could be read as symbolic title deeds – 'Skyrail Garri, Bulurru' – a claim
legitimised by the ancestor Bulurru, who is seen as 'the source of life ... the
Good Spirit that protects life and Law' (Duffin and Brim n.d.).

Although Djabugay were claiming the Skyrail land as *their* land and
non-Indigenous protesters were claiming it as belonging to the entire
world, the inconsistency does not appear to have been clearly recognised
by either group. Perhaps this was because Aboriginal and non-Aboriginal
protest against the Skyrail was expressed in terms of values that, although
they may have had different cultural foundations, required the same outcome: Skyrail had to be stopped for the sake of preserving the rainforest.
As an Aboriginal elder, Enid Boyle, tearfully said in the Cultural Awareness Workshop (3 July 1994), 'what I mean by the trees, those trees are
our culture too ... we don't like to see those trees being cut down and the
ground, the bulldozers running over it. That's what I call desecration to the
land, you know'. Moreover, they held other objections against the Skyrail
in common. Although some anti-Skyrail protesters were not locals and although the blockaders were joined by environmentalists from the south of
Australia and even from overseas, most of the protesters were in fact long
term residents of the area. For them, Skyrail did not simply pose a threat
to the rainforest, whatever the cultural basis on which it might be valued.
It also stood for an increased tourist threat to this embattled local community. Both Aboriginal and non-Aboriginal residents of Kuranda were
already feeling that the 'village in the rainforest' was no longer theirs. Developers had slowly appropriated it for the use of tourists. As an Aboriginal
woman said in the moment of protest examined above, 'We used to roam
those bloody streets in Kuranda. And where now? Kuranda's polluted with
tourists'. Loss of control over definition of place also means loss of ability to
define community identity. Skyrail provided the site for harnessing global
discourses in localised political action that might enable people to reclaim
their home place (and themselves in the process). The Djabugay in particular, as agents in their own interests, strategically drew on the power of
wider community mobilisation and environmentalist discourse to lodge a
native title claim over the Barron Gorge National Park. However, while the
Skyrail dispute provided the initial impetus for their claim, it was to take
over ten years before a consent determination was made and their native
title rights and interests in the Park were recognised (Figure 7.3). This rec-

Figure 7.3. Djabugay Elder Florence Williams Fighting for Native Title, c. 1997.
Photographer: Rosita Henry.

ognition was granted subject to the Djabugay people adopting a science-based discourse and submitting to bureaucratic environmental planning and management strategies that related to national parks. Djabugay people are expected to exercise their rights only in a manner compatible with the continued 'sustainable management' of the Park, and the determination is subject to an Indigenous Land Use Agreement (ILUA) between the Djabugay People, the State of Queensland and the Djabugay Native Title Aboriginal Corporation.

Out of His Tree: A Performance of a Performance

Like the Kuranda Market War, which generated the production of the stage play *The Three Marketeers*, the Skyrail dispute inspired dramatisation by local performers, but this time in the form of a film. The film, entitled *Out of His Tree*, was written and directed by Ricardo Rusch. It features thirty-three local actors, including three Aboriginal actors, and its production involved a local team of fifteen people. A number of these had been actual protesters during the anti-Skyrail demonstrations. The film was entered in the 1998 Short and Curly Film Festival, a part of the Adelaide Festival, and it was also screened at the Fremantle Film and Television Institute in Western Australia on 8 April 1998. The film is introduced as follows: 'All the sites to the east had fallen to yet another development aimed at the tourist dollar, but on the western flank a group of eco-warriors never gave up fighting to protect this sacred site'.

While obviously siding with the protesters, the film parodies the actions of all parties to the dispute: the protesters as well as the developers, the police and the loggers. It opens with the developer – referred to as the 'evil developer' in the credits – rolling out his plans while a number of women – referred to as 'forest nymphs' – walk through the rainforest lovingly stroking the trees. An oversized tube of super-glue is used by one of the nymphs to glue her hands together around a tree. With the help of a ground crew of other protesters, a tree sitter is then hoisted into a tree where he sits playing his piano accordion. Big fat policemen with pink curly tails and faces made up as snouts arrive on the scene. While the eco-warriors pelt the police with fruit, the police punch and kick the protesters with their heavy boots until one of them lies senseless on the rainforest floor. They then pose as a television crew to trick the tree sitter out of his tree and carry him off slung from a pole like a wild game animal.

This film is yet another example of how social dramas in Kuranda are often literally performed twice. I have referred above to the direct actions of the protesters as 'performances of protest'. The film is also a performance of protest, although a performance offered after the fact and at a level once removed. The distinction between the two types of performance is not that one involves consciousness while the other does not; rather, different modes of consciousness come to the fore in each. Theatricalised performances produced for the stage or for film are an expression of human consciousness in its reflective mode. Yet, as Kapferer (1997: 222) writes, '*consciousness* is a dimension of all human action and is not limited to that which is established reflectively or contemplatively. Human beings are conscious beings by virtue of their embodied existence in the world'. The passions involved at the height of a social drama do not allow for much reflection or contemplation, but they are nonetheless expressions of people's consciousness of their social situation.

Conflict Narratives and Binary Oppositions

Although the Skyrail protesters received some support from national and international environmentalist groups and although they drew upon what they thought of as a global environmental ethic to legitimate their claims, the campaign was essentially locally based and locally driven. The direct actions of the protesters were statements of local resistance to what were perceived as globalising strategies of power. In particular, protestors saw themselves as resisting the strategies of power and the forces of economic rationalism that support private development at the expense of communal values. Yet there were complex nuances in the social interactions of people involved in the Skyrail dispute that reveal that it was not just a matter of people being for or against communal values, for or against environment, or for or against the Skyrail. In the heat of social drama, people represent their issues in terms of oppositions. They construct and perform narratives of conflict in terms of binary identities at the same time as such binaries are continually unravelled.

I have highlighted a particular moment of protest within the Skyrail dispute. The Skyrail dispute produced many such moments of protest that allowed Kuranda people to use performance to articulate relationships among themselves and in relation to the state. In such moments of protest, people actively construct, communicate and challenge categorical identities in the context of connections to place that are contestable only because they are shared. As evidenced by the protest scene described above, actors celebrate cultural differences in the performance of protest, but they also re-fashion a sense of collective identity by engaging their differences. They produce an idea of 'community': 'We're here for one another. We're not here for ourselves'.

Although the protesters used 'rhetorical strategies which drew upon categorical and/or stereotypical identities' (Moore 1994: 5), rather than simply taking these categorical identities as given, I have focused my discussion on the discursive fields and practices that operated to *reproduce* such identities. One such discursive field was the 'language game of science' (Lyotard 1984). Both Aboriginal and non-Aboriginal protesters were caught up in a game of truth, a game that constrained them to wage their dispute with government agencies and Skyrail developers according to the universalising claims of science. Within the terms of this game, their assertions about the significance of the rainforest and the destructiveness of Skyrail were made to look foolish. Yet although the Skyrail debate was couched in terms of scientific fact, the underlying forces that drove the dispute really had nothing to do with such facts. It was not about right and wrong trees or authentic and inauthentic Aboriginal sites. Rather, it was about 'burning breasts' and 'bleeding hearts' (Keith and Pile 1993: 10). It was an assertion that there are different experiences of being in this world and experiences of place that refuse to be muted.

The Skyrail dispute involved the mobilisation of local Kuranda people against the state and the power of big business. In their performances of protest during the dispute, people constituted themselves and others in terms of their relations to place. The dispute threw into relief the ties between people and place that were symbolically expressed, as I have suggested elsewhere, by the protester's physical attachment of herself to the tree (see Henry 1995, 1998). The Skyrail dispute, like the Kuranda Market War and the disputes over the Kuranda Amphitheatre, drew people into two opposing camps and reduced a complex diversity of values to a duality. In their narratives of the conflict, people tended to represent their views and actions in terms of binary values. If one was not *against* the Skyrail, then one had to be *for* it, and being *for* the Skyrail automatically meant that one was *against* the environment. However, the development of strong binary identities along one axis in a conflict situation can mean that other oppositions become muted, if only temporarily. An examination of the performative dimensions of the Skyrail conflict reveals that the entrenched oppositions between the values of Aboriginal and non-Aboriginal people were downplayed for the sake of an alliance over place value. In their protest performances concerning place, activists made their own statements that gave voice to other ways of being in the world.

NOTES

1. Parts of this chapter have been previously published in the journal *Aboriginal History* (see Henry 1998). I thank the journal for permission to republish this material.
2. Taussig argues that identity 'has to be seen not as a thing-in-itself but as a relationship woven from mimesis and alterity within colonial fields of representation' (1993: 133).
3. I am indebted to Bruce White for his 'A Chronology of Documents, Letters, Media and Events Telling the Story of How It Is That a Cairns-Kuranda Cableway Got to Be Constructed in a Djabugay Cultural Landscape', unpublished manuscript submitted to s10 Heritage Protection Reporter Mr George Menham, 1995.
4. The Council was incorporated on 7 July 1992 and became the Djabugay Tribal Aboriginal Corporation.
5. As transcribed by White (1995) from an interview he conducted immediately following a visit to Kuranda by Mr George Menham, 17 May 1995. Damarri is an ancestral being. Guraminya and Gurabana are moiety names.
6. The Aboriginal and Torres Strait Islander Heritage Protection Act of 1984 requires that a report under section 10(4) deal with the 'particular significance of the area to Aboriginals'.

7. Damarri is also called Bulurru. Bulurru is how Djabugay refer to the Dreaming. Storywaters, or locations associated with the Dreaming, as well as the ancestral beings associated with those locations are known as Bulurru. Bulurru is considered to be 'the source and condition of all life and is ever-present in the land and people' (Quinn 1992: 16). Some Djabugay people today think of Bulurru as 'our God', as distinct from the Christian God they were taught to worship in the mission. Others think of Bulurru as simply the Djabugay name for the Christian God.
8. 'Act locally, think globally' is a slogan popularised by Rene Dubos.
9. Another example is the Todd River Dam case in Central Australia; see Jacobs 1994.
10. These comments were made during a workshop for Aboriginal people on development in Kuranda that I organised and facilitated with the aid of a grant from the Australian Institute of Aboriginal and Torres Strait Islander Studies in 1995.

Creating Place

The Production of a Space for Difference

> *To illuminate the junction between the State and space, it is*
> *necessary that we stop misrecognizing the spatial, and, corre-*
> *spondingly, that we come to recognize the importance of a theory*
> *of (social) space.*
>
> —Henri Lefebvre

This study of a small Australian town has grounded theoretical discussions about place, identity, the state, and the relationship between local and global forces in the actualities of human experience. This is not an account of an Indigenous 'Other' or of cultural differences as given, but a study of how such differences are both generated and effaced within and in relation to a transforming state system. I have shown how both Aboriginal and non-Aboriginal people in Kuranda place themselves and one another in the world via a politics of identity that expresses itself in social dramas that break out with regularity in the town. I have focused on the ways that people make themselves in relation to others through practices and performances of place and on how, in the course of their place-making activities, they confront and respond to the effects of state and corporate power. My key aim has been to demonstrate ethnographically how Kuranda people reproduce state effects at the very same time as they seek to resist those effects. However, this is not to say that their resistances are futile, for they play a vital role in enabling people to create for themselves a sense of belonging and a space for difference.

While residents represent Kuranda as a special place that is harmonious and relatively free of racism, they also think of it as riddled with social conflict. Townspeople often shake their heads and shrug with acceptance at the latest eruption, as if conflict were an inevitable part of what defines the town. The conflict tends to focus on key sites that are 'socially and ideologically demarcated and separated from other places' and that are 'differently manipulated according to specific group interests' (Kuper 2003: 258–59).

The manipulation appears to be mostly over the definition, image and representation of Kuranda as a place. Yet it is more than that. The social dramas discussed in this book have to do with the actual constitution of place, not merely its representation. The conflict situations are constitutive in that they draw townspeople out of the routine of their everyday lives into intensely participatory webs of social action and into effervescent experiences of sociality that foster the production of the narrative memories that serve as their title deeds to place.

Place Memory

The relationship between place and memory has been well discussed, and much attention has been given to the social construction of the past and the significance of place in the making of collective memories (e.g. Bender 1993; Casey 1993, 1997; Lattas 1996; Gupta and Ferguson 1997; David and Wilson 2002; Steward and Strathern 2003). More recently, the issue of memory has continued to be debated among anthropologists in relation to processes of intergenerational transmission of violent loss (e.g. Argenti and Schramm 2010). Place and landscape play an important part in the creation and consolidation of narrative memories that foster in people a sense of identification with and belonging to particular social groups (Beckett 1996). Yet the production of a sense of belonging involves spatial practices of identification and differentiation that have the potential to lead to intense social conflict. In this book, I have given ethnographic focus to 'memory in practice' (Argenti and Schramm 2010: 21). I have explored the performances of people involved in small-town conflict situations. These are played out in terms of relatively benign social dramas that are nevertheless revealing of how people respond to the structural violence of state effects.

As I argued in Chapter 1, the colonising practices that accompanied the early European settlement of the Kuranda area strategically operated to expunge Aboriginal priority in place. The country was cleared for European settlers not only by the physical removal of Aboriginal people by agents of the colonial state, but also by the memorial purging of their presence from the landscape. Yet the removal of Aboriginal people from their home places did not succeed in erasing their identity in place. Although the disciplinary practices of institutionalisation worked towards wiping out the memory of a lifeworld, there were other forces that operated to counter such practices. Among these forces were the economic demands of the mission establishment itself. Throughout its early years, the Mona Mona mission struggled to feed its population, and Aboriginal people had to supplement their rations by pursuing hunter-gatherer subsistence activities in the surrounding scrub. This allowed for the experiential accumulation of memories of the country beyond the mission compound. The forestry, railway and tourist industries also worked against practices of erasure, and the requirement for Aboriginal labour provided access to country that they would otherwise have been denied. The tourist industry created a demand for Aboriginal arts and cultural performances. This is not a recent phenomenon, but something that began before the 'round-ups' and continued intermittently during the mission period, with a heyday during the 1950s when busloads of tourists would visit Mona Mona. Thus public cultural performances have been a practice of memory and of resistance against erasure since well before the more recent tourist demands of the past thirty years and the birth of land rights and native title politics.

Another factor that operated in favour of place memory was the fact that for most of the life of the mission, there were two fringe camps on Mona Mona. Here the old people managed to maintain a certain independence of lifestyle and to continue practices that were denied their children in the dormitories. The camps themselves became symbols of resistance to missionisation and – for children in the dormitories – a reminder of a lifeworld that remained accessible as an intriguing potentiality. Although the removal of Aboriginal people to reserves left many with a profound sense of loss, their attachment to place remains as deep as the trust that they have in the abiding nature of ancestral power in country. For the descendants of Mona Mona people as with other Aboriginal people in the region (*Bama*), power continues to reside in places 'by virtue of the presence of the Old People; their spiritual Being is emplaced and their power is emplaced' (Langton 2002: 267). This continuity of being-in-place is reinforced in the present through contemporary practices and performances such as the ones I have described in this book. As Austin-Broos (2009: 269) underlines in her study on the Western Arrernte, 'continuity is made, not given ... a space of difference within the state must be worked at'.

Settler Practices of Place

While there are numerous histories that explore the relationship between early settlers and Aboriginal people in various parts of Australia, few studies have treated the non-Aboriginal settlement of Aboriginal country as a continuing process. In some places, such settlement has been gradual and unremarkable; in other places, there has been dramatic transformation due to sudden rapid influxes of large numbers of people. This was especially the case in rural areas such as Kuranda that became magnets of the counterculture exodus from the cities during the 1970s and 1980s. In this book, I have attempted to address this gap in the literature by focusing on the relationships between the wave of settlers that began to arrive in Kuranda during this period and the local Aboriginal population. I have examined the practices by which these counter-culture settlers attempted to mould Kuranda into their own imagined village community, practices that brought them into conflict with earlier settlers and the agents of state bureaucracy, the shire council and the police. In the wake of the counterculture settlers, a flood of people were drawn to the 'village in the rainforest' throughout the 1980s and 1990s in search of the tourist dollar, encroaching in turn on the hippies and challenging the freedom of movement of Aboriginal people by buying up the land surrounding their settlements. Real estate development and residential subdivisions put additional pressure on the Aboriginal population by constraining access to camping and fishing spots and to places where resources – such as particular types of grasses for weaving – had been freely available.

The responses of the hippie settlers to the individualising and atomising strategies of the state, or the 'isolation effect' (Trouillot 2001: 131), was to attempt to mobilise in the name of community and to represent Kuranda as a special place, a place set apart in space-time. They sought to create a Brigadoon-like place with its own marketplace and village common (the amphitheatre). Yet their communitarian efforts were eventually undermined by the very ideological foundations that inspired their counterculture resistance – that is, by a particular manifestation of what Kapferer (1988) has described as 'egalitarian individualism'. Moreover, in their creation of the structures that they considered to be defining of a village, such as a marketplace, an amphitheatre and a library, these new settlers drew into the heart of their domain the very thing they were attempting to resist: capitalist development and the tentacles of state bureaucratic surveillance. The strategic planning process in Kuranda provides a case study of the insidious operation of the disciplinary mechanisms of state bureaucracy at work in relation to both Aboriginal and non-Aboriginal people. In their search for empowerment, people turned to strategic planning only to experience another form of bureaucratic bondage. Yet planning, as I have described its operation in Kuranda, also generates productive social dramas that in turn provide the social memories that contribute to the creation of Kuranda as a home place.

As my ethnographic study has revealed, 'The relation between "private" interests and the activities of "public" powers sometimes involves collusion, sometimes collision' (Lefebvre 2009: 227; see also J. Kapferer 2008: 8). In the longer term, a process of commercialisation of the alternative lifestyle movement over a period of thirty years in the Kuranda region led to the gentrification of many of the original hippies, artists and craftspeople who had settled there in order to escape 'the system'. Commoditisation of their creative endeavours, in tandem with the process of state co-optation of the arts, has led to a 'cultural industry' project of urban planning and design that has transformed the streetscape of Kuranda. As Miles (2008: 109) concludes in his discussion of the rise of the culture industries: 'Culturally led urban redevelopment puts power in the hands of developers, entrepreneurs, and intermediaries. The emphasis is on the production of image and the spaces that signify that image, rather than the maintenance of extant cultures as the ways of life of the inhabitants'. Nevertheless, as one walks down the main street of Kuranda at different times of the day or night, one can observe rhythms in the spatial practices of the inhabitants that challenge this project of image production and that work to remake Kuranda as a dwelling place.

Individualism and Communitarianism

A number of common themes lie at the foundation of the social dramas involving these counterculture settlers. One of these is the contradiction between individualism and communitarian principles that resulted in the failure of many communes and tenancies-in-common and that compromised communal ventures such as the amphitheatre. The new settlers sought community, but their concept of community rested on a liberal humanist view of the human subject and on a notion of equality among individuals that assumed, indeed required, similarity. This is part of a liberal discourse with an underlying logic that imagines a level playing field. It does not admit the possibility of difference as a socio-historical product. The idea of community celebrated by Kuranda settlers is compatible with the principles of Australian egalitarian individualism where individual difference is hailed, but only if it is grounded in nature. However, unlike the settlers, Indigenous Australians are usually constructed within the state system not as individual agents, but as members of a 'natural' category with 'problems' that require massive state intervention. Australian egalitarianism thus recognises difference, including cultural difference, as essentially founded in nature, and refuses to entertain the possibility of socially and historically constituted categorical differences.

This denial of historical process underlies the glorification of culture and the state sponsorship of multiculturalism as exemplified in the government support of the Djabugay cultural revival (Chapter 6). The fact that categorical identities are historically, socially and economically constituted is masked by multiculturalism's reduction of difference to cultural difference. By emphasising cultural particularity, the discourse subtly denies the reality of colonising practices of erasure and bureaucratic bondage and the hierarchy of domination that Australian egalitarianism generates but that it cannot admit.

Empowering Place

Another contradiction revealed in Kuranda social dramas, particularly those concerning town planning and development, is the contradiction that has played out between the concepts of space and place. The triumph of space (as the 'indifferent site-space of cartography or rational geometry' [Casey 1987: 192]) over place is continually tested by the way people position themselves in the world through the agency and relationship of their lived bodies. As Casey (1987: 197) writes: 'Places are empowered by the lived bodies that occupy them; these bodies animate places, breathe new life into them by endowing them with directionality, level, and distance – all of which serve as essential anchoring points in the remembering of place'. Yet if places are empowered or animated by lived bodies, then this is done by bodies in intense and active socio-political engagement with one another rather than by bodies as individual psycho-physical objects. In other words, places are empowered by *people*. The 'world' is not something given; instead it is produced within fields of sociality and is in itself an experiential field of sociality. This is perhaps what Husserl meant by his notion of 'lifeworld'. As Jackson (1996: 16) writes: 'For Husserl, the *Lebenswelt* was the world of immediate experience, of sociality, common sense, and shared experience that exists for us independent of and prior to any reflection upon it'. Since the lifeworld is inherently social, being-in-the-world is a profoundly social activity. Being-in-the-world, I argue, means *becoming* in the world through *doing*. It is a matter of practice. However, it is also a matter of performance, and as such, it is not entirely independent of reflection.

The Power of Performance

Kuranda people use theatrical performances to explore the contradictions that give rise to conflict in the town. Such performances allow them to mediate the tensions between individualism and communalism. By taking their experiences of actual social dramas in the town into the realm of play and theatricalising them for stage or film, Kuranda people explicate the particular conditions of their existence and translate their consciousness of their situation into a more critically reflective mode. At the same time, they challenge purely mental modes of being in the world by celebrating the embodiment of memory and of place, the 'corporeal intentionality ... binding us to the life-world we inhabit' (Casey 1997: 229).

I have used the term performance in relation both to theatrical productions and social dramas, but the two are not performances of the same order. While both types of performance can be seen as forms of resistance (because through them people attempt to transcend their social situations), the relationship an audience has to actors staging a dramatisation with a scripted outcome is quite different from the relationship an audience has to actors caught up in an unpredictable situation of social conflict. In both types of performance, audiences and actors alike experience particular constellations and operations of power that they encounter on a regular basis as part of everyday life. Performances of protest – as well as the subsequent staged dramatisation of such direct actions – evidence people's consciousness of the fact that as subjects, they are constrained by power relations. This is not only a matter of critical reflection but also one of embodied recognition. Yet the scripted performances in the Kuranda Amphitheatre and at Tjapukai also employ humour and parody to defuse tensions among protagonists in the social dramas that are being dramatised. Thus they operate as a means for people to forget temporarily the burden of social conflict by suggesting ways that they might remember such conflict differently. Through re-enactments in the amphitheatre and at Tjapukai, participants produce performative memories that offer them an alternative future. As Argenti and Schramm (2010: 23) note: 'Performative genres enable their practitioners to collapse time and to shed light on the historical continuities between past and present by juxtaposing one onto the other, using deep wells of cultural knowledge to interpret contemporary injustices that are often as extreme, ineffable and inchoate as were those of the past'. Through their staged performances, Kuranda participants are able to confront the historical transformations that continue to fragment their communities, as well as to present these transformations to a wider local, national and international audience.

Aboriginal Cultural Performances

Inverting the denigration of earlier times, Aboriginal cultural performances are glorified in Australia today. While opportunities for public performance such as the Tjapukai Cultural Park and various cultural festivals provide Aboriginal people with a means of confronting and challenging the practices that keep them in a state of domination, these very opportunities arise out of and are structured and limited by the bureaucratic order. They are also undermined by 'the (market-based) democratisation of the discourse of cultural difference' (Kahn 1995: 154) that trivialises them as mere tourist products. Dominant discursive practices based on the celebration of tradition and underlying assumptions about the authenticity of cultural transmission operate to *create* the idea of cultural discontinuity. Yet as Stephen Turner (1994: 84) notes, 'discontinuity ... is a dubious phenomenon'. Within the terms of the discourse about culture and tradition, Aboriginal people are made to experience themselves as having a lack of knowledge. The idea of discontinuity is thus made possible and continually reproduced by the demand for 'indigenous alterities' (Povinelli 2002).

Given the context of a history of colonially induced mutilation of memory, it is not surprising that this celebration of traditional culture has spawned a desire among Aboriginal people to remember and preserve cultural knowledge. It is understandable that Aboriginal people might adopt essentialist concepts of culture, heritage and tradition. Morris (1989: 224) has noted the shift among Aboriginal Australians from a 'redistributive politics of equal rights and egalitarianism to the politics of difference'. Yet I argue that Aboriginal performances in Kuranda exhibit something other than a simple complicity with essentialist discourses of difference. While on the one hand they assert and celebrate cultural singularities as an essential aspect of Kuranda Aboriginal people's identity as Indigenous Australians, they also challenge and seek recognition of the historical conditions and state projects that continue to particularise them as different from mainstream Australians. This was verbally expressed, for example, in the appeal of the woman anti-Skyrail protester to the police and loggers: 'Learn your history. We're the ones that suffered not you. You don't even know our history' (Chapter 7). According to Morris (1989: 218), the historical relations of domination are mystified 'by replacing them with cultural representations of Aborigines in an essentialist form which exist outside time and space', but in Kuranda at least Aboriginal people resist such mystification.

As a form of resistance, performance involves an awareness or consciousness of the tentacles of power that operate in a particular social situation. Such awareness is not necessarily articulated cognitively. It may be articulated through bodily emplacement and in terms of bodily awareness of being in relationship with others in a lifeworld. Thus, theatricalised performances in the Tjapukai Cultural Park and elsewhere, although ostensibly for tourists, allow Aboriginal people to play a part in redefining themselves. Performances for tourists become an opportunity to challenge a paradigm that assumes that remembering is merely the recollection of intellectual knowledge. Through such performances Djabugay people celebrate the possibility of embodied acquisition of culture. This celebration is not necessarily of culture as biologically given in the body. It is a claim for recognition of the embodiment of historically produced lived experiences and of a cosmology that distinguishes 'between inner truths and outside appearances in all aspects of being' (Sansom 2001: 3). By moving into performance, Djabugay people allow this 'inner reality' to reveal itself via body memory. The potentiality of the old lifeworld remains imminent for Aboriginal people. This is expressed today in the narratives about sightings of the Old People who continue to live according to the old ways, mostly hidden in the landscape but sometimes making themselves visible. It is also expressed in the notion that cultural knowledge can be carried and transmitted through bodily engagement in contemporary cultural performances. To have been removed from country during the mission period was not for Aboriginal people a discontinuity of connection to place. Place continues to be animated and imbued with new memories, and people experience place and body as vitally connected.

Beyond States of Domination

My project has been neither to compare and contrast Aboriginal and non-Aboriginal cultural values nor to identify their differences in terms of 'culturally embedded behaviours' (Sutton 2009: 119). Rather, I have focused my discussion on the practices and performances that operate to generate and reproduce such categorical differences. Although difference is indeed apparent in the values, practices and performances of Aboriginal people, to reduce interpretation to a matter of cultural comparison operates to deny people recognition as political agents and to deny the significance of the state projects that continue through repetitive cycles of intervention to define the very terms of their existence. Histories of dispossession are not a matter of the past. The removal of Aboriginal people from Mona Mona, their brief period as independent home-owners during the 1960s and their eventual re-encompassment as state housing dependents (Chapter 1) was a cycle that was repeated forty years later in the case of the Tjapukai Dance Theatre, which shifted from initial non-Aboriginal ownership to a majority Aboriginal shareholding and then to almost total government agency ownership (Indigenous Business Australia) (Chapter 6). The experiences of Kuranda people are instructive in assessing current government policies regarding Aboriginal communities and attempts to stimulate economic development by legislating for private leasehold opportunities on communally held land. It is important to recognise the power of the identification effect of the state over the isolation effect in relation to Aboriginal Australians. While the isolation effect works to produce 'a particular kind of subject as an atomized member of a public', the identification effect continually works against the isolation effect to homogenise Aboriginal people in terms of a single governable identity category (Trouillot 2001: 131–132).

For Aboriginal people, contemporary performances of dance and music and performances of protest (such as the protests against the Skyrail, against government policy on Aboriginal housing, the sale of 'fake' Aboriginal art or the future of Mona Mona) are responses to being in 'a state of domination' (Foucault 1988b: 19). This book has described a long history of activism and protest against agents of the state among Aboriginal people of Kuranda. Yet Aboriginal people rarely get publicly involved in issues of dispute among the non-Aboriginal townspeople – particularly issues that concern town planning and development – in part because they doubt that their voices would be heard, but mainly because they are overwhelmed with the need to focus on issues that affect them more directly and immediately such as the housing crisis, chronic health problems, native title issues and rights to the land at Mona Mona. The Skyrail issue was an exception because Djabugay people were directly confronted with a challenge to their identity as rainforest people – an identity which had gained strength during the Djabugay renaissance – and to native title rights, which had become a possibility after the High Court decision in Mabo (1992). In addition, they were able to mobilise publicly because they were able to find allies among the new settlers, heirs of the counter-culture who were inspired by the holistic philosophy of life that they attributed to Indigenous peoples.

As opposed to a 'state of domination', non-Aboriginal people's performances tend on the other hand to reflect their experience of power as a matter of strategic manoeuvres among free and equal individuals who sometimes band together in opposition to a state government that continually threatens to impinge on individual freedom. The resistance activity of one of the 1970s settlers against the buses is a case in point (Chapter 5). The bus resister manifested autonomy and control in his dealings with the bus drivers and in relation to the courts. His actions, like that of the environmentalist activists described in Chapter 7, are typical of resistance where power is experienced as 'strategic games' among agents who occupy relatively equal positions but who have conflicting interests. Local activists against the Kuranda Skyrail became 'transnationalized local actors' in the process of their resistance (Ferguson and Gupta 2002: 995). They were able to draw on a globally networked environmentalist movement to enhance their strategic position and their capacity to confront both the private development company and the state agents that approved and supported the development.

Through their social engagement, people imbue place with memories and thus make it theirs. I have interpreted the various disputes discussed in this book in connection with the market place, the amphitheatre, the dance theatre and the Skyrail as social dramas of emplacement. In these dramas, contradictions between individualism and communalism, and autonomy and relatedness, as well as tensions in processes of differentiation and identification, are thrown into the limelight, allowing people to claim a role as agents in the creation and transformation of their own lifeworlds. By means of such performances, Kuranda people challenge the dominant state projects that mask colonialist interactions and bureaucratic processes and that sustain historically produced strategies of power, but in the process they also contribute to the cultivation and propagation of state effects. Through their public performances as well as their everyday spatial tactics, they both resist and reproduce state effects at the same time as they seek to develop relationships that transcend the state.

ᐒ REFERENCES ᐰ

Anderson, C. 1979. 'Aboriginal Economy and Contact Relations at Bloomfield River, North Queensland', *Australian Institute of Aboriginal Studies Newsletter* (New Series) 12: 33–37.

———. 1983. 'The Political and Economic Basis of Kuku-Yalanji Social History', Ph.D. dissertation. Brisbane: University of Queensland.

———. 1989. 'Aborigines and Conservationism: The Daintree-Bloomfield Road', *Journal of Social Issues* 24: 214–27.

Andrews, J. 1982. 'The Struggle in Kuranda: A Resume', unpublished manuscript. Kuranda: J. Andrews.

Argenti, N. and K. Schramm. 2010. 'Introduction: Remembering Violence: Anthropological Perspectives on Intergenerational Transmission', in N. Argenti and K. Schramm (eds), *Remembering Violence: Anthropological Perspectives on Intergenerational Transmission.* New York: Berghahn Books, pp. 1–39.

Attwood, B. and F. Magowan. (eds). 2001. *Telling Stories: Indigenous History and Memory in Australia and New Zealand.* Crows Nest, NSW: Allen & Unwin.

Attwood, B. and S. G. Foster (eds). 2003. *Frontier Conflict: The Australian Experience.* Canberra: National Museum of Australia.

Austin-Broos, D. 1994. 'Narratives of the Encounter at Naria', *Oceania* 65: 131–50.

———. 2009. *Arrernte Present, Arrernte Past: Invasion, Violence, and Imagination in Indigenous Central Australia.* Chicago: University of Chicago Press.

Australian Bureau of Statistics. 2003. *Regional Population Growth, Australia and New Zealand, 2002-03.* ABS Catalogue no. 3218.0.

Babidge, S. 2004. 'Family Affairs: An Historical Anthropology of State Practice and Aboriginal Agency in a Rural Town, North Queensland', Ph.D. dissertation. Townsville: James Cook University.

———. 2010. *Aboriginal Family and the State: The Conditions of History.* Aldershot: Ashgate.

Bachelard, G. 1969. *The Poetics of Space.* Boston: Beacon Press.

Banning, R. and M. Quinn. 1989. *Djabugay Ngirrma Gulu.* Kuranda.

Bateson, G. 1955. 'A Theory of Play and Fantasy', *Psychiatric Research Reports* 2: 39–51.

Beckett, J. 1994. 'Aboriginal Histories, Aboriginal Myths: An Introduction', *Oceania* 65(2): 97–115.

Beckett, J. 1996. 'Against Nostalgia: Place and Memory in Myles Lalor's "Oral History"', *Oceania* 66(4): 312–22.

Bell, D. 1998. *Ngarrindjeri Wurruwarrin: The World That Is, Was, and Will Be.* North Melbourne: Spinifex Press.

Bender, B. (ed.). 1993. *Landscape: Politics and Perspectives.* Providence: Berg.

Blau, H. 1990. 'Universals of Performance; or Amortizing Play', in R. Schechner and W. Appel (eds), *By Means of Performance: Intercultural Studies of Theatre and Ritual.* Cambridge: Cambridge University Press, pp. 250–72.

Bolton, G. C. 1963. *A Thousand Miles Away: A History of North Queensland to 1920.* Brisbane: Jacaranda Press in association with the Australian National University.

Bottomley, G. 1987. 'Cultures, Multiculturalism and the Politics of Representation', *Journal of Intercultural Studies* 8(2): 1–9.

———. 1994. 'Post-multiculturalism? The Theory and Practice of Heterogeneity', *Culture and Policy* 6(1): 142.

Bottoms, T. 1990. 'Djarrugan, the Last of the Nesting', M.A. (Qual.) dissertation. Cairns: James Cook University.

———. 1992. *The Bama, People of the Rainforest: Aboriginal-European Relations in the Cairns Rainforest Region up to 1876.* Cairns: Gadja Enterprises.

———. 1993. 'The World of the Bama: Aboriginal-European Relations in the Cairns Rainforest Region to 1876', *Royal Historical Society of Queensland Journal* 15(1): 1–14.

———. 1999. *Djabugay Country: An Aboriginal History of Tropical North Queensland.* St Leonards, NSW: Allen & Unwin.

Bourdieu, P. 1977. *Outline of a Theory of Practice.* Cambridge: Cambridge University Press.

———. 1990. 'Social Space and Symbolic Power', in P. Bourdieu (ed.), *In Other Words: Essays Towards a Reflexive Sociology.* Stanford: Stanford University Press.

Braudel, F. 1986. *The Wheels of Commerce: Civilization and Capitalism 15th–18th Century, Volume II.* Translation from the French by Sian Reynolds. New York: Harper & Row.

Briscoe, G. 2003. *Counting Health and Identity: A History of Aboriginal Health and Demography in Western Australia and Queensland 1900–1940.* Canberra: Aboriginal Studies Press.

Broughton, A. D. 1991. *A Pictorial History of the Construction of the Cairns Range Railway 1886–1891.* Cairns: The Historical Society, Cairns, North Queensland.

Brunton, R. 1991. 'Controversy in the "Sickness Country": The Battle of Coronation Hill', *Quadrant* (September): 16–20.

———. 1996. 'The Hindmarsh Island Bridge and the Credibility of Australian Anthropology', *Anthropology Today* 12(4): 2–7.

Casey, E. S. 1987. *Remembering: A Phenomenological Study.* Bloomington: Indiana University Press.

———. 1993. *Getting Back Into Place: Towards a Renewed Understanding of the Place-World.* Bloomington: Indiana University Press.

———. 1997. *The Fate of Place: A Philosophical History.* Berkeley: University of California Press.

Cassells, H. 1977. 'Djabugay: A Language of the Cairns Rainforest Area', unpublished manuscript. Canberra: Australian Institute of Aboriginal and Torres Strait Islander Studies.

Castells, M. 1996. *The Information Age: Economy, Society and Culture. Volume I: The Rise of the Network Society.* Oxford: Blackwell.

———. 1997. *The Information Age: Economy, Society and Culture. Volume II: The Power of Identity.* Oxford: Blackwell.

Chase, A. 1980. 'Which Way Now? Tradition, Continuity and Change in a North Queensland Aboriginal Community', PhD dissertation. Brisbane: University of Queensland.

Chauduri, U. 1991. 'The Future of the Hyphen: Interculturalism, Textuality, and the Difference Within', in B. Marranca and G. Dasgupta (eds), *Interculturalism and Performance*. New York: PAJ Publications, pp. 192–205.

Choong, Soon Kim. 1990. 'The Role of the Non-Western Anthropologist Reconsidered: Illusion versus Reality', *Current Anthropology* 31(2): 197–200.

Cohen, A. P. 1985. *The Symbolic Construction of Community.* Chichester, Sussex: Ellis Horwood.

Coleman, A., F. McLeod and M. Quinn. 1993. *Warrma Gurrinan: Gurrina's Corroboree.* Kuranda: The Authors.

Collins, S. 1981. 'Mona Mona: A Culture in Transition', Graduate diploma in Material Culture dissertation. Townsville: James Cook University.

Collmann, J. 1988. *Fringe-Dwellers and Welfare: The Aboriginal Response to Bureaucracy.* St Lucia: University of Queensland Press.

Connerton, P. 1989. *How Societies Remember.* Cambridge: Cambridge University Press.

Connolly, D. M. 1984. *Chronicles of Mowbray and Port Douglas and the Pioneering Saga of the Reynolds and Connolly Families: An Historical Record.* Cairns: D. M. Connolly.

Cowlishaw, G. 1988. *Black, White or Brindle: Race in Rural Australia.* Cambridge: Cambridge University Press.

———. 2004. *Blackfellas, Whitefellas and the Hidden Injuries of Race.* Carlton South, Victoria: Blackwell Publishing Asia.

———. 2009. *The City's Outback.* Sydney: UNSW Press.

Crothers, D. n.d. 'First Settlers Kuranda Township 1880 to 1903', unpublished manuscript. Cairns: The Cairns Historical Society.

Cuthbert, D. and M. Grossman. 1996. 'Trading Places: Locating the Indigenous in the New Age', *Thamyris* 3(1): 18–36.

David, B. and M. Wilson (eds). 2002. *Inscribed Landscapes: Marking and Making Place.* Honolulu: University of Hawai`i Press.

de Certeau, M. 1984. *The Practice of Everyday Life.* Berkeley: University of California Press.

Dixon, R. M. W. 1976. 'Tribes, Languages and Other Boundaries', in N. Petersen (ed.), *Tribes and Boundaries in Australia*. Canberra: Australian Institute of Aboriginal Studies, pp. 207–38.

———. 1977. *A Grammar of Yidny.* Cambridge: Cambridge University Press.

Douglas, M. 1995. 'Forgotten Knowledge', in M. Strathern (ed.), *Shifting Contexts: Transformations in Anthropological Knowledge.* London: Routledge, pp. 13–29.

Duffin, R. and R. Brim. n.d. *Ngapi Garrang Bulurru-M: All Things Come From Bulurru.* Kuranda.

Duffin, R., R. Brim and A. Coleman. 1992. *Jilli Binna Magazine* (October).

Eden, C. H. 1872. *My Wife and I Queensland: An Eight Years' Experience in the Above Colony, With Some Account of Polynesian Labour.* London: Longmans, Green & Co.

Edwards, R. and A. Edwards. 1994. *An Explorer's Guide to Kuranda.* Kuranda: The Rams Skull Press.

Eipper, C. 1990. 'Imagining Anthropology: Wherein the Author Journeyed to Exotic Ireland, was Initiated as an Ethnographer, but Questioned the Discipline's Image of Itself', *Canberra Anthropology* 13(1): 48–77.

Eliot, Mark. 1989. *My Place, My Land, My People – People of Kuranda* (videorecording – VHS). Film directed and produced in association with NQTV for Queensland Satellite Television. Point Leo, Vic.: Eliot Jarvis Productions.

Fahim, H. (ed.). 1982. *Indigenous Anthropology in Non-Western Countries.* Durham: North Carolina Academic Press.

Fergie, D. 1996. 'Secret Envelopes and Inferential Tautologies', *Journal of Australian Studies* 48: 13–24.

Ferguson, J. and A. Gupta. 2002. 'Spatializing States: Toward an Ethnography of Neoliberal Governmentality', *American Ethnologist* 29(4): 981–1002.

Finlayson, J. 1991. 'Don't Depend on Me: Autonomy and Dependence in an Aboriginal Community in North Queensland', PhD dissertation. Canberra: Australian National University.

———. 1995. 'Aboriginal Employment, Native Title and Regionalism', *CAEPR Discussion Paper No. 87.* Canberra: Centre for Aboriginal Economic Policy Research, Australian National University.

———. 1997. 'Aboriginal Tradition and Native Title Representative Bodies', in D. E. Smith and J. Finlayson (eds), *Fighting over Country: Anthropological Perspectives.* Canberra: Centre for Aboriginal Economic Policy Research, Australian National University, pp. 141–52.

Foucault, M. 1967. *Madness and Civilization: A History of Insanity in the Age of Reason.* Trans. Richard Howard. London: Tavistock.

———. 1970. *The Order of Things: An Archaeology of the Human Sciences.* New York: Pantheon Books.

———. 1977. *Discipline and Punish.* Trans. Alan Sheridan. Harmondsworth: Penguin.

———. 1979. *Power, Truth, Strategy,* eds. M. Morris and P. Patton. Sydney: Feral Publications.

———. 1986. 'Of Other Spaces', *Diacritics* 16(1): 22–27.

———. 1988a. 'Nietzsche, Genealogy, History', in D. F. Bouchard (ed.), *Language, Counter-memory, Practice: Selected Essays and Interviews.* Trans. Donald F. Bouchard and Sherry Simon. Ithaca, New York: Cornell University Press.

———. 1988b. 'The Ethic of Care for the Self as a Practice of Freedom', in J. Bernauer and D. Rasmussen (eds), *The Final Foucault.* Boston, Mass.: MIT Press.

Friedman, J. 1992a. 'The Past in the Future: History and the Politics of Identity', *American Anthropologist* 94(4): 837–59.

———. 1992b. 'Myth, History, and Political Identity', *Cultural Anthropology* 7(2): 194–210.

Fuary, M. 2000. 'Torres Strait and Dawdhay: Dimensions of Self and Otherness on Yam Island', *Oceania* 70(3): 219–30.

Geertz, C. 1973. *The Interpretation of Cultures*. London: Fontana Press.

Gell, A. 1982. 'The Market Wheel: Symbolic Aspects of an Indian Tribal Market', *Man* (New Series) 17: 470–91.

Genocchio, B. 1995. 'Discourse, Discontinuity, Difference: the Question of "Other" Spaces', in S. Watson and K. Gibson (eds), *Postmodern Cities and Spaces*. Cambridge, Mass: Blackwell Publishers, pp. 35–46.

Glowczewski, B. 1989. *Les Rêveurs du Désert*. Paris: Plon.

Gluckman, M. 1971 [1940]. *Analysis of a Social Situation in Modern Zululand*. Rhodes-Livingstone Paper no. 28. Manchester: Manchester University Press.

Goffman, E. 1974. *Frame Analysis: An Essay on the Organization of Experience*. Cambridge, Mass.: Harvard University Press.

Greed, C. H. 1994. *Women and Planning: Creating Gendered Realities*. London: Routledge.

Greer, S. and R. Henry. 1996. 'The Politics of Heritage: the Case of the Kuranda Skyrail', in J. Finlayson and A. Jackson-Nakano (eds), *Heritage and Native Title: Anthropological and Legal Perspectives*. Canberra: Native Title Research Unit, Australian Institute of Aboriginal and Torres Strait Islander Studies, pp. 16–27.

Greer, S. 2009. 'Portals in a Watery Realm: Cultural Landscapes in Northern Cape York', *Historic Environment* 22(1): 38–43.

———. 2010. 'Heritage and Empowerment: Community-Based Indigenous Cultural Heritage in Northern Australia', *International Journal of Heritage Studies* 16(1–2): 45–58.

Grewal, I. and C. Kaplan. (eds). 1994. *Scattered Hegemonies: Postmodernity and Transnational Feminist Practices*. Minneapolis: University of Minnnesota Press.

Gruzinski, S. 1990. 'Mutilated Memory: Reconstruction of the Past and the Mechanisms of Memory among 17th Century Otomis', in M. Bourguet, L. Velensi and N. Wachtel (eds), *Between Memory and History*. Chur, Switzerland: Harwood, pp. 131–47.

Gupta, A. and J. Ferguson. 1997. *Culture, Power, Place: Explorations in Critical Anthropology*. Durham: Duke University Press.

Halbwachs, M. 1992. *On Collective Memory*. Chicago: University of Chicago Press.

Hale, K. 1976. 'Tya:pukai (Djaabugay)', in P. Sutton (ed.), *Languages of Cape York*. Canberra: Australian Institute of Aboriginal Studies, pp. 236–42.

Haley, B. D. and L. R. Wilcoxon. 1997. 'Anthropology and the Making of Chumash Tradition', *Current Anthropology* 38(5): 761–94.

Handler, R. 1985. 'On Dialogue and Destructive Analysis: Problems in Narrating Nationalism and Ethnicity', *Journal of Anthropological Research* 41: 171.

Handler, R. and J. Linnekin. 1984. 'Tradition, Genuine or Spurious', *Journal of American Folklore* 97(385): 273–290.

Harvey, D. 1985. *Consciousness and the Urban Experience: Studies in the History and Theory of Capitalist Urbanization*. Baltimore: Johns Hopkins.

Hastrup, K. 1996. 'Anthropological Theory as Practice', *Social Anthropology* 4(1): 75–81.

Heidegger, M. 1971. *Poetry, Language, Thought*. New York: Harper and Row.

———. 1973. *Being and Time*. Oxford: Blackwell.

Henry, R. 1994. 'Kuranda at War: Contested Space and the Politics of the Market-place', *The Australian Journal of Anthropology* 5(3): 294–305.

———. 1995. 'Environmental Values and the Politics of Identity: The Kuranda Skyrail', *Northern Radius* 2(2): 6–8.

———. 1998. 'Performing Protest, Articulating Difference: Environmentalists, Aborigines and the Kuranda Skyrail Dispute', *Aboriginal History* 22: 143–61.

———. 1999. 'Confronting Ethnographic Holism: Field Site or Field of Sociality', *Canberra Anthropology: The Asia Pacific Journal of Anthropology* 22(2): 51–61.

———. 2000. 'Dancing into Being: The Tjapukai Aboriginal Cultural Park and the Laura Dance Festival', *The Australian Journal of Anthropology* 11(3): 322–32.

———. 2008. 'Engaging with History by Performing Tradition: The Poetic Politics of Indigenous Australian Festivals', in J. Kapferer (ed.), *The State and the Arts: Articulating Power and Subversion*. New York: Berghahn Books, pp. 52–69.

Henry, R. and A. Daly. 2001. 'Indigenous Families and the Welfare System: The Kuranda Community Case Study, Stage Two', *CAEPR Discussion Paper No. 216*. Canberra: Centre for Aboriginal Economic Policy Research, Australian National University.

Herzfeld, M. 1982. *Ours Once More: Folklore, Ideology, and the Making of Modern Greece*. Austin: University of Texas.

Hobsbawm, E. and T. Ranger. (eds). 1983. *The Invention of Tradition*. Cambridge: Cambridge University Press.

Holden, A. and R. Duffin. 1998. 'Negotiating Aboriginal Interests in Tourism Projects: The Djabugay People, the Tjapukai Dance Theatre and the Skyrail Project', *Aboriginal Politics and Public Sector Management Research Paper* 4. Brisbane: Centre for Australian Public Sector Management, Griffith University.

Hollingsworth, D. 1992. 'Discourses on Aboriginality and the Politics of Identity in Urban Australia', *Oceania* 63: 137–55.

Hughes, Major W. E. 1982. 'Early Pioneers – Thron and Elizabeth Mattisen', *The Historical Society, Cairns, North Queensland Bulletin*, 267.

Humston, S. 1988. *Kuranda: The Village in the Rainforest*. Kuranda: The Centenary Book Committee.

Ingold, T. 1993. 'The Temporality of the Landscape', *World Archaeology* 25(2): 152–74.

Jackson, M. 1996. 'Introduction: Phenomenology, Radical Empiricism, and Anthropological Critique', in M. Jackson (ed.), *Things as They Are: New Directions in Phenomenological Anthropology*. Bloomington: Indiana University Press, pp. 1–50.

Jacobs, J. M. 1993. '"Shake 'im this country": The Mapping of the Aboriginal Sacred in Australia – the Case of Coronation Hill', in P. Jackson and J. Penrose (eds), *Constructions of Race, Place and Nation*. London: University College London.

——. 1994. 'Earth Honouring: Western Desires and Indigenous Knowledge', *Meanjin* 53: 305–14.

Jessop, B. 1990. *State Theory: Putting the Capitalist State in its Place.* Cambridge: Polity Press.

Jones, D. 1976. *Trinity Phoenix.* Cairns: Cairns and District Centenary Committee.

Kahn, J. S. 1995. *Culture, Multiculture, Postculture.* London: SAGE.

Kapferer, B. 1986. 'Performance and the Structuring of Meaning and Experience', in V. Turner and E. Bruner (eds), *The Anthropology of Experience.* Urbana: University of Illinois Press.

——. 1988. *Legends of People: Myths of State: Violence, Intolerance, and Political Culture in Sri Lanka and Australia.* Washington: Smithsonian Institution Press.

——. 1995a. 'The Performance of Categories: Plays of Identity in Africa and Australia', in A. Rogers and S. Vertovec (eds), *The Urban Context: Ethnicity, Social Networks, and Situational Analysis.* Oxford: Berg, pp. 55–79.

——. 1995b. 'Bureaucratic Erasure: Identity, Resistance and Violence – Aborigines and a Discourse of Autonomy in a North Queensland Town', in D. Miller (ed.), *Worlds Apart: Modernity through the Prism of the Local.* London: Routledge, pp. 69–108.

——. 1996. 'Preface to the 1996 Edition', in V. Turner, *Schism and Continuity in an African Society: A Study of Ndembu Village Life.* Oxford: Berg, pp. vii–xiii.

——. 1997. *The Feast of the Sorcerer: Practices of Consciousness and Power.* Chicago: University of Chicago Press.

Kapferer, J. 1996. *Being All Equal: Identity, Difference and Australian Cultural Practice.* Oxford: Berg.

——. 2008. 'Introduction: The Architectonics of State Power – Complicity and Resistance', in J. Kapferer (ed.), *The State and the Arts: Articulating Power and Subversion.* New York: Berghahn Books, pp. 1–12.

Keith, M. and S. Pile. 1993. 'Introduction Part 1: The Politics of Place', in M. Keith and S. Pile (eds), *Place and the Politics of Identity.* London: Routledge, pp. 1–21.

Kidd, R. 1997. *The Way We Civilise: Aboriginal Affairs – The Untold Story.* St Lucia: University of Queensland Press.

——. 2002. 'Queensland Stolen Wages Fact Sheet', *Journal of Australian Indigenous Issues* 5(2): 26–30.

Kolig, E. 1995. 'A Sense of History and the Reconstitution of Cosmology in Australian Aboriginal Society: The Case of Myth versus History', *Anthropos* 90(1–3): 49–67.

——. 2000. 'Social Causality, Human Agency and Mythology: Some Thoughts on History-consciousness and Mythical Sense among Australian Aborigines', *Anthropological Forum* 10(1): 9–30.

Küchler, S. 1993. 'Landscape as Memory: The Mapping of Process and Its Representation in a Melanesian Society', in B. Bender (ed.), *Landscape, Politics and Perspectives.* Oxford: Berg, pp. 85–106.

Küle, M. 1997. 'Home: a Phenomenological Approach', in A. Tymieniecka (ed.), *Passion for Place, Book II.* Dordrecht: Kluwer Academic Publishers, pp. 97–112.

Kuper, Hilda. 2003. 'The Language of Sites and the Politics of Space', in S. M. Low and D. Lawrence-Zuniga (eds), *The Anthropology of Space and Place: Locating Culture*. Malden: Blackwell, pp. 247–263.

Kuranda Amphitheatre. 1989. *Artstarters (Community Arts Information Kit)*. Brisbane: Queensland Community Arts Network.

Laclau, E. and C. Mouffe. 1985. *Hegemony and Socialist Strategy: Towards a Radical Democratic Politics*. London: Verso.

Langton, M. 2002. 'The Edge of the Sacred, the Edge of Death: Sensual Inscriptions', in B. David and M. Wilson (eds), *Inscribed Landscapes: Marking and Making Place*. Honolulu: University of Hawai`i Press, pp. 253–269.

———. 2003. 'The "Wild", the Market, and the Native: Indigenous People Face New Forms of Global Colonization', in S. Vertovec and D. Posey (eds), *Globalization, Globalism Environments, and Environmentalism*. Oxford: Oxford University Press, pp. 141–70.

Lattas, A. 1992. 'Wiping the Blood off Aboriginality: The Politics of Aboriginal Embodiment in Contemporary Intellectual Debate', *Oceania* 63(2): 160–64.

———. 1993. 'Essentialism, Memory and Resistance: Aboriginality and the Politics of Authenticity', *Oceania* 63: 240–66.

———. (ed.). 1996. *Articulations of Memory: The Politics of Embodiment, Locality, and the Contingent*, special issue of *Oceania* 66(4).

———. 1997. 'Aborigines and Contemporary Australian Nationalism: Primordiality and the Cultural Politics of Otherness', in G. Cowlishaw and B. Morris (eds), *Race Matters: Indigenous Australians and 'Our' Society*. Canberra: Aboriginal Studies Press.

Lefebvre, H. 1991. *The Production of Space*. Oxford: Blackwell.

———. 2004. *Rhythmanalysis: Space, Time and Everyday Life*. London: Continuum International Publishing.

———. 2009. *State, Space, World: Selected Essays*. Minneapolis: University of Minnesota Press.

Levi-Strauss, C. 1966. *The Savage Mind*. Chicago: University of Chicago Press.

———. 1992. *Tristes Tropiques*. Harmondsworth: Penguin Books.

Long, N. 1996. 'Globalization and Localization: New Challenges to Rural Research', in H. L. Moore (ed.), *The Future of Anthropological Knowledge*. London, New York: Routledge, pp. 37–59.

Loos, N. 1982. *Invasion and Resistance: Aboriginal-European Relations on the North Queensland Frontier, 1861–1897*. Canberra: ANU Press.

Lyotard, J. 1984. *The Postmodern Condition: A Report on Knowledge*. Manchester: Manchester University Press.

McGregor, R. 1997. *Imagined Destinies: Aboriginal Australians and the Doomed Race Theory, 1880–1939*. Carlton, Victoria: Melbourne University Press.

McConnel, U. 1939–40. 'Social Organization of Tribes of Cape York Peninsula', *Oceania* 10(1): 54–72.

McIntyre-Tamwoy, S. R. 2004. '*Places People Value: Social Significance and Cultural Exchange in Post Invasion Australia*,' in R. Harrison and C. Williamson (eds), *After Captain Cook: The Archaeology of the Recent Indigenous Past in Australia*. Walnut Creek, California: Altamira Press, pp. 171–90.

Macdonald, G. 1997. 'Recognition and Justice: The Traditional/Historical Contradiction in New South Wales', in D. E. Smith and J. Finlayson (eds), *Fighting Over Country: Anthropological Perspectives*. Canberra: Centre for Aboriginal Economic Policy Research, Australian National University, pp. 65–82.

Mackett, P. J. 1989. 'Aboriginal Notes' [extracted from various registers, letterbooks and documents held at the Queensland State Archives], unpublished manuscript. Brsibane: Queensland State Archives.

Maddock, K. 1987a. 'Yet Another 'Sacred Site' – the Bula Controversy', in B. Wright, G. Fry and L. Petchkovsky (eds), *Contemporary Issues in Aboriginal Studies: Proceedings of the First Nepean Conference*. Sydney: Firebird Press, pp. 119–40.

———. 1987b. 'God, Caesar and Mammon at Coronation Hill', *Oceania* 58(4): 305–10.

———. 1988. 'Myth, History and a Sense of Oneself', in J. Beckett (ed.), *Past and Present: The Construction of Aboriginality*. Canberra: Australian Institute of Aboriginal Studies, pp. 11–30.

Magowan, F. 2007. *Melodies of Mourning: Music and Emotion in Northern Australia*. Oxford: James Currey Publishers.

Marcus, J. 1996. 'New Age Consciousness and Aboriginal Culture: Primitive Dreaming in Common Places', *Thamyris* 3(1): 37–54.

———. 1997. 'The Journey Out to the Centre: The Cultural Appropriation of Ayers Rock', in G. Cowlishaw and B. Morris (eds), *Race Matters: Indigenous Australians and 'Our' Society*. Canberra: Aboriginal Studies Press, pp. 29–51.

Mareeba Shire Council. 1993. 'Kuranda Village Planning Study', 9 vols. [C&B Consultants Pty Ltd.] Mareeba.

———. 1995. 'Draft Development Control Plan 2 – Kuranda Village', 6 vols. [C&B Consultants Pty Ltd.] Mareeba.

———. 1997. 'Kuranda Traffic Study'. [Connell Wagner Pty Ltd.] Mareeba.

Marika, W. and J. Isaacs. 1995. *Wanjuk Marika: Lifestory as told to Jennifer Isaacs*. St Lucia, Queensland: University of Queensland Press.

Martin, D. F. 1993. 'Autonomy and Relatedness: An Ethnography of Wik People of Aurukun, Western Cape York Peninsula', Ph.D. dissertation. Canberra: Australian National University.

———. 1997. 'The Incorporation of "Traditional" and "Historical" Interests in Native Title Representative Bodies', in D. E. Smith and J. Finlayson (eds), *Fighting Over Country: Anthropological Perspectives*. Canberra: Centre for Aboriginal Economic Policy Research, Australian National University, pp. 153–63.

———. 2001. 'Is Welfare Dependency "Welfare Poison"? An Assessment of Noel Pearson's Proposals for Aboriginal Welfare Reform', *CAEPR Discussion Paper No. 213*. Canberra: Centre for Aboriginal Economic Policy Research, Australian National University.

Martin D. F. and J. Finlayson. 1996. 'Linking Accountability and Self-determination in Aboriginal Organisations', *CAEPR Discussion Paper No. 116*. Canberra: Centre for Aboriginal Economic Policy Research, Australian National University.

May, D. 1994. *Aboriginal Labour and the Cattle Industry: Queensland from White Settlement to the Present*. Cambridge: Cambridge University Press.

Merlan, F. 1991. 'The Limits of Cultural Constructionism: The Case of Coronation Hill', *Oceania* 61(4): 1–12.

———. 1994. 'Narratives of Survival in the Post-colonial North', *Oceania* 65: 151–74.

———. 1999. *Caging the Rainbow: Places, Politics, and Aborigines in a North Australian Town.* Honolulu: University of Hawai`i Press.

Messerschmidt, D. A. (ed.). 1981. *Anthropologists at Home in North America: Methods and Issues in the Study of One's Own Society.* New York: Cambridge University Press.

Meston, A. 1897. 'Queensland Aboriginals: Outline of Work in 1897. New Systems of Improvement, Their Future Welfare. Special Protective Legislation; to W. H. Ryder Esq. Principal Under Secretary', unpublished manuscript. Brisbane: Queensland State Library.

Miles, M. 2008. 'The Culture Industries: Symbolic Economies and Critical Practices', in J. Kapferer (ed.), *The State and the Arts: Articulating Power and Subversion.* New York: Berghahn Books, pp. 98–112.

Mitchell, J. C. 1956. *The Yao Village.* Manchester: Manchester University Press.

Mjöberg, E. 1918. *Bland Stenaldersmanniskor I Queenslands Vildmarker.* Stockholm: Albert Bonniers Forlag. [As translated by Dymphna Clark, unpublished manuscript held in the library of James Cook University.]

Moore, H. 1994. *A Passion for Difference.* Oxford: Polity Press.

———. 1996. 'The Changing Nature of Anthropological Knowledge: An Introduction', in H. L. Moore (ed.), *The Future of Anthropological Knowledge.* London: Routledge, pp. 1–15.

Morphy, H. 1995. 'Landscape and the Reproduction of the Ancestral Past', in E. Hirsch and M. O'Hanlon (eds), *The Anthropology of Landscape: Perspectives on Place and Space.* Clarendon: Oxford, pp. 184–109.

Morphy, H. and F. Morphy. 1984. 'The "Myths" of Ngalagan History: Ideology and Images of the Past in Northern Australia', *Man* 19(3): 459–78.

Morris, B. 1989. *Domesticating Resistance: The Dhan-Gadi Aborigines and the Australian State.* Oxford: Berg.

Morton, J. 1999. 'Anthropology at Home in Australia', *The Australian Journal of Anthropology* 10(3): 243–58.

Motzafi-Haller, P. 1997. 'Writing Birthright: On Native Anthropologists and the Politics of Representation', in D. E. Reed-Danahay (ed.), *Auto/Ethnography: Rewriting the Self and the Social.* Oxford: Berg, pp. 195–222.

Mulligan, J. V. 1877. *Guide to the Palmer River and Normanby Gold Fields, North Queensland.* Brisbane: George Slater and Company.

Munn, N. 1970. 'The Transformation of Subjects into Objects in Walbiri and Pitjantjatjara Myth', in R. M. Berndt (ed.), *Australian Aboriginal Anthropology.* Perth: University of Western Australia, pp. 141–63.

———. 1973. *Walbiri Iconography: Graphic Representation and Cultural Symbolism in a Central Australian Society.* Ithaca: Cornell University Press.

Munro-Clark, M. 1986. *Communes in Rural Australia: The Movement since 1970.* Sydney: Hale & Iremonger, in association with the Ian Buchan Fell Research Centre.

Myers, F. R. 1986. *Pintupi Country, Pintupi Self: Sentiment, Place and Politics among Western Desert Aborigines.* Canberra: Australian Institute of Aboriginal Studies Press.

Narayan, K. 1993. 'How Native is a "Native" Anthropologist?' *American Anthropologist* 95(3): 671–83.

Nasar, J. L. and B. Fisher. 1993. '"Hot Spots" of Fear and Crime: a Multi-method Investigation', *Journal of Environmental Psychology* 13: 187–206.

Natanson, M. 1970. *The Journeying Self.* Menlo Park, California: Addison-Wesley.

Newton, J. 1988. 'Aborigines, Tribes and the Counterculture', *Social Analysis* 23: 53–71.

Okely, J. 1992. 'Anthropology and Autobiography: Participatory Experience and Embodied Knowledge', in J. Okely and H. Callaway (eds), *Anthropology and Autobiography.* London: Routledge, pp. 1–28.

———. 1996. *Own or Other Culture.* London: Routledge.

O'Meally, R. and G. Fabre. 1994. 'Introduction', in R. O' Meally and G. Fabre (eds), *History and Memory in African-American Culture.* New York: Oxford University Press, pp. 3–17.

Patz, E. 1978. 'A Sketch Grammar of Dyabugay', B.A. (Hons) dissertation. Canberra: Australian National University.

Pearson, N. 2000. 'Passive Welfare and the Destruction of Indigenous Society', in P. Saunders (ed.), *Reforming the Australian Welfare State.* Melbourne: Australian Institute of Family Studies, pp. 136–55.

Peters, J. D. 1997. 'Seeing Bifocally: Media, Place, Culture', in A. Gupta and J. Ferguson (eds), *Culture, Power, Place: Explorations in Critical Anthropology.* Durham: Duke University Press, pp. 75–92.

Pike, G. 1984. *Conquest of the Ranges.* Mareeba: Pinevale Publications.

Plattner, S. 1989. 'Markets and Marketplaces', in S. Plattner (ed.), *Economic Anthropology.* Stanford: Stanford University Press, pp. 171–208.

Povinelli, E. A. 1993. *Labor's Lot: The Power, History and Culture of Aboriginal Action.* Chicago: University of Chicago Press.

———. 2002. *The Cunning of Recognition: Indigenous Alterities and the Making of Australian Multiculturalism.* Durham: Duke University Press.

Queensland, Parliament. 1896. *Report on the Aboriginals of Queensland; to the Honourable Horace Tozer, Home Secretary (by Archibald Meston, Special Commissioner Under Instructions From the Queensland Government).* Brisbane: Government Printer.

———. 1900. *Annual Report of the Northern Protector of Aboriginals for 1899; to the Under Secretary, Home Secretary's Department.* Brisbane: Government Printer.

———. 1905. *Annual Report of the Chief Protector of Aboriginals for 1904; to the Under Secretary, Department of Public Lands.* Brisbane: Government Printer.

———. 1913. *Annual Report of the Chief Protector of Aboriginals for the Year 1912; to the Under Secretary, Home Department.* Brisbane: Government Printer.

———. 1915. *Annual Report of the Chief Protector of Aboriginals for the Year 1914; to the Under Secretary, Home Department.* Brisbane: Government Printer.

———. 1951. *Report Upon the Operations of Certain Sub-Departments of the Department of Health and Home Affairs: Native Affairs – Annual Report of the Director of Native Affairs for the Year Ended 30th June, 1951.* Brisbane: Government Printer.

———. 1952. *Report Upon the Operations of Certain Sub-Departments of the Department of Health and Home Affairs: Native Affairs –Annual Report of the Director of Native Affairs for the Year Ended 30th June, 1952.* Brisbane: Government Printer.

———. 1960. *Report Upon the Operations of Certain Sub-Departments of the Department of Health and Home Affairs: Native Affairs –Annual Report of the Director of Native Affairs for the Year Ended 30th June, 1960.* Brisbane: Government Printer.

———. 1962. *Report Upon the Operations of Certain Sub-Departments of the Department of Health and Home Affairs: Native Affairs –Annual Report of the Director of Native Affairs for the Year Ended 30th June, 1962.* Brisbane: Government Printer.

Quinn, M. 1992. *Djabugay: A Djabugay -English Dictionary.* Brisbane: Queensland Department of Education.

Quinn, M. and R. Banning. 1991. *Buda:dji Miya-Miya Djada.* Kuranda.

———. 1992. *Nganydjin Bulmba: Our Country.* Kuranda.

Rabinow, P. 1986. 'Representations are Social Facts: Modernity and Post-modernity in Anthropology', in J. Clifford and G. E. Marcus (eds), *Writing Culture: The Poetics and Politics of Ethnography.* Berkeley: University of California Press, pp. 234–61.

Reynolds, H. 1982. *The Other Side of the Frontier: Aboriginal Resistance to the European Invasion of Australia.* Ringwood, Victoria: Penguin.

———. 1987. *The Law of the Land.* Ringwood, Victoria: Penguin.

Roach, J. 1995. 'Culture and Performance in the Circum-Atlantic World', in E. K. Sedgwick and A.Parker (eds), *Performitivity and Performance.* New York: Routledge, pp. 45–63.

Roberts, R. B. 1986. 'The Early Work among the Aborigines', in A. J. Ferch (ed.), *Symposium on Adventist History in the South Pacific, 1885–1918.* Wahroonga, NSW: South Pacific Division of Seventh Day Adventists, pp. 141–51.

Rose, D. 1984. 'The Saga of Captain Cook; Morality in European and Aboriginal Law', *Australian Aboriginal Studies* 2: 24–39.

———. 1994. 'Ned Kelly Died for Our Sins', *Oceania* 65: 175–85.

Rowley, C. D. 1972. *The Destruction of Aboriginal Society.* Harmondsworth: Penguin.

Rowse, T. 1998. *White Flour, White Power.* Melbourne: Cambridge University Press.

Rubin, C. T. 1994. *The Green Crusade: Rethinking the Roots of Environmentalism.* New York: Free Press.

Ruddick, S. 1990. 'Heterotopias of the Homeless', *Strategies* 3: 183–202.

Rumsey, A. 1994. 'The Dreaming, Human Agency and Inscriptive Practice', *Oceania* 65: 116–30.

Rumsey, A. and J. Weiner. 2001. *Emplaced Myth: Space, Narrative, and Knowledge in Aboriginal Australia and Papua New Guinea.* Honolulu: University of Hawai`i Press.

Sackett, L. 1991. 'Promoting Primitivism: Conservationist Depictions of Aboriginal Australians', *The Australian Journal of Anthropology* 2(2): 233–46.

Sansom, B. 1980. *The Camp at Wallaby Cross.* Canberra: Australian Institute of Aboriginal Studies.

———. 2001. 'Irruptions of the Dreaming in Post-colonial Australia', *Oceania* 72(1): 1–32.

Schieffelin, E. 1985. 'Performance and the Cultural Construction of Reality', *American Anthropologist* 12(4): 707–24.

Seaton, D. 1952. 'A Legend of Durren Dae (Dream Time)', *North Queensland Naturalist* 20(101): 18–19.

Shils, E. 1981. *Tradition.* Chicago: University of Chicago Press.

Sharp, R. Lauriston. 1938–39. 'Tribes and totemism in north-east Australia', *Oceania* 11: 254–75, 439–61.

Smith, B. R. 2000. '"Local" and "Diaspora" Connections to Country and Kin in Central Cape York Peninsula', *Native Title Research Unit Issues Paper* 2(6). Canberra: Native Title Research Unit, Australian Institute of Aboriginal and Torres Strait Islander Studies.

Sourial, M. 1994. 'Protesters, Credible or Farcical?' *Cairns Post*, 5 August: 8.

Stafford, E. 1984. 'The Multiplier Effect in the Arts: the Kuranda Amphitheatre Example', *Community Arts Network News* (April): 4–5.

———. 1994. 'Kuranda Amphitheatre', in A. McArthur and D. Ellenby (eds), *Report of the Kuranda Amphitheatre Future Search Workshop, Saturday 22 January 1994.* Kuranda.

Steward, P. and A. Strathern (eds). 2003. *Landscape, Memory and History: Anthropological Perspectives.* London: Pluto Press.

Strang, V. 1997. *Uncommon Ground: Cultural Landscapes and Environmental Issues.* Oxford: Berg.

Strathern, M. 1987. 'The Limits of Auto-Anthropology', in A. Jackson (ed.), *Anthropology at Home.* London: Tavistock, pp. 16–37.

Strauss, J. 2009. 'Indigenous Community Staying Put at Mona Mona', *Green Left Weekly*, 17 January 2009. Last accessed 30 April 2011, http://www.greenleft.org.au/2009/779/40153.

Sutton, P. 1988. 'Myth as History: History as Myth', in I. Keen (ed.), *Being Black: Aboriginal Cultures in Settled Australia.* Canberra: Aboriginal Studies Press, pp. 251–68.

———. 1995. *Country: Aboriginal Boundaries and Land Ownership in Australia.* Canberra: Aboriginal History Monograph 3.

———. 2000. 'The Politics of Suffering: Indigenous Policy in Australia since the 1970s', *Anthropological Forum* 11(2): 125–73.

———. 2009. *The Politics of Suffering: Indigenous Australia and the End of the Liberal Consensus.* Carlton, Victoria: Melbourne University Press.

Swain, T. 1993. *A Place for Strangers: Towards a History of Australian Aboriginal Being.* Melbourne: Cambridge University Press.

Taussig, M. 1984. 'Culture of Terror – Space of Death: Roger Casement's Putumayo Report and the Explanation of Torture', in N. B. Dirks (ed.), *Colonialism and Culture*. Ann Arbor: University of Michigan Press, pp. 135–74.

———. 1993. *Mimesis and Alterity: A Particular History of the Senses*. London: Routledge.

Taylor, P. (ed.). 1988. *After 200 Years: Photographic Essays of Aboriginal and Islander Australia Today*. Canberra: Aboriginal Studies Press.

Tindale, N. 1938–1939. *Harvard and Adelaide Universities Anthropological Expedition, Australia, 1938–1939*. [Contents of Vol. II, unpublished notes on contents for cards N.332–N.945 of the expedition series]. Canberra: Australian Institute of Aboriginal and Torres Strait Islander Studies.

———. 1974. *Aboriginal Tribes of Australia*. Los Angeles: University of   California Press.

———. 1976. 'Some Ecological Bases for Australian Tribal Boundaries', in N. Petersen (ed.), *Tribes and Boundaries in Australia*. Canberra: Australian Institute of Aboriginal Studies, pp. 12–29.

Trigger, D. S. 1992. *Whitefella Commin': Aboriginal Responses to Colonialism in Northern Australia*. Cambridge: Cambridge University Press.

———. 1996. 'Contesting Ideologies of Natural Resource Development in British Colombia, Canada', *Culture* 16(1): 55–69.

———. 1997. 'Mining, Landscape and the Culture of Development Ideology in Australia', *Ecumene: A Journal of Environment, Culture, Meaning* 4(2): 161–80.

———. 1999. 'Nature, Work and "The Environment": Contesting Sentiments and Identities in the Southwest of Western Australia', *The Australian Journal of Anthropology* 10(2): 163–76.

Trouillot, M. 2001. 'The Anthropology of the State in the Age of Globalization', *Current Anthropology* 42(1): 125–38.

Turner, T. 1991. 'Representing, Resisting, Rethinking: Historical Transformations of Kayapo Culture and Anthropological Consciousness', in G. Stocking (ed.), *Colonial Situations: Essays on the Contextualization of Ethnographic Knowledge*. Madison: University of Wisconsin Press, pp. 285–313.

Turner, V. 1974. *Dramas, Fields, and Metaphors: Symbolic Action in Human Society*. Ithaca: Cornell University Press.

———. 1996. (1957) *Schism and Continuity in an African Society: A Study of Ndembu Village Life*. Oxford: Berg.

Ulin, R. C. 1995. 'Invention and Representation as Cultural Capital', *American Anthropologist* 97(3): 519–27.

Veivers, W. 1988. *Pioneers of a Trackless Land: The Veivers Family in Australia*. Gold Coast: Wayne Veivers.

van Velsen, J. 1964. *The Politics of Kinship*. Manchester: Manchester University Press.

———. 1967. 'The Extended-case Method and Situational Analysis', in A. L. Epstein (ed.), *The Craft of Social Anthropology*. London: Tavistock.

von Sturmer, J. R. 1984. 'The Different Domains', in Australian Institute of Aboriginal Studies (eds), *Aborigines and Uranium*. Canberra: Australian Institute of Aboriginal Studies, pp. 218–37.

Wearne, H. 1980. *A Clash of Cultures: Queensland Aboriginal Policy, 1824–1980.* Brisbane: Uniting Church of Australia.

Weiner, J. 1995a. 'Anthropologists, Historians and the Secret of Social Knowledge', *Anthropology Today* 11(5): 3–7.

———. 1995b. 'The Secret of the Ngarrindjeri: The Fabrication of Social Knowledge', *Arena* 5: 17–32.

Wheatley, D. K. 1969. 'Get out, Hippies! You're Not Wanted in the North', *Pix Australia,* 6 September 1969: 6.

White, B. 1995. 'A Chronology of Documents, Letters, Media, and Events Telling the Story of How It Is That a Cairns-Kuranda Cableway Got to Be Constructed in a Djabugay Cultural Landscape', unpublished manuscript. Cairns: Bruce White.

White, H. 1973. *Metahistory: The Historical Imagination in Nineteenth Century Europe.* Baltimore: John Hopkins University Press.

Wilson, Sir R. Darling. 1997. *Bringing them Home: Report of the National Inquiry into the Separation of Aboriginal and Torres Strait Islander Children from their Families.* Sydney: Human Rights and Equal Opportunity Commission.

Windschuttle, K. 2002. *The Fabrication of Aboriginal History: Volume One, Van Diemen's Land 1803–1847.* Sydney: Macleay Press.

Wolf, E. R. 1982. *Europe and the People without History.* Berkeley: University of California Press.

Wood, R. 1990. 'Aboriginal Interests in Port Douglas and Environs: A Report to Environment Science and Services', unpublished manuscript.

Woolston, F. P. and F. S. Colliver. 1967. 'Christie Palmerston – A North Queensland Pioneer, Prospector and Explorer', *Queensland Heritage* 1(7): 30–34.

———. 1968. 'Christie Palmerston - A North Queensland Pioneer, Prospector and Explorer', *Queensland Heritage* 2(1): 26–31.

Wynhausen, E. 1971. 'A Way Out', *The Bulletin,* 6 November 1971: 38–41.

Yiftachel, O. 1995. 'The Dark Side of Modernism: Planning as Control of an Ethnic Minority', in S. Watson and K. Gibson (eds), *Postmodern Cities and Spaces.* Oxford: Blackwell, pp. 216–42.

Zablocki, B. 1980. *Alienation and Charisma.* New York: Free Press.

Legislation and Legal Authorities

Aboriginal Councils and Associations Act of 1976 (Cwlth).
Aboriginal Land Act of 1991 (Qld).
Aboriginals Preservation and Protection Act of 1939–1946 (Qld).
Aboriginals Protection and Restriction of the Sale of Opium Act of 1897 (Qld).
Aboriginal and Torres Strait Islander Affairs Act of 1965 (Qld).
Aboriginal and Torres Strait Islander Commission Amendment Act of 2001 (Cwlth).
Aboriginal and Torres Strait Islander Heritage Protection Act of 1984 (Cwlth).
Co-operative and Other Societies Act of 1967 (Qld).

Cultural Record (Landscapes Queensland and Queensland Estate Act) of 1987 (Qld).
Jean Anderson and Ors v. Mareeba Shire Council and Maytrend Pty Ltd (Kuranda Shooting Gallery Appeal) (1997) Appeal no. 48.
Koowarta v. Bjelke-Petersen (1982) 153 CLR 168.
Local Government (Aboriginal Land) Act of 1978 (Qld).
Mabo v. State of Queensland (1992) 66 ALJR 408.
Mareeba Shire Council By-Laws. Queensland Government Gazette, 30 December 1976, vol. CCLIII, no. 92.
Native Title Act of 1993 (Cwlth).
Racial Discrimination Act of 1975 (Cwlth).
The Members of the Yorta Yorta Aboriginal Community v. State of Victoria (1998) FCA 1606.

⊰ INDEX ⊱